PRAISE FOR *FIGURING*

'In *Figuring Out Thirty*, Bridget examines the modern woman's experience with fresh eyes. This book is funny, feminist and authentic in exploring the questions we all harbour through some of the most confusing years of our lives. It's the big sister you need, blazing a trail that challenges the institutions, expectations and insecurities women and girls are facing.'

Hannah Ferguson, CEO of Cheek Media

'No one likes admitting that they're afraid of turning thirty, even though so many of us are. This book will validate your feelings – whether you're approaching thirty and bricking it or feel like you have it all figured out. I steamed through it in one sitting. Bridget welcomes everyone in, and is generous in sharing her story, and wise in knowing it will help other women who are unlearning the script we've been told to memorise.'

Lucinda 'Froomes' Price, author of *All I Ever Wanted Was to Be Hot*

'Tender, heartfelt and joyful, *Figuring Out Thirty* is a millennial's modern-day toolkit wrapped in a warm hug. This memoir-style self-help book is full of feeling and will leave you feeling seen and comforted. Bridget's infectious personality and bright-eyed enthusiasm shines through, as do her honest and quiet self-reflections. It's Bridget as you've never seen her before.'

Maggie Zhou, writer and co-host of the *Culture Club* podcast

'A refreshingly real blueprint for the reality of turning thirty. So grateful for Bridget's generosity in sharing so deeply – I felt so seen.'

Laura Henshaw, co-founder of Kic

'*Figuring Out Thirty* will speak to so many of us when it comes to navigating life, love and loss! A vulnerable and honest book, and one we all need on our bedside tables.'

Allira Potter, author of *Wild & Witchy*

'We're excited for every milestone birthday, until the big 3-0 arrives ... Why? Well, Bridget perfectly sums it up in this hilariously heart-touching, honest read.'

Steph Claire Smith, co-founder of Kic

'Turning thirty is like realising no one really has it all figured out, and that's okay. This book is your go-to for laughing, crying and feeling seen as you navigate the messy, beautiful chaos of figuring out life in your thirties.'

Brooke Blurton, author of *Big Love*

'A relatable and enlightening guide to your thirties and why the decade is something to be embraced instead of feared.'

Alexandra Hourigan and Sally McMullen,
hosts of the *Two Broke Chicks* podcast

FIGURING OUT THIRTY

Bridget Hustwaite

DECODING THE DECISIVE DECADE

(and what really matters)

FIGURING OUT THIRTY

Bridget Hustwaite

The information contained in this book is for general purposes only. It is not intended as and should not be relied upon as medical advice. A medical practitioner should be consulted if you have any concerns about your mental or physical health.

PENGUIN BOOKS

UK | USA | Canada | Ireland | Australia
India | New Zealand | South Africa | China

Penguin Books is part of the Penguin Random House group of companies whose addresses can be found at global.penguinrandomhouse.com

First published by Penguin Books, 2025

Copyright © Bridget Hustwaite, 2025

The moral right of the author has been asserted.

All rights reserved. No part of this publication may be reproduced, published, performed in public or communicated to the public in any form or by any means without prior written permission from Penguin Random House Australia Pty Ltd or its authorised licensees.

Cover and text design by George Saad © Penguin Random House Australia Pty Ltd
Typeset in Adobe Garamond Pro by Midland Typesetters, Australia

Printed and bound in Australia by Griffin Press, an accredited
ISO AS/NZS 14001 Environmental Management Systems printer

 A catalogue record for this book is available from the National Library of Australia

ISBN 978 1 76134 486 2

penguin.com.au

We at Penguin Random House Australia acknowledge that Aboriginal and Torres Strait Islander peoples are the Traditional Custodians and the first storytellers of the lands on which we live and work. We honour Aboriginal and Torres Strait Islander peoples' continuous connection to Country, waters, skies and communities. We celebrate Aboriginal and Torres Strait Islander stories, traditions and living cultures; and we pay our respects to Elders past and present.

To all the female writers, thinkers and visionaries whose work has shaped my understanding of life and growth – you freakin' rule.

INTRODUCTION 1

SUDDENLY
(AND UNSOBERLY)
THIRTY 9

THE BIG BREAK-UP 27

SATURN RETURN 51

THINGS I HAVE LEARNED
ABOUT BEING SINGLE
IN MY THIRTIES 65

WHY AM I LIKE THIS? 79

THINGS I HAVE LEARNED
ABOUT RELATIONSHIPS
IN MY THIRTIES 115

TO BABY OR
NOT TO BABY 127

I DO ... NEED TO TALK ABOUT MARRIAGE 159

BODY BETTER 189

I QUIT 209

A NEW DIAGNOSIS (OR TWO) 235

FOR THE LOVE AND LOSS OF FRIENDSHIP 259

THIRTIES: A VIBE CHECK 278

THIRTY-THREE 281

ACKNOWLEDGEMENTS 293

ENDNOTES 295

ABOUT THE AUTHOR 310

INTRODUCTION

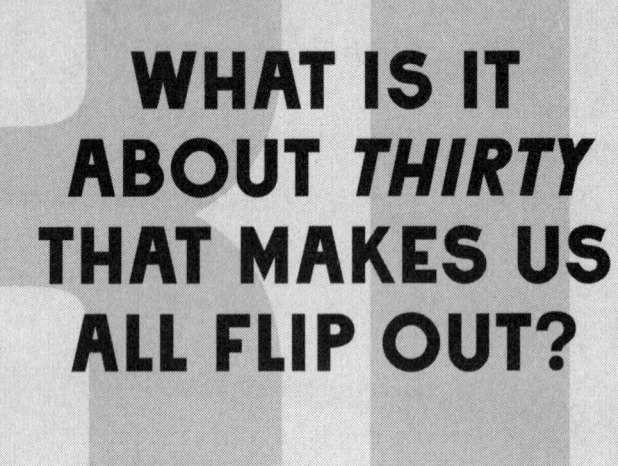

"WHAT IS IT ABOUT *THIRTY* THAT MAKES US ALL FLIP OUT?"

As a defining new decade loomed on the horizon, I thought I had everything figured out. I was in a long-term relationship with aspirations to settle down. I was financially independent and working a job I loved but had also found purpose outside of it with my endometriosis advocacy. I thought I was on the right track to having everything we are told we should have by the time we hit that milestone of the big 3-0. When we become a *real* adult.

These past few years, however, have proven otherwise. I'm thirty-three, and nothing is as I thought it would be. Shit kind of (read: really) hit the fan six weeks before I turned thirty and, as it turned out, heartbreak was only the beginning.

Between the ages of twenty-nine and thirty-three, I (inhale):

- was dumped by my partner of five years
- published my first book, *How to Endo*
- grieved the passing of a mentor
- had my second endometriosis surgery
- lived through six COVID-19 lockdowns
- relapsed into body image obsession
- became a single dog mum

- went on my first dating app date
- fell in love with someone five years my junior
- quit my dream job
- moved house five times and ended up interstate, 3417 kilometres from home
- received (and grieved) two new diagnoses, for ADHD and PMDD
- embraced new connections and experienced the demise of friendships
- delved into the complexities of generational trauma within my family
- pondered my sexuality, as well as my marital and maternal desires.

(Exhale.) All of these things have made me question who I am and what I really want in life versus what I thought I *should* want. And let me tell you, such confrontation with oneself is Pretty Fucking Terrifying!

I was being paid to have conversations about music as a radio presenter on a national network but off air, I yearned to discuss the tumult of turning thirty and find out if I was alone in the chaos and confusion of it all. So, like with my endometriosis experience, I created a platform to talk about it. Except this time around, it wasn't an Instagram account like @endogram, it was a podcast. Looking back on an entry in my Notes app, it was exactly five days prior to being dumped by my ex that I brain-dumped the concept in my phone:

I'm about to turn thirty and I'm freaking out. I know age is just a number and it's not like your life suddenly changes the day you transition into a new decade, but there's just something there that's making me worry. An existential crisis of sorts. On paper, I'd be looking pretty successful at my age. I host a live national radio program. I'm about to be known as an author. I'm in a long-term relationship. I'm doing well. But something feels

INTRODUCTION

off. I don't own a house. I don't have a kid. I've never fully raised my own pet. As a woman in music, I feel like I have an expiry date.

The timestamp was 1.16 a.m., which tells me that I was quietly smashing out my thoughts and feels in bed with my back turned on the snores of my ex-boyfriend. It's wild to me that I was typing that out just days before we broke up. Maybe I could sense that something was about to happen.

I'M THIRTY-THREE, AND NOTHING IS AS I THOUGHT IT WOULD BE.

On my 31st birthday, I launched *Figuring Out 30* with ten episodes exploring heartbreak, career, fertility, dating, divorce, finance and astrology. I treated this project as a pilot season to see whether I enjoyed the podcast format and if anyone vibed this kind of content from me. I was quickly met with countless messages, mostly from women, who felt like they were the only ones dealing with uncertainty as they transitioned into their thirties. Listening to my podcast made them feel less alone and they also got a better sense of who I was beyond radio.

But there was still more I wanted to explore. What is it about *thirty* that makes us all flip out? From *Bridget Jones's Diary* to *Sex and the City*, pop culture has wielded significant influence in shaping our perception of what it means to turn thirty – especially for women. Maybe it was sold to you as 'Thirty, flirty and thriving' by Jenna Rink in *Suddenly 30*.[1]

Or perhaps you know it as a distressed Rachel Green refusing to leave her bedroom in season 7, episode 14 of *Friends*, 'The One Where They All Turn Thirty'.

We have been raised in a milestone culture, encouraged to tick our way through life in a heteronormative fashion:

University. *Tick.*

Career. *Tick.*

Husband. *Tick.*

House. *Tick.*

Baby. *Tick.*

But the world is not the same as it was when our parents were growing up. And a lot has changed as *we* have grown up. Yet we still seem to be subconsciously tied to these life markers. As we cross the threshold into our thirties, we often find ourselves standing at a place where our elaborate dreams collide with the stark truths of adulthood.

I wrote this book not only to delve deeper into my own personal journey, but also to explore new voices and perspectives on the things that so many of us struggle with at this point in our lives. Unlike *How to Endo*, this is not a guide with tips and tricks. In fact, this book might leave you with more questions than answers (sorry!). But I want to offer my reflections to remind you that it is okay to still be figuring things out. That you are not alone in feeling scared, confused or frustrated. I want to take you through my highs and lows and rage at the bullshit but also empower you to reject any societal pressures of this decade. I want you to celebrate the lessons and the privilege that is ageing, thirty and beyond.

Speaking of, I also want to acknowledge my privilege as a middle-class, cisgender white woman and that my experience is not every experience. I know the hardships I have faced are minute compared

INTRODUCTION

to everything else happening in the world and within marginalised communities, but I do hope my words might resonate in some small way.

So, let's get into it! Starting with my 30th birthday, which, let's just say, went completely off script ...

SUDDENLY
(and unsoberly)
THiRTY

THIRTY IS LIKE A MIDYEAR REPORT CARD EXCEPT WE'RE GRADING OURSELVES ON HOW WELL WE ADULT.

Bridget Hustwaite
15h

Hello, dear friends. I'm turning 30 (?!) on the 10th of April and I'd really like to go out for dinner and drinks the night before. Doesn't have to get feral, although I will be drinking. But I can't get totally cooked as I need to be in Ballarat the next day lol.

Reader, I got totally cooked.

Waking up on my 30th birthday felt like I had washed up on a deserted island. The light through my bedroom blinds stung my eyes as I slowly regained consciousness, disoriented and completely unaware of the time. An ache pulsed through my skull, dull but persistent like a drum, each beat amplifying my discomfort and dehydration. It was a doof I absolutely could not get around. The stale scent of alcohol lingered in the air and I realised I could still taste it, a pungent medley of spirits clinging to the back of my tongue. Red wine. Espresso martinis. Gin and tonics. Shots. Rookie error. More indefensible, however, was drunk me failing to plug my phone into the charger. *You had one fucking job.*

FIGURING OUT THIRTY

My semi-naked body protested every movement as I tried to unravel the tangled sheets cocooning me. The room felt as wobbly as my attempt to walk up my apartment stairs a few hours earlier. That was one thing I remembered – kind of. My friend Georgia had dropped me home and waited patiently in the car as another friend, Charlie, helped me get inside. I couldn't remember the code to the door of my apartment building. It was like I was detached from my own body, swaying and entering random numbers as Charlie watched on, a helpless but humoured spectator. All he could do was hope I would snap out of my drunken trance. Which I did, eventually. 'I'm gonna say a good fifteen minutes,' he wrote on the Facebook event page I had created for the dinner, where I later asked for recollections of the night. 'It only took you about 106 attempts.'

The Facebook event was humbly titled 'Little 30th Dinner' with an innocent emoji hugging a love heart as the cover image. Innocent … or perhaps naive. After a tumultuous six weeks entailing a break-up, the tragic and unexpected death of a friend on the same day my debut book was released, and the upheaval of moving homes twice within a single month, this was supposed to have been a tame evening of celebration. The vomit hiding underneath my green Zara dress on the bathroom floor suggested otherwise. *I'll deal with that later*, I thought as I stumbled to the kitchen in frail pursuit of hydration. My trembling hands raised a glass of water to my lips, each sip holding the potential for some much-needed relief. After two forced swallows, I knew this hangover wasn't going to leave quietly.

The last day of my twenties had been a busy one. I was recording the audiobook for *How to Endo* and had taken the week off from working my evening radio show on triple j. With just over an hour to spare, I'd rushed home to my two-bedroom Brunswick apartment, which I was

SUDDENLY (AND UNSOBERLY) THIRTY

still unpacking from my second move in a month. With Justin Bieber's *Justice* playing through my phone speakers, I curled my hair and applied make-up. That was another thing I thought I would have figured out by thirty: how to apply make-up beyond the basic 2004 look entailing just foundation, bronzer and mascara. Even as I write this, I am still considering signing up to a make-up masterclass.

My birthday dinner dress from Zara had been purchased a few weekends earlier. It was a vibrant shade of green with a flowy skirt and a plunging neckline that required boob tape. Matched with a pair of cheap gold earrings, black ankle-strap heels and my black teddy bear jacket because, well, Melbourne. It was by no means an extravagant ensemble but it gave me the right dose of confidence I needed after The Big Break-Up. The colour popped in photos from that night and if there was one thing that past Bridge had done right, it was making the conscious effort to take a photo with each friend at dinner before things escalated. On my bathroom floor, though, the dress repped a less promising hue.

I was scheduled to be in Fitzroy by midday to collect some dining chairs I'd purchased on Facebook Marketplace, before driving home to Ballarat for dinner with my parents. Collapsing back into bed, I updated my Facebook status, seeking help with the errand: 'Friends of Facebook in Melbourne, I need a huge favour'.

A few replies came through, mostly to say happy birthday and sorry they couldn't help. One comment stung: 'Where's Mark in this dire situation?!' Nobody except my closest friends knew we had broken up. Our Facebook relationship status had been quietly removed and not shared on my feed, as it didn't feel like the kind of flex it would have been in my early twenties. I wasn't keen to flaunt my new-found singleness. I wasn't ready to mingle. I was gutted and embarrassed. But we'll get to that later.

I ended up confessing my hungover state to the seller from Facebook Marketplace who, to my surprise, applauded my efforts. 'Only way to bring in your thirties!' she wrote. We arranged another day for the chair collection. After sending a few shaky voice memos to some friends while staring at the ceiling, I went back to sleep before summoning the strength to seek refuge in the shower bathtub. Surely this would improve my state? Surely the warm water would cleanse my body and thoughts and bring an ounce of coherence to the fragmented memories of my birthday celebrations?

My birthday dinner had been at the Green Man's Arms, a charming corner pub nestled on the outskirts of Melbourne's renowned Lygon St, where its entirely vegetarian menu could seemingly cater to everyone's tastes and dietary requirements. The drinks flowed in my direction and, soon enough, I lost track of what I was consuming. The waitress carried out a small pudding-like dessert with a single green candle and everyone broke out into 'Happy Birthday'. I couldn't stop laughing – nothing was funny, I was just overwhelmed with joy and shock that I was even celebrating my 30th birthday. Six weeks ago, I'd had no intention of doing so, planning nothing more than a quiet dinner with my now ex-boyfriend. No fuss. But I needed this. I didn't want to make a speech but I stood up and told those twenty people just how much it meant to me that they were there for me. Someone then recommended a sassy dive bar down the road. I'd had no plans to head out, but I wasn't ready to leave the bubble of elation for my quiet apartment. Besides, where was the harm in one more drink?

It was the pickleback shot that sealed my fate. The final hour of my twenties was a blur. I remember sitting on a bar stool, telling a friend from work how badly I wanted her to take over my radio show when I was ready to move on. I remember sitting in the beer garden under

FOR SO LONG, WOMEN HAVE FOUGHT FOR MORE CHOICE, BUT CHOICE CAN PRESENT ITSELF AS A DOUBLE-EDGED SWORD. BECAUSE WITH THIS CHOICE COMES PRESSURE.

the fairy lights with another friend from my travel agent days, telling her how much I appreciated her friendship. I remember the flamboyant bartender carrying a pot glass with a sparkler out to me at midnight and everybody gathering around to sing 'Happy Birthday' once more.

I was thirty.

Apparently we hopped to another bar, fittingly called Bad Decisions. Georgia said we didn't stay long but had a little dance. It was the first time I had been drunk with my friends since being dumped and I wasn't sure where my emotions were going to take me. I could have easily swerved into Sad Girl territory, but instead I was Buoyant Birthday Bridge. I was also annoying, insisting to Charlie I'd lost my keys and wallet despite holding both in my hand. Sorry, Charlie! I knew he and Georgia were the only reason I got home when I did.

Now, the shower wasn't helping. I crawled out feeling even more fatigued than before. I texted Mum, who was awaiting my arrival in Ballarat: 'I'm hungover. I vomited on my bathroom floor. I'm still in bed and won't be able to drive until the afternoon.'

Her reply was somewhat sympathetic: 'I'd prefer if you tell Dad that you want us to come and get you, we are on holidays [school holiday break from work]. Was worried about you xo.'

I went back to sleep.

At around eleven, I ordered Uber Eats. One three-piece Chicken McNugget Happy Meal. Small Sprite with ice. Small fries. No dipping sauce. Keep it small, keep it bland. Due to COVID-19, delivery drivers weren't permitted to drop off straight to your door. You had to meet them outside. I could barely make the return trip to my kitchen, let alone all the way to the front entrance of my apartment building. But I was determined, convinced that the nuggets would cure me. Usually, the salty aroma would have been welcomed by my senses as a beacon of hope, but I felt my stomach churn. The ultimate betrayal from my body. I wailed and called Mum to tell her I couldn't muster the strength or sobriety to drive to Ballarat. 'We will come and get you. We've organised a surprise dinner for you,' was her response.

My heart sank with guilt. My parents and my oldest friend, Katie, had booked a private dining room with some of my closest hometown girlfriends. Balloons. Cake. One friend had even travelled two hours to be there. There was no getting out of this. I dragged myself to the bathroom for a second shower attempt and returned to my deathbed, awaiting my parents' arrival and judgement.

This was not the birthday I had envisioned for myself. My 30th birthday was supposed to mark a productive start to my thirties. I mean, a whole new decade in front of me, a fresh start after the shitshow of recent weeks … I had great expectations about making it count and couldn't help but feel like I had started on the wrong foot.

So, what is the big deal about *thirty*?

Well, it is probably the first time in our lives that we stop and reflect on everything we have done up until this point, how we feel about ourselves and what we want to do moving forward. It's natural to want to see how we're tracking with our life, relationships and goals. Thirty is like a midyear report card except we're grading ourselves on how well we adult. Most of us fear approaching it simply because we fear failure. Or rather, what society deems as failure.

Speaking to *British Vogue*, actress Emma Watson revealed she never understood why everyone made such a big fuss about turning thirty until approaching it herself. 'Cut to twenty-nine, I'm like, "Oh my god, I feel so stressed and anxious." And I realise there is suddenly this bloody influx of subliminal messaging around if you have not built a home, if you do not have a husband, if you do not have a baby, and you are turning thirty, and you're not in some incredibly secure, stable place in your career, or you're still figuring things out, there's just this incredible amount of anxiety.'[1]

Another reason why we fear thirty? The patriarchy. Duh! Still rearing its ugly head is the system that thrives on devaluing women as they age, deeming youthfulness as more desirable and tying our worth to our ability to fulfil more traditional, domestic roles. As America Ferrera expressed in her role of Gloria in Greta Gerwig's (award-winning, box-office-smashing, world-slaying) film *Barbie*: 'It is literally impossible to be a woman ... You have to never get old, never be rude, never show off, never be selfish, never fall down, never fail, never show fear, never get out of line.'[2]

Such a mood, hey?

NO WONDER DEPARTING OUR TWENTIES FEELS LIKE SUCH A RUDE AWAKENING.

It's the bit about never getting old that stuck out for me, because it seemed that as kids *all* we wanted to do was hit fast-forward and enjoy the perks of life as a grown-up. My first taste of FOMO was when we were approaching the new millennium and everyone was turning ten except me. 'I want to be ten! I want to turn ten in the year 2000 with everyone else!' I whined one night as I sat on the lap of my dad's mum, Nanny, in her quaint South Geelong flat. She would have thought

SUDDENLY (AND UNSOBERLY) THIRTY

I was being so dramatic, yet she provided comfort and a loving embrace as I wondered how I could possibly survive what felt like the biggest hardship of my life – youth.

FOMO crept in again during Year 12, but this time it felt more socially punishing than Y2K, as I scrambled for a somewhat convincing fake ID while my friends drove freely into their eighteenth year on their newly acquired P-plates and uploaded excessive photo albums of wild nights at clubs and bars to Facebook. The parties continued into our twenties as I farewelled home-cooked meals in Ballarat and embraced the independence of criminally overpriced student accommodation in Melbourne, where my diet mainly consisted of instant noodles and goon bags with cheap orange juice. Turning twenty-five came with jokes of a quarter-life crisis and an emerging limbo of feeling like an adult, but also … not. Almost like an entry-level adult, not yet *fully* qualified. It's 'The Space Between', as Michelle Andrews and Zara McDonald famously coined in their bestselling book of the same title, when you're 'still intimidated by quince paste but can appreciate the eclectic cushion arrangements at West Elm'.[3]

No wonder departing our twenties feels like such a rude awakening. Author Nell Frizzell described this transition as a period of personal crisis created by the world around us, which forces us to reassess, transform and make change. 'While in the midst of it, you feel as though you are twisting through a web of impossible decisions – about work, money, love, location, career, contraception and commitment' – she wrote in her bestselling book *The Panic Years* – 'each one pulling like a thread on all the others, impossible to untangle or move through without unravelling the whole thing.'[4]

Such impossible decisions are commonly considered to be the 'usual' markers of adulthood and they can be hella overwhelming, particularly when you don't know if you can see yourself veering towards those milestones, or as you scroll your Instagram feed and see highlight reel after highlight reel from those around you who appear to have it all together. We now not only grapple with comparison but also have to deal with something that women have not always possessed: choice. As society has progressed and gender norms have been challenged, women have had increased opportunities within the workforce, and been able to exercise more freedom within their relationships and general lifestyle. For so long, women have fought for more choice, but it can present itself as a double-edged sword. Because with it comes pressure.

While researching for this book, I came across an intriguing concept called the 'paradox of choice'.[5] Popularised by American psychologist Barry Schwartz, the paradox of choice refers to the idea that while having many options can initially be perceived as positive, too much choice can lead to negative consequences and decision-making difficulties. Choice can liberate but it can also debilitate. Often where there is choice, there is also sacrifice. This is reflected in a theory described by David Sedaris called the Four Burner Theory.[6] Imagine a stovetop with four burners. These burners represent different aspects of your life:

Family: This burner is our time and energy devoted to partners, children, parents, siblings and other extended family members.
Friends: This burner refers to social relationships outside of the family, such as friendships, social circles and community involvement.
Health: This burner is our physical and mental wellbeing – exercise, nutrition, stress management and overall self-care.
Work: This burner symbolises our career, professional ambitions and financial stability derived from work-related pursuits.

SUDDENLY (AND UNSOBERLY) THIRTY

The Four Burner Theory suggests that we often struggle to keep all four burners running optimally because there's a finite amount of time, energy and resources available. So, in order to really slay in one area, we may need to tone it down somewhere else. Have you ever felt a pull between progressing in your career and your capacity as a caregiver or your desire to start a family? Have you ever feared that embracing a fitness routine might compromise nights out with friends and result in you drifting apart? These are the kinds of multifaceted challenges that aren't considered when we are told by people like American writer and editor Helen Gurley Brown that 'women can have it all'.[7]

If we're supposed to have it all – and have it all figured out by thirty – this puts immense pressure on the milestone itself. Now add the confusion of turning thirty in the midst of a global pandemic. While a lot of my friends were very happy to have their 30ths fly under the radar, they didn't feel the effects of entering a new decade until a new normal way of life had resumed. New York writer Katy Schneider dubbed this the 'pandemic skip', which is defined as the strange sensation that our bodies might be a step out of sync with our minds.[8] Schneider wrote about her friend who had started the pandemic at age twenty-nine and now wanted to make up for the time she had lost. Travel, work, dinners – she wanted to do all the things a young and carefree city gal would want to do. But she also wanted children and felt like she needed to settle down soon. 'I'm really thirty-one in my head [but thirty-three in age], which is a problem, because now I actually don't have time for my brain to catch up with my body,'[9] Schneider's friend said.

For each interview that I record for my podcast, I start by asking my guests to think back to when they were growing up and what they envisioned for themselves at the age of thirty. Then I ask them to share the reality of their life at thirty. I love watching them pause and ponder everything they have achieved and experienced in life so far. I love seeing their thoughts play out in their facial expressions, wondering if this is where they thought they would be by now, and how different it is to what they had pictured. Some guests answer quickly, others need more time. But there is a common thread – not one guest so far has been able to perfectly reconcile their expectations with their reality.

It's also important to acknowledge just how heteronormative this whole idea of the thirty-year milestone is, especially when we are talking about marriage and children. Despite how much society has progressed, we still seem to subscribe to this archaic ideal of a white picket fence and nuclear family, a vision that no longer resonates with many people.

A particularly sobering response came from Sean Szeps, who is a podcast host and author of *Not Like Other Dads*. When Sean had imagined his thirties, he'd come up with two scenarios. The first was living a lie: getting married and having children with a woman. 'The second option, which I guess is the darker one, is that I wouldn't be here by my thirties. I wouldn't survive. The narrative surrounding gay people when I was a kid was death. When I was a really young kid, all I wanted was exactly what I have now in my thirties, but for such a long time, for decades, I just didn't allow myself to dream of it.'[10]

I posed the same question to my listeners on Instagram.

EMMA, 30
Expectations: Happily married with kids
Reality: Forever single and still in a share house

CHRISTINE, 30
Expectations: Married, kids, home ownership, stable career and have travelled
Reality: Some travel, figuring out career, long-distance relationship

ALEISHA, 31
Expectations: Stay-at-home mum with three kids
Reality: Married (kept last name), no kids but a rescue dog, focusing on career and travel

KATE, 32
Expectations: Married and mother of two kids, happy with job
Reality: Engaged, unhappy with job, endometriosis diagnosis and a miscarriage

ROSE, 32
Expectations: Married with two kids
Reality: Living in London, chasing career goals

LIZ, 31
Expectations: Engaged
Reality: Single, living in lockdown at parents' house

AMY, 32
Expectations: Married, teacher, mother of two children
Reality: De facto, teacher, endometriosis diagnosis and fertility issues

CLAIRE, 39
Expectations: Dead due to cystic fibrosis
Reality: Engaged, needing new lungs

BROOKE, 32
Expectations: Established career
Reality: Still finishing master's degree

JENNA, 36

Expectations: Married, homeowner with children

Reality: Divorced, renting and freezing eggs solo

ELLE, 34

Expectations: Married with kids, still in Brisbane

Reality: New boyfriend seven years younger, two dogs, supporting each other to build our respective careers

NIKKI, 31

Expectations: Married with kids

Reality: Homeowner, two dogs, dating again

As for me, by thirty I thought I would have bigger boobs, longer nails (sadly still a biter), children, a husband, a house and a uni degree. Instead, I had a five-year relationship break down, endometriosis, anxiety, a national live radio show, a bestselling book and two rental leases bleeding my wallet dry.

You know what else I had? One of the worst hangovers of my life.

Eventually, Mum and Dad arrived at my door. There was no judgement, just determination to get me home. I moved as slowly as a sloth, trying to gather some clothes to pack as Mum guided me to the car. I slumped against the back seat and applied a face sheet mask like a lifeline. Mum handed me a Hydralyte and we sat in gentle silence until we reached Ballarat, where I collapsed on the couch until it was time to get ready.

That night, as I stepped into the private dining room where my friends and two big silver balloons in the shape of 3-0 awaited me, I feigned a look of surprise. They wouldn't know I had prior knowledge of the dinner unless they happen to be reading this now. So, to my friends: sorry for the charade, but also, thank you for coming ILYSM!

Seated at the table, I looked on as everybody ordered delicious chicken parmas and pastas but could barely bring myself to touch the steamed vegetables and chips in front of me. It was a grim sight, but I was grateful.

What I lost in brain cells on my 30th birthday I gained in a newfound appreciation of the magic and complexity that is the spectrum of human emotion. I was feeling *so* many things. Grieving expectations that hadn't been met and what could have been. Feeling the pain of loss and change. Mourning a relationship, lifestyle and routine. But simultaneously, I felt so damn full with the support and kindness of friends and family who reminded me of my worth and the potential of starting a new decade completely afresh. This was the sign I needed. Sure, there would be struggles and things not going to plan, but I was hopeful that there would also be some lovely surprises along the way.

THE BIG BREAK-UP 2

> **HEARTBREAK HITS DIFFERENT, ESPECIALLY WHEN YOU'RE SIX WEEKS SHY OF TURNING THIRTY.**

They say the older you get, the higher the stakes.

I was twenty when my first serious boyfriend and I ended things after nearly two years together. There were tears and there were silly drunken nights where we would reunite for a casual hook-up, followed by some dumb, insignificant (and incoherent) argument, but at the end of the day, I never saw myself marrying the guy. The end of that relationship never felt like the end of the world.

Fast-forward nearly a decade and I have learned that break-ups involve more than throwing out the spare toothbrush, collecting whatever clothes you left at theirs and moving on. This time around, there was a whole house of shared possessions to divide up, a brand-new rental contract to break and a new home to find. The unravelling of routines and habits that were built together across five years. A love was lost and, perhaps more significantly, a sense of self.

Heartbreak hits different, especially when you're six weeks shy of turning thirty.

Let me take you back to that fateful night in 2021. I was sitting in the taxi on my way home from work, my arms crossed tightly across my abdomen, nursing the cramps kindly provided by day two of my period.

It was the last Wednesday in February and despite the hellish aches, I was relieved they were happening now rather than in six days, coinciding with the official release of my first book, *How to Endo*. With full-time radio commitments and press interviews filling the upcoming month, I had little (read: zero) patience for such discomfort. Plus, there was still a lot to unpack in the new townhouse that my boyfriend, who we shall call Mark, and I had just moved into three weeks prior.

In the lead-up to our five-year anniversary, we had decided to move slightly further north of Melbourne, from Coburg to Reservoir. For the past two years, our home had been a modern two-bedroom apartment within the walls of Pentridge Prison. Yep, a jail. It closed in 1997 but the giant bluestone walls remained, our balcony overlooking a set of outdoor cells. Bit of character, ya know?

Throughout the process of inspecting, applying and moving into our new townhouse, things had felt tense and distant between us. We weren't affectionate, our backs facing each other as we slept. Mark kept to his study, even when I came home from work, and I was struggling to regulate my stress leading up to the release of my book. I would not have been fun to be around, especially when I had period and endometriosis pain, but I never expected what was to come.

As my taxi driver made his way across the Bolte Bridge, I stared out of the window at the glimmering Melbourne skyline and thought about how keen I was to turn things around. I decided I would be more explicit in expressing my gratitude to Mark and to push through my period pain. I would be more positive. Earlier that day, I had received an email from a local artist who sounded like a modern version of Oasis and YUNGBLUD, sharing an advance stream of his next single. Mark *loved* this guy and I had been counting down the hours until I could wrap up work and play him the new song. My cramps worsened as we continued

THE BIG BREAK-UP

north of the city so I messaged Mark, asking if he could start running a bath for me.

'Hello!' I chirped as I walked inside.

I heard Mark's footsteps come down the stairs from the bathroom. 'Hey. Can we talk?'

He sounded distant. I could hear it in his voice before he even spoke the words.

We entered the kitchen and stood on either side of the benchtop, the tap upstairs running in the background.

'I can't do this anymore,' he said softly.

> **BREAK-UPS INVOLVE MORE THAN THROWING OUT THE SPARE TOOTHBRUSH, COLLECTING WHATEVER CLOTHES YOU LEFT AT THEIRS AND MOVING ON.**

Tears fell down his face as he told me his heart was no longer in it and he had been feeling this way for a while. I asked why he hadn't said something four months ago when I had expressed my own unhappiness, or on one of the other occasions I'd checked in to see if he was happy for us to move and commit to a brand-new lease. He said he couldn't bring himself to acknowledge how he was feeling. He said he knew that I could be happier without him.

I asked if there was anything I could do to change his mind.

'No. I'm not flipping like last time.'

Ouch.

We'd met while we were both living in share houses six years prior, mine in the suburb of Burnley and his in Alphington. After joining the casual roster on triple j, I wanted to fully commit to my new role so I moved back home to Learmonth, a small country town twenty minutes out of Ballarat, to shack up with the parents. It was no longer viable to bounce between a demanding full-time stint at Student Flights and the graveyard radio shift I usually did. And I wanted to be available whenever triple j needed someone to fill in for a show.

Mark relocated back to his parents' home, about an hour north of Melbourne, to be closer to his work and save money. The distance between us was just shy of a two-hour drive, but we made it work and spent most of our weekends together. Then, at the end of 2017, I was offered the hosting role of my dream program. The catch? I would have to move to Sydney, where the main headquarters of the station was based.

If you know me from triple j, you will know I obviously accepted it, but there was no way Mark was going to move with me. I didn't blame him. He had a secure job teaching music at the high school he'd attended and had spent years building up a loyal base of guitar students. It would have been too much for him to ditch that and start from scratch in Sydney.

Two weeks before my interstate move, Mark dropped an unexpected bombshell: he wanted to break up. It happened right after I had finished a summer evening shift, a timeslot mirroring what I would soon be undertaking in my new role as host of *Good Nights*. I'd got into my car to drive back to Ballarat and dialled his number. My enthusiasm was met with a palpable sense of unease.

'I feel sick.' He sounded faint over the phone.

'Oh, what kind of sick, babe? Tummy?'

There was a pause. 'About us.'

Panic surged through me. 'Oh, we're going to make this work, it's going to be fine,' I insisted.

'I'm sorry.'

The weight of those words hit me like a ton of bricks. 'What? You can't just break up with me over the phone. I'm coming over.'

'I'm sorry,' he repeated, his voice heavy with regret.

I felt as though I had been sucker-punched, left winded by the suddenness and gravity of the situation.

Slamming my foot on the accelerator, I sped along the Hume Highway to his parents' house. I was sobbing when his mum opened the door. She hugged me before I went to Mark, who took me into his room. The rest of the visit was a blur. Mark wouldn't let me drive home to Ballarat in such a heightened emotional state, so I stayed the night.

Instead of focusing and preparing for my move to begin my dream job, the next couple of weeks were spent trying to convince Mark that we could make it work. I was suffocating in my sadness but I tried to be understanding, patient and supportive, giving him time to think things through.

To my shame, I recognised that there was another way I could potentially save the relationship: sex. Driven by desperation and fuelled by my profound insecurities and fear of abandonment, I threw on my horny hat, hoping that physical intimacy would persuade Mark to stay. It's a sad reality and one I'm not proud to admit to, but unfortunately it's something many women understand all too well: the extent to which we equate our value with our ability to satisfy men's desires. Lo and behold, Mark had a change of heart and decided he wanted us to spend New Year's Eve together with his family down by the beach. He would fly with me to Sydney and help me settle into my new share house that I'd found on Flatmate Finders, and we would pursue an interstate relationship.

We vowed to make it work but Sydney left me feeling depressed – to the point where a doctor diagnosed me with seasonal depression. After four months in my new role, I approached management and informed them of my decision to move back to Melbourne by the end of the year. They had eight months to determine whether I could take the show with me. In the meantime, I made the journey home to Melbourne once a month, and at times even twice, for a brief 48-hour period to be with Mark. A cycle that involved finishing work at 10.30 p.m. on the Friday night, flying to Melbourne at 6 a.m. and returning to Sydney at 6 a.m. on the Monday morning, before starting work at midday.

At the end of 2018, I was allowed to return to Melbourne with my radio show in tow, and Mark and I moved in together. It was fun and exciting; we often had music playing and were building a joint collection of vinyl. If we weren't out at a gig, we would be home playing Mario Kart or Tony Hawke Pro Skater. There were also some adjustments, like our differing schedules. I would usually get home from work between 9.30 p.m. and 10.30 p.m., which was when Mark would be getting ready for bed, as he needed to get up at 5 a.m. I wouldn't join him in bed for another hour or two after I had fully unwound and, honestly, it was difficult for me to get to sleep with his relentless snoring every night, which he wasn't interested in fixing. We only had one car space and Mark needed a vehicle due to his daily commute, so I gave up my car and found myself relying on him whenever I needed to go and do something. Sure, first-world problems, but it evoked a sense of regression, akin to the feeling of being dependent on your parents to get around. This was a dynamic I struggled to reconcile at the age of twenty-eight.

The onset of COVID-19 lockdowns in 2020 brought forth numerous

> AS HEARTBROKEN AND OVERWHELMED AS I FELT, I HAD TO PUT ON MY GAME FACE AND TACKLE THE LOGISTICS OF WHAT WAS TO COME.

challenges. As schools toggled between on-site and remote learning, our second bedroom morphed into a makeshift music room, the strumming of guitars echoing through the walls. Meanwhile, I found myself writing *How to Endo* primarily from the couch in our living area. It wasn't all bad and we did our best, but as the days wore on, I began to feel increasingly confined and irritated. Despite appearing outgoing on air, I often require moments of solitude. In our apartment, I felt trapped and, like for many others, the pandemic exacerbated existing tensions in our relationship. I knew Mark was stressed about his work and felt pressure to show up for his students as a positive, encouraging figure, despite feeling just as uncertain about it all. And I was also in pain. My endometriosis felt like it had become worse following my surgery in 2018, and I went in for a second procedure, which had me off work for a month. There had also been moments of unease around how we valued honesty that made it difficult for me to feel completely secure in our relationship.

Four months prior to The Big Break-Up, I confronted Mark about my unhappiness and admitted I had been looking at one-bedroom rentals, contemplating the prospect of living alone. I knew this was a red flag, yet I was unwilling to concede that our relationship might be faltering. Doing so felt like failure and I wanted to make it work. Although Mark said he wouldn't stop me from moving out on my own, I suggested finding a larger space, preferably on the north side to ease his commute. He agreed, and so I took on the task of searching for suitable properties, eventually finding a modern three-bedroom townhouse twenty minutes north.

Back in the kitchen that night though, my cramps were getting worse and the bathwater was still running upstairs. Mark said he would stay at his parents' house and left. Little did I know that this would be our last face-to-face conversation.

THE BIG BREAK-UP

I pulled myself up the stairs and immediately messaged a few of my closest friends. I also messaged my boss to let her know I needed the next two days off. In the space of twenty-four hours, I had gone from crying on Mark's shoulder due to my period pain, to crying alone in the bathtub, nursing my cramping stomach and mourning the end of a five-year relationship. I thought we'd figure it out. I was prepared to take responsibility for my part in the tension and to really make an effort. But Mark was done.

My emotions unravelled when I started thinking about the next steps. I felt so hurt and angry that he was doing this to me before another huge professional milestone, this time six days before my book came out. We still had boxes to unpack and I had spent thousands of dollars on new furniture. Why was he doing this now, when we were previously on a month-to-month lease and could have made a smooth exit? What was our new real estate agent going to think of us breaking this contract three weeks after signing it? Where was I going to live? As heartbroken and overwhelmed as I felt, I had to put on my game face and tackle the logistics of what was to come.

The next morning, I went to pick up my brand-new car that I had purchased a few weeks earlier. Perhaps Mark had been waiting for me to get my own vehicle before dumping me, so I at least had a way of getting around. As I jumped into the Uber, 'Save Your Tears' by The Weeknd was playing. *For fuck's sake*, I thought. Tears streamed down my cheeks, hidden behind my face mask. They wouldn't stop. When the car dealer insisted on snapping a photo of me beside my new car, I feigned a smile and attributed my teary eyes to hayfever. Determined to keep pushing through, I went to the physio to have my wrist checked for carpal tunnel, a consequence of writing my book on my laptop from the couch, then drove home to Ballarat, where I would allow myself two days of mourning. I needed to get it out of my system so I could focus on my book and celebrate my hard work.

As I passed through the town centre of Ballarat, I popped into a bookstore and bought their last copy of Zoë Foster Blake's *Break-up Boss*. I got a pedicure, debriefed with my oldest friend, Katie, as we walked the local lake, and cried into the bowl of pasta that Mum made for dinner. I was also quick to jump onto the real estate app to look for a new rental; there was absolutely no way I was going to stay in this Reservoir townhouse. I had to find a small apartment where I could live alone and start fresh. I signed up to inspect a small two-bedroom apartment in Brunswick for the following Saturday.

I woke up that morning and made my way back to Melbourne, the sun rising as I drove my new car along the quiet freeway with my friend Georgia's playlist blaring through the speakers. She had named it 'delete men', featuring all of our girls – Miley, Dua, Cher, Ariana and Little Mix, to name a few. Tears rolled down my face as Miley belted the chorus of 'Midnight Sky', which I repeated out loud like words of affirmation.

While I was scared to leave the safety net of my parents' house and familiarity of my hometown, I had no choice but to put on my Big Girl Pants and return to the harsh reality that awaited me in Melbourne. The repercussions of my failed relationship loomed large and felt like time wasted, but Queen Miley helped me replace my devastation with determination. I was not going to waste a second more. I was going to be the kind of break-up boss that Zoë Foster Blake would be proud of. I was going to get this rental. I was going to smash out this book press. I was going to come into this new era like a bloody wrecking ball.

The week of my book release began on a positive note with news that I had been approved for the Brunswick apartment. But on that same morning, I found myself confronting our existing real estate agent, who had received an email from Mark informing her of our decision to break the lease. 'What is going on?!' she exclaimed, clearly taken aback. I didn't know what else to say so I fessed up and disclosed The Big Break-Up.

Her reaction was unexpected and lowkey iconic. One moment she was a professional real estate agent and the next she was hyping me up, much like what you do with strangers in the girls' bathroom of a nightclub. Her energy shifted dramatically as she launched into a rant about men, even divulging details of her own love life and encounters with a 'toy boy'. While her openness caught me off guard, I had no choice but to stan how hilariously unhinged and supportive she was.

Tuesday came around and my book hit the shelves. It would be a big day of back-to-back radio interviews before hosting my own show. I received a message from Mark at 4.49 a.m. His message of congrats was the first I received that day, and in it he acknowledged how hard he had made things for me and how sorry he was that this was all happening at the same time. It was a really lovely message. I didn't expect to hear from him again at 8.01 a.m.

'Did you hear the news? I'm really sorry to hear about Gudinski.'

I didn't know what he was talking about. For the past six-odd months, I had been working with Michael Gudinski on a music TV show called *The Sound* and he would frequently call for a yarn. He was arguably the most influential person in Australian music and a huge supporter of mine, who had welcomed me into his Mushroom record label family. I discovered through a Google search that he had unexpectedly passed away. Our last phone call was only a fortnight earlier. My chest felt heavy. I was at work early to do some breakfast radio interviews, so thankfully nobody was around to see me break down in one of the meeting rooms. Quickly composing myself, I headed into the Tardis booth to chat with an interstate ABC program about my book.

The rest of the day was a blur: my eyes were literally blurry with tears. I remember receiving flowers and continuing the trend of crying into my food, this time a cake that my friend Moon had organised. I was exhausted and fragile but had to get my own radio show done. All I remember of it was breaking down on air when I spoke about Michael's death. Beyond his professional mentoring, he had my back on a personal level. At a live music recording a few months prior, he'd sought out Mark, who was playing guitar for another artist. 'Right, which one of you is Bridget's partner?' he'd bellowed across the stage of the Sidney Myer Music Bowl during soundcheck, to which Mark stepped forward and nervously raised his hand. 'Don't you fuck her around. She's a good woman,' Gudinski asserted, lightly tapping Mark across the cheek. 'I hope the ghost of Gudinski haunts you,' I half-jokingly texted my new ex.

In *Break-up Boss*, Zoë Foster Blake insists that the only way to truly move on from heartbreak is by cutting all ties with your former lover.[1] I remember reading this during my pedicure, just around the corner from my parents' house, and initially thinking it was a bit extreme. It was also not currently possible in my case, as Mark and I had so much to organise with the lease and the division of our belongings. Beyond that, we had gone through so much together. How do you just let all that go? *Surely* we could be friends one day, right?

Wrong. As the weeks passed, I became more and more frustrated with how much I was doing in terms of real estate correspondence, selling and dividing furniture, and organising the cleaning. Mark had told me he would make this process as easy as possible for me, but I felt like he was letting me down with his lack of initiative. The real estate agent couldn't find anyone to take over our lease so I was paying double rent and stressing the fuck out as this dragged on and on. The cherry on top came two months after The Big Break-Up, when Mark soft-launched his new relationship with the dance teacher at the school he taught music at. When I confronted him about this particular timeline of events I was blocked by him everywhere except email, where we had to continue correspondence for *another* two months until our lease break was finally settled. By this point, I couldn't have been more excited to embrace Zoë's rule.

While I'm sure we hold differing perspectives, I think it's safe to say that we both had our flaws in this relationship. I can recognise where I projected my insecurities, struggled to regulate my emotions and ultimately set myself up to fail by convincing myself that Mark was The One. I had placed him on a pedestal with unrealistic expectations. Deep down, I knew that I had settled in this relationship because that's what I thought I had to do by thirty. In fact, it was quite easy to realise that I too had been unhappy. I hadn't even challenged Mark when he said he thought that I would be happier without him. What was hard was deciding what to do with that knowledge. Because the older you get, the higher the stakes.

Let's quickly unpack that.

In the realm of relationships, patriarchal structures have ingrained a fear in women of navigating life independently. Media and pop culture have further reinforced this by promoting the notion that true fulfilment can only be achieved through romantic love. There is no happy ending without it. As we age, the pain of staying in a less than satisfying relationship seems more manageable than the pain of leaving, and settling down seems less scary than a new beginning. Forget FOMO, it's the fear of *starting over*. Forty-five per cent of singles surveyed by dating blog Plenty of Fish reported experiencing FOSO, with 44 per cent indicating it was the reason for prolonging a doomed relationship.[2] Starting over not only can be emotionally overwhelming, but also can be made nearly impossible for some women because of logistical challenges.

FIGURING OUT THIRTY

Consider the economic and historical barriers to education, employment opportunities and property ownership. In the 1960s, Australian women couldn't apply for a mortgage or obtain a chequebook without their husband's permission. The 2016 Census revealed that older women were the fastest-growing demographic experiencing homelessness in Australia, with a 10 per cent increase in women and girls experiencing homelessness by 2021.[3] As the Mercy Foundation notes, women over fifty-five are at great risk of financial and housing insecurity due to systemic and compounding factors, such as lack of superannuation, working part-time or casually throughout their lives, taking time out of the workforce to care for family and bearing the brunt of the gender pay gap.[4] Understandably, a lot of women for a long freaking time have been shitting themselves at the thought of starting over, because the systems that have been in place have historically never supported doing such a thing.

Despite always being firm in the belief that a failed relationship does not make *you* a failure, on the cusp of the big 3-0, a time where I thought I should have all this shit ticked off and figured out, I felt like a complete fuck-up. So many people around me were getting engaged or building homes and here I was getting my ass dumped. Even though I had been unhappy with Mark, it still hurt to face the ultimate rejection by the one person who knew me better than anyone else. I was embarrassed to say that I was broken up with, because it made me feel like there was something wrong with *me*. But if you asked now whether I'd rather have my heart broken or break his, I'd choose the former. I needed him to end the relationship, because I couldn't do it myself. Entering a new decade amplified the fear of the unknown and consequently the fear of navigating it alone, so I held on for dear life, unable to take that leap. He had to push me. Yes, the fall was slow and painful. Yes, it was disruptive to my life and my self-imposed timeline, but my god it was necessary.

THE BIG BREAK-UP

Plus, imagine the fuckery if we'd had more to deal with beyond a lease break and splitting our belongings. Imagine if we'd had a mortgage, a bank account or a child together. It could have been waaay messier. The stakes could have been much higher! It didn't take too long to realise that I had been gifted the opportunity to treat my thirties as a much-needed reset and canvas for self-discovery.

Charlotte Ree, author of *Heartbake*,[5] echoed a similar sentiment on my podcast when she spoke about break-ups and what changed when she split up from her husband. 'I spent so long trying to be everything to everyone else that I didn't realise I can actually be what I need,' she said. 'Even my work in therapy at the moment is my therapist saying to me, "You know, if this relationship doesn't work out, you know you're going to be okay, right? You've just gone through these three years of actually realising you do have to look after yourself." And I do ... I'm so excited to meet my future self, and I mean that in every sense of the word. Failing is so exciting. I have fucked up so much in the last three years and been so mad at myself in so many different ways. But I kid you not: every single day I say to myself, "I am so proud of you, Charlotte," because we're all just doing our best. Broken people in a broken world doing our best, and for me, all I want to do is find joy. I'm going to stuff up along the way, but I'll have fun while I'm doing it.'[6]

So yeah, heartbreak does hit different on the cusp of thirty. Emotionally, logistically and (annoyingly) societally. A love was lost, but you know what was gained? A whole lotta growth. And with that, a newer, *truer* sense of self.

Turns out that The Big Break-Up would in fact be The Big Break-Through that I needed.

> **HEARTBREAK IS AN OPPORTUNITY TO GET TO KNOW YOURSELF AND TO LOVE YOURSELF.**

BRIDGE'S *unsolicited* PEP TALK ON HEARTBREAK

- **Tell your friends.** As soon as I was dumped, I messaged five of my closest friends and told them I wasn't okay and that I would be leaning on them for support. They were all SO amazing, because that's what friends are for, right? Make sure you have a solid support network around you because you will need it.

- **Journal.** I've never been one to journal but after getting dumped, I whipped out an empty notepad straight away and jotted down my thoughts and feelings. I just needed to get them out of my system. Journalling is such a healthy outlet, so write whatever you need to write! I mostly journalled every night when I jumped into bed and even started compiling lists like 'Things to love about being single' and 'Why he wasn't good for me'. I would write the most superficial stuff, like how I could now buy pink bedding! Journalling can provide a safe space to prioritise your fears and concerns, help with processing emotions and give you a sense of control over your feelings. It might even save you from sending an impulsive message that you later regret.

- **Out of sight, out of mind (kinda).** I didn't agree with Zoë Foster Blake at first, but I think she was right. Cut off all ties with your ex. Remove them from your socials. Adopt a no-contact rule. It really does help speed up the healing process and can help you regain your strength, self-esteem and confidence. Plus, you won't be able to see if they have a new partner or if they're on holidays and living their best life. You don't need to see that shit. Obviously it's harder if kids and pets are involved, but if you don't have that stuff, just cut ties straight away. In her book, Foster Blake talked about how we might want to keep communication open to get closure. But she also noted the very true reality that we may just never get it.[1] A lot of how we respond to a break-up comes back to us and how we value ourselves.

- **Immerse yourself in books and podcasts.** I found books to be a powerful escape during The Break-Up, especially in the still of night, and podcasts were great little pep talks on my daily walks. One podcast I loved in particular was *Do You F*cking Mind?* by Alexis Fernandez. Alexis feels like that honest friend who will give you tough love. She's about facts, she doesn't beat around the bush, and I think that's something we need when coming out of a relationship. A lot of the content Alexis was covering helped me realise how I was viewing myself and valuing my own worth and how that has played into my relationships. She's also got a master's in neuroscience so she's not talking out of her ass!

- **Exercise.** I'm not saying you need to go smash an F45 class, but if you want to, by all means slay. For others, the simple act of walking can be so, so powerful – Chrissie Swan is an epic example of this. Speaking on *The Imperfects* podcast, Chrissie said she had a realisation at the age of forty-five that she was halfway to dying and wondered whether she was really happy with what she was doing with her life. So, she started walking every day. Chrissie said it changed her entire life, giving her an outlet to process tough decisions and situations. 'Every day I walk, if there's anything troubling me.'[2]

- **Consider avoiding alcohol.** I don't want to sound condescending when I say this, but I didn't want to reach for a bottle of wine during The Big Break-Up – even though I probably deserved fifty bottles! I knew drinking would make me feel worse about myself and I wanted to tackle all of the heartache and rejection with clarity and a sober mind. The only messy night was my 30th, but other than that, I was proud of my desire to push through the discomfort and uncertainty on my own. Of course, there are probably going to be some nights where you're like, *Fuck I really need a drink*. And that's okay. I would just encourage you to sit with the feeling for a moment first and ask yourself: Why do I want to drink? How is this going to make me feel? How am I going to feel in the morning? Is this worth it?

    I had a great podcast chat with author and journalist Jill Stark about sobriety. She said the worst thing about sobriety is that you get to feel all your feelings, and the best thing about sobriety is that you get to *feel* all your feelings! 'Sobriety doesn't remove your problems, it illuminates them. It shines a flashlight on them and you have to have the courage to look at that,' she told me. 'Yes, I feel all the other feelings, the tough feelings, but I'm so much more equipped to deal with them.'[3]

- **Therapy!** I totally acknowledge that this isn't the most accessible tip given the stressed, underfunded and under-resourced state of our healthcare system, but if you can, get a mental healthcare plan from your GP. Sitting and speaking with a professional and learning more about myself and why I react to things the way I do has been a game changer. In a way, I wanted to take control of The Big Break-Up and turn it into my Personal Debrief. It was a time in my life when I could solely focus on me and gain confidence, and identify my strengths and weaknesses.

- **Time, take it!** Let's not sugarcoat it, break-ups are a Really! Big! Experience! In fact, there is such a thing as broken heart syndrome. Yep, also known as stress cardiomyopathy or takotsubo syndrome, it's a temporary heart condition triggered by intense emotional or physical stress. It can even mimic the symptoms of a heart attack, like chest pain and shortness of breath, but typically doesn't involve blocked arteries. The condition is believed to be caused by a surge of stress hormones that temporarily disrupt the heart's normal pumping function, leading to the characteristic shape of the left ventricle resembling a Japanese octopus trap, or 'takotsubo', on imaging scans.[4]

    Plus, ignore what Charlotte York said on *Sex and the City*: that it apparently takes half the total time you went out with someone to get over them.[5] Such an oversimplified calculation fails to recognise any complexity of human emotion or context. No relationship is the same! Some people might only need a few months while some people might need a few years. There is no singular, straightforward frame of reference here: heartbreak is a highly personal journey.

To sum up, there will be moments when you will feel devastated and crushed and like everything is falling apart and you're never going to recover. That said, not to get all Toxic Positivity on you, but heartbreak is also an opportunity. An opportunity to get to know yourself and to love yourself. To establish your true needs and what you want moving forward. I absolutely believe that with every relationship breakdown, there comes a breakthrough. I recommend using this time on *you*

THE BIG BREAK-UP

because you won't always get that time to spend on yourself. Honour your feelings. Be kind to yourself and – just like the Leona Lewis song I heard as I roamed the shopping aisles for cleaning products upon obtaining the keys to my apartment, aka a sign from the universe – it will all get better in time. Promise!

SATURN RETURN

> **SATURN RETURN IS LIKE BEING MET WITH THE FEELING THAT YOU'RE NO LONGER WHO YOU ONCE WERE, BUT YOU AREN'T QUITE SURE OF WHO YOU ARE YET EITHER.**

Fair to say that there was a bit going on for me in the lead-up to turning thirty, but the good news was that I found out a name for all the shit hitting the fan! Yay!

I came across it one night after work when I was curled up in bed with a book. Man, books *really* saved me during The Big Break-Up. Although it happened during one of the busiest periods of my life, my hectic schedule still wasn't enough to distract me from the stillness of the nights. Sometimes I would *really* take my time finishing up work just to avoid the quiet that met me upon entering my new rental apartment. Transitioning from the lively studio, where music filled the air for three straight hours and listeners engaged through calls and messages on the text line, to the eerie silence of my new living space became my nightly struggle.

It was during these late hours on my own that negative thoughts would creep in, plunging me into a spiral of self-doubt and despair. I dwelled on every misstep, questioned my worth and concluded that I must be utterly unlovable for someone to literally walk out on me. I wanted to hold myself accountable for how I had acted during the relationship, but the hatred and blame I placed on myself was next level.

To ward off these toxic narratives, I turned to books as an escape alongside journalling: I needed to keep my broken heart and mind busy. From Dolly Alderton's *Ghosts* and *Everything I Know About Love* to Jessie Stephens's *Heartsick*, I was desperate to find solace in someone else's story. Except I wouldn't recommend reading *Heartsick* straight after a break-up – brilliant book but damn, I was probably too raw for it.

One book I held close was *Of Gold and Dust* by Australian jewellery designer and entrepreneur Samantha Wills. We shared the same publication date and, less fortunately, an endometriosis diagnosis. Samantha posted about my book and I posted about hers, which was really nice. We both wanted to see a fellow endo warrior succeed!

Samantha's memoir gave such a heartfelt and intriguing insight into her creative life, but it also revealed more personal truths about her upbringing and relationships. Halfway through the book, I came across a chapter called 'Saturn return'. Underneath the title, beautifully handwritten in calligraphy by Samantha, was the definition: 'In horoscopic astrology, an astrological transit that occurs when the planet Saturn returns to the same place in the sky it occupied at the moment of a person's birth; the influence of the Saturn return is considered to start in the person's late twenties.'[1]

My eyes were fixed on the final two words: late twenties. I dog-eared the page and continued reading as Samantha detailed how she had found it hard to make friends amid all her global travel, and how she had made the biggest mistake of her entire career by changing everything about her jewellery brand to try to fit into a new market. 'Rather than staying true to who we were, I started to design products for who I thought we should be.' When I look back on that sentence, I can see how it can be applied to so many things, like how we might try to design our lives a certain way in our late twenties, attempting to follow the script that society tells us to follow as opposed to making decisions based on who we really are.

The book transported me back to the end of 2011, when Samantha was twenty-nine. She had returned home to Australia for Christmas and was catching up with an old friend she used to work with at the local surf shop. Seven years of lost time was condensed into a few drinks at a bar in Bondi and led to Samantha's friend recommending a clairvoyant named Sandra. The following week, Samantha drove an hour to the western suburbs of Sydney to meet Sandra and her tarot cards. At first, Samantha was sceptical and made sure not to share her surname so that there would be no sneaky googling of her profile. But the things Sandra knew were not things you could find online – from Samantha's business partner, Geoff, to the nickname that her grandpa gave her, and even the prediction that Samantha would make a new friend in New York called Freya, who she ended up meeting shortly after her reading. Sandra was bang-on.

It was Sandra who alerted Samantha to her Saturn return. 'The good news is, it's all going to work out fine, exactly as it's meant to,' Sandra assured her as she shuffled her cards. 'But before it does, there's a bit of ... universe fuckery ahead.' Sandra went on to describe Saturn return as a 'scheduled crisis' that brings us face to face with our deepest fears. 'Everything we thought we wanted comes into question and it's like the universe tests us to see how much we really want it.'

I paused on these words as I sat in bed, realising full well that this was exactly what I was going through. Having a name for it excited me. Eager to learn more, I pulled out my laptop and typed 'Saturn return' into my Google search, and devoured article after article. Learning about it gave me a sense of control at a time when I felt like I didn't have any. There was comfort in knowing it was something that a lot of people at that age encountered and, most importantly, that it would pass.

FIGURING OUT THIRTY

Seven months following my discovery of Saturn return, British singer Adele announced her new album. A lot was riding on this record; it would be Adele's first in six years and the follow-up to *25*, the fastest-selling album of 2015.² Beyond the hits, one striking feature of Adele's celebrated discography is that each record has been titled as the age Adele was when she started writing it. The new album would be called *30*.

Across her social media platforms, Adele shared a candid message about the new record: 'I was certainly nowhere near where I'd hoped to be when I first started it nearly three years ago. Quite the opposite, actually.'³ Even Adele's reality of turning thirty did not reflect her expectations, it seemed. Five days before the album release, Adele performed live at Griffith Observatory for a TV concert special called *Adele One Night Only*. With big gold Saturn earrings hanging from her lobes and a tattoo of Saturn on her left wrist, girly was committed to the cause. She went on to tell *Vogue* that her Saturn return was where she 'lost the plot'. 'When that comes, it can rock your life,' she said. 'It shakes you up a bit: Who am I? What do I want to do? What makes me truly happy? All those things.'⁴

Adele wasn't someone we played at triple j, but I'd always been a fan and had even seen her perform live at Glastonbury in 2016. Above all, I loved her relatable demeanour. I was hell invested in hearing what Adele had to say about transitioning into her thirties and if she was mentioning Saturn return, then some shit must have gone down. Coming to know that Adele's journey through Saturn return, particularly her divorce, mirrored a lot of my own struggles with heartbreak felt super comforting.

When I started mapping out the first ten episodes of my podcast, I knew I had to dedicate one to Saturn return. My launching episode was just me on the microphone, talking about what was happening in my life as I approached thirty, and for the next instalment I welcomed my first guest, astrologer Natasha Weber.

I had been an avid online reader of Natasha's horoscopes so I was lowkey fangirling to meet her for a crash course in Saturn return via Zoom. 'It gets a bit of bad wrap sometimes!' she said with a grin, a giant star constellation adorning the wall behind her. Natasha described the cosmic entryway into adulthood as an evolution of the soul. 'It's about coming of age and learning lessons. But if you choose to ignore the lessons, that's when Saturn return can come and kick you in the pants!'[5]

Saturn return occurs approximately every twenty-nine and a half years, coinciding with the duration of Saturn's orbit around the sun, and typically spans a period of two and a half to three years. According to Natasha, Saturn creates mini growth moments in seven-year increments, which are known as squares or oppositions – like cosmic jolts to keep you in check. 'Every seven years, you pretty much get an opportunity for personal growth and to tweak your direction in life. And this will culminate at the return moment, around the age of twenty-nine.' However, anything in astrology that has a profound effect or evolution of the soul will also be in effect in the year preceding it and then ease off in the following year as well. It's like a build-up and then a falling away. So for a lot of people, shit can start to kick off as early as twenty-seven or twenty-eight. 'If you deny those seven-year lessons or opportunities for growth and instead are clinging on to your youth, outdated stale patterns or behaviour that isn't serving your growth and future development, when it comes time for your Saturn return, the accumulation of all of those years and moments can come back and bite you in the butt,' Natasha said.

I was curious as to why so many people felt so blindsided by this

> **WHILE I FOUND COMFORT IN THE CONCEPT OF SATURN RETURN AND ENJOYED DELVING INTO ITS INTRICACIES, I HAD ONE LINGERING QUESTION: WHEN WILL I KNOW IT'S OVER?**

period and why we didn't tend to hear as much about it in comparison to the eclipses and retrogrades. For Natasha, Saturn return is more complex than other astrological events and to fully understand how it might affect you personally, you need to know your birth chart, which maps the positions of astrological points at a person's birth. Astrologers use birth charts to analyse personality traits, strengths, weaknesses, life patterns and potential outcomes according to astrological principles. While there are broad themes that we may all encounter, it's important to note that Saturn's specific impact will be unique to you, depending on where it sits in your birth chart.

So, what kinds of things can go down during one's Saturn return? Although I was dumped and Adele got divorced, heartbreak isn't necessarily a prerequisite. It can be anything from changing jobs, moving cities, ending friendships or taking on a greater financial responsibility.

My friend Sam told me that she discovered Saturn return on TikTok: 'I'm too online.' 'I never thought I actually had a Saturn return but then I remembered when I was twenty-nine, I quit my longstanding job, ended a ten-year on-and-off relationship, ended some bad friendships and met my husband. So I guess I did! Good year. A lot of trash was taken out.'

Dating columnist Jana Hocking said her Saturn return entailed packing in her high-paying TV job for a low-paying radio gig, moving from Sydney to Newcastle, breaking up with a 'dud dude', getting a dog and dying her hair hot pink. 'It really was a rollercoaster ride!'[6]

Saturn return is like being met with the feeling that you're no longer who you once were, but you aren't quite sure of who you are yet either. So yes, we are all Britney standing on the edge of a clifftop, singing, 'I'm Not a Girl, Not Yet a Woman'. Seriously, though, Saturn return can be really tough for people, but Natasha is firm that if you step up to the responsibility instead of shying away from it, it can also bring incredible rewards and accolades.

'Saturn always rewards effort, hard work and discipline,' she assured me. 'If you're the type of person where that comes more easily, you'll probably breeze through your Saturn return, whereas if you're someone who wants to live a really frivolous life and it isn't in your best interest, then Saturn is going to make you grow up really fast and that can sometimes be pretty painful.'[7]

While I found comfort in the concept of Saturn return and enjoyed delving into its intricacies, I had one lingering question: when will I know it's over? Will I simply wake up one morning, embraced by a new sense of calm and clarity?

'Well, the funny thing about astrology is that once Saturn return ends you've usually got a Mars return or Venus return or something!' Natasha joked.

Birth charts can help you grasp when you can expect your Saturn return to pass, but Natasha warned of the possibility of a potential double whammy: Saturn retrograde. Turns out that Saturn might go retrograde at any time in someone's life – even before, during or after their Saturn return. It doesn't always line up with the Saturn return, though, because retrograde periods are just part of how planets move naturally.

When Saturn is retrograde in someone's birth chart, it might affect them on a more internal, introspective level. But whether Saturn is retrograde or not during a Saturn return, the big ideas about growing up, taking responsibility and learning life lessons from Saturn are still important. As writer, performer and astrologist David Odyssey wrote for *NYLON*, 'At this point, an unstoppable force may be exactly what's necessary to shake you out of the social, familial, and societal obligations which keep you in a perpetual child-state: Are you really going to spend the rest of your life with *this* person? Do you *want* to be in medical school, or do you just want your father to like you? Saturn will come to smash the juvenile attachments you cling to, for the sake of awakening you to your own authority, agency, and power.'[8]

There's no other way to put it: millennials and gen Z are vibing *hard* with astrology. And I get it. Understanding astrological events can provide a sense of control and a community for people. I can't scroll through Instagram without seeing a caption or meme on star signs and it's a compulsory addition to my friends' dating profile bios. And, of course, ol' mate capitalism is catching on and cashing in on people's growing fascination. According to Allied Market Research, the value of the global astrology industry went from US$2.2 billion in 2018 to US$12.8 billion in 2021. By 2031, it's expected to rise to US$22.8 billion.[9]

But it's not for everyone. In a piece for the *Sydney Morning Herald*, Melbourne comedian Alice Tovey described Saturn return as 'like whenever Toadie comes back to *Neighbours*, but for the sky'. Tovey deemed it all a bit silly. 'If there's one thing my generation likes to do, it's blame interplanetary forces for our problems.'[10]

I mean, fair point. But I'm going to do it anyway.

SATURN
in song

As a music presenter, I love analysing how music can capture universal experiences and Saturn return is no exception. Not only that, I love giving recommendations! If you are looking to expand your Saturn return soundtrack beyond Adele, here are three other albums to listen to.

ANGIE MCMAHON, *LIGHT, DARK, LIGHT AGAIN* (2023)

The second record from Melbourne singer-songwriter Angie McMahon is an earnest and meditative ode to self-discovery, as so poignantly captured in the opening track, 'Saturn Returning'. Sonically, you can expect a beautiful dance between big crunching guitars and drums and softer, intimate arrangements. I love how Giselle Au-Nhien Nguyen from *The Guardian* regarded Angie's songs as 'an invitation to slow down, to listen, to observe, to accept, to exist among the madness of it all'.[1] Big mood!

NO DOUBT, *RETURN OF SATURN* (2000)

The new millennium saw Gwen Stefani and co return to the scene with not only their first album in five years but also arguably Gwen's most confessional songwriting work, ever. Obviously 'Ex-Girlfriend' is the big hit of the record and 'Artificial Sweetener' contains a direct reference to Saturn, but I'm obsessed with how Gwen bares all on 'Simple Kind of Life', grappling with the conflicting desires of starting a family and pursuing her career as an independent artist. Utterly relatable.

SATURN RETURN

KACEY MUSGRAVES, *DEEPER WELL* (2024)

If you're after self-care and healing through the means of folk-pop, Kacey's sixth studio record is the match for you. A real cosiness is evoked through raw-plucked guitars, and while Kacey's vocals are always soothing, she's firm in her message: my Saturn has returned and I've got to take care of myself. Sing it, sister.

4 THINGS I HAVE LEARNED ABOUT BEING SINGLE

in my thirties

> YOU SHOULD ALWAYS, ALWAYS, *ALWAYS* BE THE LOVE OF YOUR OWN LIFE.

SINGLE SHAMING IS REAL, FROM OTHERS AND WITHIN

Even though I can now look back at The Big Break-Up and see that it needed to happen (albeit not in *that* way), the fact that it took place six weeks before I turned thirty amplified my doubts about my own desirability. When I had last been single, at twenty-five, I'd felt empowered and free with no sense of urgency to seek out a relationship. In fact, it took me quite a few months to warm to my ex before we started seeing each other, because I was so content being single. But as I approached thirty, I realised I viewed my single status as inferior and incomplete.

I was curious about going on the dating apps, but I also felt like I was too old to be on them. I carried shame at seeing 'Bridget, 30' attached to my profile, inadvertently reinforcing broader cultural narratives and gender norms that equate a woman's worth with her relationship status. My single shaming signalled a poor understanding of my own value and right to authentically exist in the world and revealed internalised misogyny and ageism. But can you blame me? Patriarchy has done a slay job of telling women that their happiness and worth relies on romantic partnerships, and that we can't have a truly fulfilling life without a man. Rarely are we made to feel bad about being in a relationship, but we are often made to feel bad about being single – *especially* being single in our thirties. Just ask Bridget Jones.

It made me realise ...

SOCIETY IS STILL UNCOMFORTABLE WITH THE IDEA OF A WOMAN BEING SINGLE AND HAPPY

We often hear the phrase 'single and ready to mingle', but what if we don't want to mingle? What if we are completely content with our own company and seek fulfilment in other aspects of our lives, through our friendships, career, travel or fitness?

We are deeply rooted in the idea of coupling being a destination and singledom being the transitional phase. But it goes even further for women. For us, singledom is a misfortune rather than a choice (and a conscious, empowered choice at that). Consider the language used to describe single women compared to men. In the late Middle Ages, the term 'spinsters' emerged to describe women who professionally spun wool, many of whom were unmarried.[1] These women often held lower-status jobs as the higher-status roles were typically reserved for married women who could afford the materials through their husbands. Meanwhile, single men have been characterised as 'bachelors', with more positive connotations – fun, carefree, suave and in their prime. Single men thrive, but apparently single women are in their flop era.

When I was single, I had interactions with friends and acquaintances who often made my dating life the central topic of conversation, which I leaned into at first. I was happy to divulge stories of who I was messaging and meeting, but by doing so, I fuelled their amusement and allowed other facets of my life to be overlooked. While my friends' intentions were well meaning, their insistence that I would find someone soon or when I least expected it carried an underlying tone of pity. Even when

THINGS I HAVE LEARNED ABOUT BEING SINGLE IN MY THIRTIES

I said I was in no rush to find a new relationship, some people couldn't fathom that I could be single and not in pursuit, or that I might be content on my own, which was what I needed at that time.

I think back to Melbourne's second COVID-19 wave lockdown rules, which were among the strictest globally. According to the Australian Bureau of Statistics (ABS), 521,828 Victorians lived alone during that period.[2] Couples living apart were allowed visits, while other visitors were banned, leaving many single individuals who lived alone isolated for weeks. Fortunately, a single bubble was established after public outcry and petitioning. Despite having an equal right to social connection, the initial exclusion of single people underscored the perception that they are inferior to those who are in relationships.

RUPAUL WAS RIGHT: 'IF YOU CAN'T LOVE YOURSELF, HOW IN THE HELL YOU GONNA LOVE SOMEBODY ELSE?'

While I was keen to have a lil stickybeak on the dating apps to see what the fuss was about, it was crystal clear to me that I had some shit to unpack first. I needed to cultivate a deep, healthy relationship with myself, so I started therapy and put time into understanding what I had learned from my last relationship and what I needed to change and work on before pursuing another. I established what I wanted and expected in a relationship, and where else I could seek happiness and fulfilment. It was through therapy and listening to podcasts that I learned to experience real love – *self*-love.

Self-love can be a little cringe and it's a concept that has been heavily cashed in on (cc: capitalism), but truly, the way in which you conduct the relationship you have with yourself will inform the quality of all your other relationships. It's a simple truth: we don't protect and take care of what we don't hold in high regard. If you lack self-like and self-love, you're essentially devaluing yourself, leading to lower standards in how others treat you. You should always, always, *always* be the love of your own life.

This leads into my next lesson ...

YOU DO NOT HAVE TO FUCK SOMEONE JUST BECAUSE YOU'RE SINGLE

One thing I thought I would look forward to upon returning to single status was sex. I thought I was going to have sooo much sex and live my best Samantha Jones life. Perhaps even form my own roster of guys! But the more conversations I had with my psychologist and with people on dating apps, the more I realised that wasn't gonna happen. This was due to a few reasons, starting with the need to unpack my aforementioned shit.

Secondly, nobody knew me when I was last single. I wasn't on triple j, I didn't have a book out. Now, I had a new-found visibility and I didn't know what to do with it. The messages I received were nice; some people said they loved my work and others were convinced it was a spam account. There was also the fear and paranoia of becoming the subject of gossip or ridicule if someone slept with me. So I laid low and accepted very few matches.

Thirdly, COVID-19. With such strict restrictions in Melbourne, it would have been near impossible to bring anyone back to my apartment. And even if it had been permitted, catching COVID-19 for the sake of a (likely mediocre) bang simply was not worth the risk to me.

Now, each to their own. If you want to embark on a single sex spree and get a roster going, I absolutely salute and love this for you. But addressing my personal issues took precedence over sex – and especially over seeking sex as solace or a way of filling a void. Instead, I bought more vibrators and filled a pink box I called my treasure chest. ☺

> **PATRIARCHY HAS DONE A SLAY JOB OF TELLING WOMEN THAT THEIR HAPPINESS AND WORTH RELIES ON ROMANTIC PARTNERSHIPS, AND THAT WE CAN'T HAVE A TRULY FULFILLING LIFE WITHOUT A MAN.**

The first and only person I had sex with following The Big Break-Up was the person I went on to have my next relationship with (spoiler alert!). So yeah, my 'drought' lasted over a year. I share this because I feel like a lot of single people feel pressure to be going out and getting some, even when they don't feel ready, and that's always a yucky feeling. If you don't want to have sex, or maybe you do want to but you're not having any luck, don't beat yourself up over it. Everyone's running a different race.

BEING ALONE IS BETTER THAN BEING IN THE WRONG COMPANY

In 2017, Everyday Health surveyed 3000 women aged twenty-five to sixty-five on wellness priorities, how they keep healthy and what they worry about. According to the study, about one-third (32%) of respondents across all age groups were more afraid of loneliness than a cancer diagnosis. Specifically, 42 per cent of millennial women said that, compared to 29 per cent of gen Xers and 27 per cent of baby boomers.[3]

My generation has been ingrained with a fear of loneliness, a sentiment I've personally grappled with. Yet, if you ask me, we hear too much about the loneliness we feel without others and far too little about the loneliness we can endure when we're with the wrong people. I can pinpoint instances in my relationships where I have felt profoundly isolated, even when we have physically been in the same room.

Being on the dating apps made me realise I would rather be alone than settle for someone whose profile I'd only half-ass swiped on, or someone who was giving me a half-ass conversation. Dating has become more instant and disposable, but that doesn't mean you need to dispose of your standards. My advice is simple: don't date, and don't settle on a date, just because you feel pressured by societal timelines.

THINGS I HAVE LEARNED ABOUT BEING SINGLE IN MY THIRTIES

NON-MALE DATING PROFILES > MALE DATING PROFILES

The best way I can describe the state of guys' dating profiles is by likening them to viral footage of two televised performances of Hilary Duff's 2007 single 'With Love', from which thousands of users on TikTok have re-created the (low energy) choreography. The most popular reaction is 'Go girl, give us nothing!'

This comment perfectly embodies how too many men treat their dating profiles. From the poorly curated collection of photos, either taken seven years ago or including group pics so you have no fucking idea who you're matching with, to answering prompts like 'My favourite love language is …' with 'English', men are really out there screaming IDGAF. It's funny that the motto of one of the dating apps is 'Designed to be deleted' because the quality of some men's profiles on the app made me want to delete it instantly. Like, even with PROMPTS, they still gave sweet fuck-all.

It frustrated me so much that I decided to include girls in my search. To no surprise, they were giving far more. Hot solo profile pictures. Considered and witty responses. For some time, I just matched with the girlies. I never went on a date, but I had some cute convos and established that gender wasn't the defining factor of what I'm attracted to. Pansexuality it is!

In analysing behaviour patterns on Tinder for the *Sydney Morning Herald* in 2017, social psychologist Jeanette Purvis concluded that men send out more messages to more potential partners but tend to put in less effort or are less committed to their matches. 'Women may feel flattered by the frequency of matches, but they may also feel disappointed when trying to follow up and have deeper conversations,' she wrote.[4] For so many men, it really does seem to be about quantity over quality.

YOU CANNOT APPROACH EACH MATCH AS POTENTIALLY BEING 'THE ONE'

Look, I know it can be fun to ponder what a future with someone would look like, and it can be an important consideration. But if you are out there internally planning your wedding with every match, you gotta chill a bit! If you do this, you are setting unreasonable standards that no prospective partner will ever live up to and therefore setting yourself up to fail. Research conducted by Dr C. R. Knee, a social psychologist at the University of Houston, revealed that placing excessive faith in romantic destiny can have detrimental effects on both individuals and the longevity of their relationships. Dr Knee's studies indicated that harbouring the belief that you have found 'The One' often results in brief, infatuation-driven relationships characterised by unrealistic expectations of perfection. He contended that individuals who subscribe to 'destiny beliefs', which posit that relationships are either meant to be or not, are more inclined to end relationships at the first sign of trouble, interpreting challenges as indications of the latter.[5]

> **DATING HAS BECOME MORE INSTANT AND DISPOSABLE, BUT THAT DOESN'T MEAN YOU NEED TO DISPOSE OF YOUR STANDARDS.**

THINGS I HAVE LEARNED ABOUT BEING SINGLE IN MY THIRTIES

Rather than viewing each match on the apps as a potential relationship, I approached each one as an opportunity for some good ol' personal development. I started by sliding into the DMs of someone I was following, purely for the sake of initiating my first conversation with a guy post break-up. I was in the taxi on the way home from work one night, scrolling away, and decided to reply to a photo he'd shared of his sports diary. All I did was ask about his day-to-day schedule but we ended up having a good conversation with long, considered replies. He was really nice! And he showed interest in what I did. It didn't go any further and I didn't need it to. It was about baby steps, which helped me to manage my expectations and not feel like I was rushing into anything or doing it because I felt like I had to.

IF A GUY LEAVES YOU ON READ AFTER ASKING 'HOW OLD ARE YOU HAHA?' TO WHICH YOU REPLY '30', HE'S A PIECE OF SHIT

That is all, no notes. (Yes, this happened to me.)

IF I HADN'T BEEN DUMPED, I WOULDN'T HAVE MADE IT TO TROYE SIVAN'S HOUSE

Iconic story time! Just over a month after The Big Break-Up, I downloaded my first dating app. Except it wasn't just a regular dating app – we're talking the dating app that sets you back about $25 a month, created for people in the public-facing industries (mostly entertainment) to connect with like-minded individuals all around the world. Yeah, ya girl was on Raya, the 'private' community featuring celebrities, entrepreneurs, influencers, athletes, that kind of crowd. I came across a few musicians too – one being the favourite child of my employer, meaning that every single of his would be rinsed on the radio. Let's call him FC.

Upon 'connecting', my first message to FC was along the lines of 'Can't believe this is how we are crossing paths and not through work.' He also thought it was funny and we got chatting. It turned out FC was going to be in Melbourne that weekend picking up his dog from the airport. He gave me his number and said to text him with a plan to catch up. After a gym class that Saturday morning, I did as requested but didn't receive a reply.

Eight hours later, I was sitting on the couch in my pyjamas watching *Drag Race* when FC replied. He apologised for the delay, casually sharing that he had been head down in the studio with Troye Sivan and G Flip. I already knew G Flip quite well but hadn't met Troye Sivan before although I had been a long-time stan. Okay, that's playing it down. I was *obsessed* with his music. FC then invited me over to Troye's house. My leap off the couch and into the shower would have been worthy of an Olympic gold medal. I tried to keep my tone cool but eager in my reply: 'That's quite a supergroup you've got going on there! Keen to drop by, as long as Troye is cool with it.' He was. Cue internal screams.

I got myself ready, voice memo'ed a few friends ('I'M GOING TO TROYE SIVAN'S HOUSE WTF'), picked up a bottle of red wine and Ubered to one of the most stylish homes I have ever set foot in. It had, after all, been featured in *Architectural Digest* only a few weeks prior. There were candles the size of pot plants, for Christ's sake! We all sat around the sleek living area, joined by G's partner at the time and a friend, as well as another music mate, Grace aka Mallrat. We decided to walk to a bar on Brunswick Street, with a few people stopping FC on the way to say hi. It was literally one of the most chill, wholesome nights ever. Plus, I got to know FC beyond his music as we spoke candidly about entering our thirties and his desire to return home to Australia.

THINGS I HAVE LEARNED ABOUT BEING SINGLE IN MY THIRTIES

I have no spice to share. We didn't go home together, we didn't kiss. I ended up interviewing FC a year later, and although I was told I only got the interview because the breakfast and drive team couldn't do it, it ended up being one of my best. The interview nearly exceeded an hour and I don't think it would have gone so well if we hadn't met the previous year. Whenever people said 'sorry' after hearing about The Big Break-Up, I would tell them it was all good because of this night. Had I not been dumped, I would not have formed a respectful connection with FC and hung out with one of my all-time favourite artists.

Love! That! For! Me!

5
WHY AM I LIKE THIS?

Content warning: this chapter discusses suicide, and emotional and physical abuse.

> IN ORDER FOR ME TO START WORKING TOWARDS THE POTENTIAL OF MY FUTURE, I HAD TO REFLECT ON THE PAST.

Turning thirty made me feel like a toddler again.

Hear me out. Thirty-year-old Bridget had the toilet training down pat, let's just get that straight. But I loved a nap (still do). Tantrums? Hanger is a real emotion! The constant seeking of explanations? Abso-freaking-lutely. All I seemed to do was ask, 'Why, why, why?'

For toddlers, the question 'Why?' stems from a place of innocence.

'Put your gumboots on.'

'Why?'

'Because it's wet outside.'

'Why?'

'Because it's been raining.'

'Why?'

'Because the clouds are full.'

'Why?'

'Errr ... because they drank too much water?'

'Why?'

For me, at thirty, the question 'Why?' came from a place of frustration. It was also personal.

Why am I like this?

FIGURING OUT THIRTY

I have The Big Break-Up to thank for this question. Heartbreak sucks, sure, but it also prompts some hardcore and necessary self-reflection. As overwhelming as it was to do this on the cusp of my thirties, there could not have been a better time, because I could focus on *me*. No partner, no child, no pet. My own Personal Debrief. I knew I had to practise self-love and I also knew I had to be real with myself. I had my own demons and flaws that needed to be acknowledged and worked on.

With the help of my psychologist, I identified where I'd fallen short as a partner – mainly, my inability to regulate my emotions and control my stress – and how I had developed such challenging traits in the first place. Of course, we sussed my attachment style and schemas (anxious-avoidant representtttt). I also recognised how I had used my particular relationship with Mark to fill a void that I'd never taken the time to process – the void of estrangement.

In order for me to start working towards the potential of my future, I had to reflect on the past. Up until this point, I'd never considered just how much my family had affected who I was and who I wanted to be, but it made sense. Our parents are generally the first people we interact with in our life and their relationship is usually the first one we are exposed to. They help shape our values, our interests and the ways in which we approach and manage our own connections, express emotions and handle conflict.

My dad's earliest memory of his life is, ironically and sadly, fearing for it. One Mother's Day, my parents and I were driving through the country back roads of the greater Ballarat region to a winery when Dad pointed out his childhood home. He casually shared his memory of being dangled over the water tank as a child by his father, thinking he was going to die. My eyes widened. It was not what I was expecting to hear but, at the same time, not all that surprising given the sprinkles of

WHY AM I LIKE THIS?

details I had gathered over the years about his father, who was severely abusive – a proper piece of shit. Dad's last memory of his father is of having to identify his body after a neighbour discovered him slumped in his car with a cup of coffee. He killed himself by carbon monoxide poisoning, nine years before I was born.

I hesitate to grant airtime to a man who I will never acknowledge as my grandfather, but the biggest realisation I have made as an adult is that he is the root cause of the dysfunction and estrangement within my family. Even decades later, the trauma of his abuse persists. It wasn't until I turned thirty that I fully grasped the extent of the damage he has inflicted and how profoundly it has shaped how I process my feelings, deal with conflict and manage my relationships.

Growing up, my three siblings and I often feared our dad. He always seemed angry and it didn't take much for him to launch into a fit of rage. At the time, I wondered if it was the stress of raising four children on one minimum wage. During these outbursts, Dad would say, 'You don't know what it was like for me growing up.' He never said any more about it, and I always questioned if that was to protect us or if it was a threatening tactic to instil more fear.

Dad seemed to chill out a bit as we got older and moved out of home, although my twin sister and older brother cut ties with him, and my older sister kept her distance. My own relationship with Dad was at its best when I was between twenty-six and thirty, but it wasn't always smooth sailing. We relapsed just a few months after The Big Break-Up when I returned home for the June long weekend.

We had just attended my friend's gender reveal party for her firstborn, and as I was packing to drive back to Melbourne, I asked Mum if she had retrieved the letter that my nanny (Dad's mum) wrote to my twin sister when we were born. Nanny passed away when we were twelve, but

FIGURING OUT THIRTY

I only discovered these letters when my parents and I had been going through old cards and photos before I moved to Sydney. My twin and I were temporarily on talking terms at this time, and I told her I would get hers when I was back at Mum and Dad's.

Mum had forgotten to pull the card out of storage and I expressed my disappointment. My dad got defensive and, for the first time in years, his emotions suddenly escalated to the kind of rage I'd often witnessed when I was younger. I was shocked and sad because I thought he was past that. And then came that line again.

'You don't know what it was like for me growing up.'

I barked something along the lines of 'Well, go on, tell me.' Dad ignored me and I suggested he seek a therapist like I had, which is highkey one of the *worst* things to say to someone. I regretted it immediately. He said he'd seen one in the '80s and it didn't do jack, then stormed out with the dog. I was left crying tears of anger, with Mum trying to console me. Dad messaged a few days later to apologise but I didn't return home for a few months after that.

My parents had been incredibly supportive throughout The Big Break-Up, so for us to have a falling-out was real shit. But I was fed up. I was doing so much work on myself, I felt like Dad should be doing the same.

I decided to reach out to one of my first cousins on my dad's side of the family. I hadn't seen her in more than fifteen years, but we were connected on Facebook and I had a gut feeling she would be happy to chat with me. I was right. Our video call ended up lasting two hours and she told me everything she knew about my dad and his twin sister – her mum – and their upbringing. (Yep, turns out twins do run in the family!)

I ended that call feeling a mix of emotions. It filled my heart to reconnect with my cousin, who was hoping I would get in touch someday, yet it was fucking devastating to hear about her violent upbringing, which was no doubt a reflection of her mother's own difficult childhood. My cousin's strength and empathy deeply moved me – how she had managed to reshape her life despite her own trauma and break the cycle, so that her own children could experience the safety and love she'd never received.

It's funny, she told me she'd always looked at my family and thought we were fully functioning and normal in comparison to how she and her brother were being treated – and I'd thought the same about her. I had no idea about the true dynamic between her and her mum. Even though the conversation was difficult and sad, I was grateful we could finally talk about it.

In my experience, there seems to be a clear generational difference in coping strategies with stuff like that. I think millennials are the first generation who want to normalise having conversations about mental health, especially those that include men. My parents' generation, and the generations before them, were raised in environments where mental health issues were even more stigmatised and misunderstood, and they consequently lack the language or awareness to discuss mental health openly.

I wanted Dad to know I'd spoken with my cousin, but I didn't want to make him feel exposed or vulnerable about what I had learned about his father. It took some time and several sessions with my psychologist to figure out the best way to approach this topic with Dad, to make sure he felt safe and supported. Like my cousin, I had a strong desire to break the trauma cycle, and I hated how I could recognise certain traits within me that I despised in my dad. That I too could have a short fuse and was unable to regulate my emotions. How easily I became stressed and anxious. I could see how that had affected my relationship with Mark and even how I had treated my twin sister growing up, often not

> **FAMILIES ARE MESSY AND COMPLICATED, AND NO ONE REALLY KNOWS WHAT'S GOING ON UNDER THE SURFACE UNLESS YOU'RE IN IT.**

speaking kindly to her. Discovering more about Dad's trauma was an ugly but necessary unveiling of the emotional inheritance within me.

Emotional Inheritance is the title of a book by American psychoanalyst Galit Atlas, referring to the passing down of emotional patterns, behaviours and coping strategies from one generation to the next within a family. These patterns affect how individuals respond to stress, express emotions, communicate and interact in relationships. Essentially, emotional inheritance suggests that people may unconsciously adopt and replicate emotional patterns and reactions observed in their parents or other family members, influencing their own emotional wellbeing and relationship dynamics.

According to Atlas, it was after World War II when psychoanalysts first began examining the impact of trauma on the next generation. 'Many of those analysts were Jews who had escaped Europe. Their patients were Holocaust survivors and later the offspring of those trauma survivors, children who carried some unconscious trace of their ancestor's pain.'[1] In the '70s, neuroscience confirmed the findings that survivors' trauma – even the darkest secrets they never discussed – had a legitimate impact on their children's and grandchildren's lives. Epigenetic studies in the '90s analysed how trauma can leave a chemical mark on a person's genes, which is passed down to the next generation. Atlas saw in her clinical work how traumatic experiences could invade the psyche of the next generation and show up in often surprising ways. 'The people we love and those who raised us live inside us; we experience their emotional pain, we dream their memories, we know what was not explicitly conveyed to us, and these things shape our lives in ways that we don't always understand.'

In many ways, I was born into estrangement. Due to his childhood, my dad never had strong or close relationships with his three siblings, especially given his twin sister moved overseas. I think she just wanted to GTFO and be as physically far away from the past as possible. One of Dad's older brothers lived in Tasmania but then travelled around. He randomly showed up at our house once when I was in Grade 6, and again when I was eighteen. Dad's other brother lived about an hour and a half away. We would see him every now and then, but he and Dad had a huge falling-out after Nanny died. I remember him rocking up one night, wanting to fight my dad. I stood by the side gate with a firm grip on my brother's cricket bat, ready to defend Dad, who was trying to defuse the situation. I haven't seen that uncle since.

Things were far from rainbows and butterflies on Mum's side of the family, too. Her own mother was verbally and physically abusive towards her and Grandpa, and when he passed away in my teens, Mum decided to cut ties with her mother and had a falling-out with her brother.

My twin and I used to say that we would never have the kind of estranged dynamic that our parents had with their siblings, but the last time my three siblings and I were all together was for my 21st birthday party. In my thirties, I have no relationship with any of my siblings. I have no relationship with any of my aunts and uncles. For the past eight years, Christmas has been just me and my parents. Well, our dogs too. And my partner, if I was in a relationship. I'm the only child to have regular contact with my parents and to stay at their house.

I'm not sharing my situation as a 'woe is me' type thing, but rather to highlight that estrangement is much more common than we may realise. I mean, we've even seen it play out publicly with Prince Harry and his brother and father. It's a conversation we need to normalise and, thankfully, we are seeing more hard topics like this in the mainstream, such as through the success of Jennette McCurdy's book *I'm Glad My Mom Died*, and Emmy award-winning TV series *This Is Us*, which have both generated more conversation around parental/child abuse and estrangement.

Research from social worker and academic Dr Kylie Agllias in 2017 revealed that about one in twenty-five Australian adults have been estranged from their family at some point in their lives.[2] But I reckon there is even more than that and research supports my suspicions. In a poll from 2022, YouGov found that more than one in four Americans (29%) reported being estranged from an immediate family member, including siblings, parents, children or grandparents.[3] This figure was slightly higher for men, with 31 per cent reporting estrangement compared to 27 per cent of women. Additionally, people between the ages of thirty and forty-four were the age group most likely to report estrangement from a family member, possibly because they were more likely to have family members in those varying age groups. Sexual orientation also appeared to be a factor, with higher rates of estrangement reported by gay men (49%), lesbian women (55%) and bisexual people (38%), compared to heterosexual people (27%).

Taking to Instagram, I did a little study of my own with my podcast community. Two hundred people responded to the question: 'Are you estranged from a family member?' with 57 per cent saying 'Yes' and 43 per cent saying 'No'. Out of the 'Yes' respondents, 18 per cent said they were estranged from a sibling, 42 per cent said they were estranged from a parent, and 40 per cent said they were estranged from a grandparent, cousin, aunt or uncle.

As Alana Schetzer wrote for *SBS*, for many people, family is the centrepiece of their life. For that reason alone, talking about estrangement can feel taboo.[4] Being estranged from a family member – or your entire family – can feel like failure, and you might feel like you're to blame for the toxic, unsafe or un-nurturing environment you have found yourself in, even if the rational part of your brain knows it's not your fault. That said, sometimes it does mean people are ultimately happier. 'Family estrangements are often portrayed in the media as being a regretful last resort for people at their wit's ends. However, for some people, family estrangements are necessary for their own health and happiness, and they have no regrets about no longer having a certain family member, like their mother or father, in their lives,' Schetzer wrote. Case in point: Jennette McCurdy's book title![5]

Any decision to estrange is not taken lightly, and according to Dr Agllias, it can take years of family stress for someone to actually action it.[6] This idea is echoed by Stephanie Foo, author of *What My Bones Know*.[7] By age thirty, Foo was successful – on paper, at least. She had her dream job as a radio producer and a loving boyfriend. But behind the scenes, she was battling panic attacks and sobbing at her desk every morning. After years of questioning what was wrong, she was diagnosed with complex PTSD, a condition that occurs when trauma happens continuously over the course of years. Both of Foo's parents had abandoned her when she was a teenager after years of physical and verbal abuse and neglect. She thought she'd moved on, but her new diagnosis shed light on the way her past continued to threaten her health, relationships and career. It also confirmed her desire to be fully estranged from her father.

Foo spoke to Kristina Scharp, Assistant Professor at the University of Washington, about the myths of estrangement for her book. 'It's more of a continuum where you can either be more or less estranged and actually people often go through multiple times of trying to create distance before they're able to maintain a level of distance that's right for them.' Foo highlighted that people aren't always happier as a result, but it might be something they need to do. 'Estrangement is not freeing. It has not felt joyful. It has not been happy. It has only felt necessary,' she wrote.

WHY AM I LIKE THIS?

Foo's book was recommended to me by a high school friend who I hadn't seen in twelve years. In Sydney for an interview with UK artist Griff, I opened Facebook to find a message notification and was pleasantly surprised to see Anna's name appear.

Anna (not her real name) and I first met at the end of Grade 6 when we attended our high school orientation day. We were assigned the same homeroom for Year 7, which meant most of our classes would be together except for a few electives. I vividly remember this short girl strutting over to my table, which she dramatically sprawled across before introducing herself: 'Hi, I'm Analiese but you can call me Anna.' I initially thought she was a bit full-on, a real sassy pants, and incredibly determined. If you could liken Year 7 Anna to anyone, it would be Hermione Granger.

We ended up being on the same debating team from Year 7 right through to Year 12, and we were a very successful one at that, winning a handful of local competitions and becoming state champion debaters in Year 9. I was second speaker, which meant my speech comprised a rebuttal of the opposition's arguments as well as presenting a new arguing point for my team. Anna was our third speaker and her role was to summarise our team's case and rebut the opposition. The thing was, Anna didn't just rebut. She tore the opposition to shreds. She was an absolute menace when it came to dissecting and dismissing their arguments.

Debating was a huge part of my adolescence and I don't think I would be a radio and TV presenter had I not been involved with it. The school library was our second home and our debating coach, Mrs Marshall, was like our second mother. Perhaps more so for Anna, as her mum passed away when she was just two years old. We would spend many an afternoon in the library after school preparing for our next debate, ordering hot chips from the fish and chip shop across the road and bringing in a few sneaky packets of Arnott's Crown biscuits from the IGA next door. Every Wednesday we would travel in a minibus to a different Melbourne school and relish our victories against the posh private schools. As co-ed public school kids from regional Victoria, we felt like we had something to prove. While we lacked their money and privilege, we made up for it with our determination and preparation.

After high school, Anna and I went our separate ways. There was no falling-out, just a natural drift as we ventured out to the real world. In her twenties, Anna spent a year in Europe and studied Arts and Law in Melbourne. She then got her Master's in Education and moved to Western Australia, where she featured in a national TV series that followed Australia's brightest minds in schools serving low socio-economic communities, where many students were falling behind.

The year the program aired was the same year I started hosting *Good Nights* on triple j, and I was so proud to see Anna not only on TV but also working a job I knew she was perfect for. She sent me messages of support whenever she heard me on the radio and when my first book came out, and more recently we had discussed plans to try to track down our debating coach for a catch-up. But it had been two years since our last conversation and I was curious as to what awaited me in this Facebook message.

> Hey mate, oh man, no excuses – just clicked in here and realised I didn't reply to the last message, I'm sorry! How are you? I hope you're well. Can't believe it's been years (!) since this last little thread. I've kept a few tabs from afar and it's been so nice seeing you flourish in the freelance (I think that's what it's called??) space.
>
> This is going to be a bit of a random one and I'm honestly so not offended if you just send me a polite thanks but no

WHY AM I LIKE THIS?

> thanks line or two ... I've been on a bit of a journey in the last year deciding to go no contact with my dad and fully coming to terms with the abuse in our relationship (it's been a lot, but overall I am well/safe).
>
> I think something I've felt frustrated about in the later parts of the journey is how little messaging, education and conversation there is about parent/child abusive dynamics vs romantic partner relationships. I feel like I'm fairly well educated/progressive in the space and always very open to these conversations, and I feel a little silly that it took until thirty-two to really see it a bit more clearly. I've also really struggled to find any podcasts or books that explore it. Anyway, I suppose in that feeling of frustration I felt a little like I might want to write an essay or share the message via a podcast, etc. and I guess I was wondering if it would be a topic/interview appropriate for a *Figuring Out 30* crowd or if you have any other suggestions. As I said earlier, really open to a 'no, thanks' so no worries/pressure if that's your take on it.

My thoughts came in thick and fast. I was stoked to hear from Anna but obviously felt concern. As much as my heart ached for her, I was so glad that despite having not seen each other in twelve years, she not only trusted me with her story but also felt I could provide her with a platform to voice her experience. This was something I was more than willing to do – in fact, the timing was wild. I was already exploring the topic of abusive relationships and family dynamics for this book, so it felt like a sign from the universe that Anna should be a part of it. Lacking the patience to type out a reply, I hit the microphone icon and recorded a voice memo, which went for three and a half minutes.

Anna responded an hour and a half later with her own voice memo – six minutes, this time, which surprised me, but then again we were state champion debaters. Her voice sounded smaller than I remembered, her footsteps echoing against the pavement. She took her time speaking and it was like I could hear her thinking and reflecting on the fraught area that is familial abuse. 'Isn't it crazy that as teenagers we didn't really know this stuff about each other?' She said she would be happy to share her story and that she was coming to Perth (where I now live) soon to catch up with some old friends and former students. 'There's so much about this that's not talked about,' she said. 'I'm genuinely very much looking forward to a *very* overdue reconnect. Okay, bye!'

Three weeks later, I picked up Anna from the Fremantle ferry dock. She had spent the day snorkelling off Rottnest Island so we pencilled in that late afternoon to catch up and grab a bite near my place. As I waited in the car, I re-read an email she had sent that further detailed her story. 'A relationship with a parent is one which is unusual in that, as the child, there is so little initial choice: you don't choose your parents, the relationship that they have with each other, the expectations they have of parenthood or of you as a person and where and how you live,' she wrote. 'You have no say over the power dynamic or the rules that are established in the absolute foundation of your relationship. Every person's relationship with their parents is unique, and it can be so difficult to appreciate and understand another person's relationship with their parent.'

I heard a casual 'Hi!' from the outside of the passenger window. She looked exactly the same, a 33-year-old version of the girl I knew in high school. I jumped out of the car and gave her a hug. The vibe was comfortable and relaxed but I sensed a slight tension, perhaps due to the anticipation of our conversation.

WHY AM I LIKE THIS?

The drive was only nine minutes and the conversation was light, mostly about Anna's time in Perth. Daisy, my black toy cavoodle, greeted us upon our arrival and we headed straight for the outdoor living area to keep chatting, trying to figure out the last time we had seen each other and laughing at our respective boyfriends at the time. We shared which high school friends we were still in touch with and wondered how our debating coach was going – this served as the segue into what we had planned to talk about. Suspecting this could be a lengthy conversation, we opted for takeaway Thai. I grabbed a beer from the fridge.

'In my twenties, there were many things about myself that were challenging and I wished they weren't there,' Anna began. 'My inability to cope with people being upset with me, the way I would spiral into the worst-case scenario when things went wrong, the extent to which I would painfully overthink interactions with everyone around me because I just wanted people to like me so, so much.' It was in the early years of this decade that Anna stumbled upon therapy. 'I certainly wasn't against it; I just didn't really have a sense of why I needed it.' Sure, Anna possessed a range of anxious traits (read above!) but she always considered herself a fairly happy person. However, when faced with an interstate career move at the end of university, Anna really spiralled. 'So I turned up at my therapist's office, giving her eight weeks to "fix" me before the move.'

While she didn't remember much about what her 23-year-old self discussed with her therapist, she recalled having her 'aha' moment. 'In those early sessions, I told my therapist the narrative of my story I had held until that point: yeah, sure, my childhood was a bit challenging and unique. After six months of dating, my 29-year-old mother received a cancer diagnosis and fell pregnant to my 23-year-old father, who was fresh out of the Navy after dropping out of high school. She died two years later and I was raised by a single father who struggled with the

> ABUSE IN ROMANTIC RELATIONSHIPS WAS REFLECTED IN THE NEWS, IN FILMS AND BOOKS, BUT FAMILY VIOLENCE AND ABUSE BETWEEN OTHER MEMBERS OF A FAMILY UNIT MUCH LESS SO.

world: struggled with his emotions, to have positive relationships with anyone, to find friends or a partner and to hold down a job.' Sadly, Anna saw herself as the partial cause of those challenges in many ways. 'My dad was unconventional, yes, but wasn't I so lucky? He had always sacrificed so much for me and put me first. Choosing to live in the regional town my mother was from even though he hated it and had less career prospects there, allowing me to have close relationships with my family members even though they hated him. Choosing not to date because I would be upset if he did as a young child. He always put me first. People would always remark on how much he loved me, was proud of me and I was the thing he cared about most.'

Anna recalled with vivid clarity her therapist saying, 'This is our eighth session together and this is the first time you've acknowledged that there may have been some bad things about the way your dad parented you.' When she said that, Anna felt shocked and challenged. 'And, in some ways, stupid. Because when she stepped it out for me, I could see it. But how had I spent twenty-three years so blind to the reality in front of me?'

Anna described her dad's emotions as strong, scary and unpredictable, which she experienced regularly from a young age. 'He would scream, call people names, swear, hit and throw items. I often preface an explanation of my dad by hurriedly making it clear that he never physically abused me, not really. It's as if I feel like I'm not entitled to that level of sympathy and like it wasn't that bad.'

It wasn't until Anna read a particular line in the book *See What You Made Me Do* by Australian writer Jess Hill which said, 'Domestic perpetrators don't need physical violence to maintain their power – they only have to make their victims believe they are capable of it'[8] that Anna realised this was exactly what her dad did. 'While he never physically punched me with a fist, he created a fear in me that I wouldn't be surprised if he did and believed that he could.' She recalled him pushing her into couches, shaking her while her back painfully hit the sink behind her, and once being slapped on the face. There was a time when he held their foreheads so close together that it hurt while screaming in her face, and another when he drove in a rage, swerving into lanes and speeding. 'I believed I could die. That I feared him hitting me or killing me holds equivalency to the fear that someone has when they actually experience it. I continue to have regular nightmares where he hurts me.'

> **I'D NEVER CONSIDERED JUST HOW MUCH MY FAMILY HAD AFFECTED WHO I WAS AND WHO I WANTED TO BE.**

There was also the emotional abuse. How her dad was jealous and dismissive of her relationships with others. Anna was in primary school when her dad first told her he was suicidal. In high school, he told her he had questions about her biological paternity. He was highly critical, enjoying embarrassing her and riling her up and constantly saying she was too sensitive. When Anna's partner first met her dad, she was floored to hear that her partner's main takeaway was how critical her father had been of her during the visit. 'I hadn't noticed it once.'

Anna's dad would also tell her inappropriate and uncomfortable things. Like how he'd had a fight with her mother when she was pregnant

WHY AM I LIKE THIS?

with Anna and had threatened to pour a pot of boiling water on himself if she left him. Or the sexual encounter he'd had as a young man where the woman initially said no, but he later persuaded her that her refusal actually meant yes.

Then there was the neglect. Sometimes Anna would spend hours waiting at the school gate to be picked up while her dad played video games. When she was five, Anna would have to wake him up multiple times to be taken to school. 'I remember my teachers telling me I needed to do more to try and get us to school on time, and I felt so much shame and unfairness,' she told me. 'I didn't know how it was possible for me to do more. When I had the lead role in the kindergarten play, he lost track of time and we missed it completely. He didn't remember my friends' names. When I went into his bedroom the morning I received my ATAR score, to excitedly tell him my news, he asked me what I was talking about.' This broke my heart. I had seen how hard she'd worked in class and I now realised this was likely because she wanted her dad to be proud of her.

Anna's dad also made it clear that he had wanted to kill himself when she was a child but hadn't done so 'for her'. In her teens and early adulthood, this turned into a threat, and he explicitly stated that if she cut him out of his life, it would be a choice he might make.

Even though Anna had completed courses on family violence across multiple university degrees and taught it to young people, she spent most of her life not quite understanding the nature and gravity of her father's abuse. 'When we discussed our relationship, his view was that even though he had made mistakes in the past, the main reason we had relationship issues as adults was because I was too sensitive, and my mental health was at fault. And while I knew this wasn't true – mental health professionals had commented that I was 'remarkably normal for my childhood' and my experiences didn't amount to a diagnosis or need for medication – his comments still made me doubt myself in small ways.' This goes to show that even the smartest, most observant and open people can struggle to accept that they have been victims of abuse. It's also reflective of how abusive people will often try to 'flip the script' to make you question your reality and blame yourself.

Anna recalled how she desperately asked her therapist to rate the abuse out of ten, to help her understand just how bad it really was. Her therapist, very professionally, declined to provide a number but said, 'Your dad was extremely abusive and it had a profound impact on you.'

When Anna decided to take time out from her relationship with her dad, she found herself opening the gate slowly whenever she left her house, carefully scanning the street as she walked to her car and looking in the mirrors once she got in. She mentioned this to her therapist, who said, 'I have to be honest – you sound like someone leaving a romantic partner relationship that was violent.'

'I felt like someone had dropped a ton of bricks on me,' Anna said. 'How and why was this so surprising? In my twenties, I understood that my father engaged in family violence. So why was it such a shock when someone pointed out to me the ways in which there was overlap with abuse in a romantic partner relationship?'

I thought back to the initial message Anna had sent me and how she referenced society's better understanding of abuse in romantic relationships – I saw her point. Abuse in romantic relationships was reflected in the news, in films and books, but family violence and abuse between other members of a family unit much less so. 'Instead, we have strong cultural and societal pressures to accept, tolerate and excuse abusive behaviour by family members,' Anna said. 'From a young age, both sides of my family impressed on me the importance of and need to prioritise families and that cutting someone out of the family was unacceptable. Abusive behaviour by parents is often conflated with challenging but reasonable or acceptable behaviour.'

As we picked through the numerous containers of Thai stir-fry and rice, Anna recalled a time when she was five years old, reading a book to her dad. 'I got a word wrong. He was clearly in a bad mood for other reasons, but I had no way of understanding that. He flew into a huge rage, screaming and swearing, and he grabbed a large metal fire poker and smashed it repeatedly into the fire. As he swung it back, it caught my face, resulting in me being rushed to hospital and requiring emergency surgery. The injury was millimetres away from causing blindness.' Five-year-old Anna saw it as her mistake and learned that mistakes were dangerous and something to try to avoid at all costs.

Scientific studies have shown that children raised with family violence show the same hypervigilance as soldiers who have been to war.[9] 'My experience as a child was that bothering or upsetting my father was both my fault and could result in something terrifying happening,' Anna said. 'As an adult, I sometimes experience debilitating anxiety and shame if I make a mistake that might upset someone. That shame makes you feel like there is something deeply wrong with you. That you can't trust that people will like or love you in the long term.'

As a result, Anna would constantly scan her environment and interactions, looking for signs of upsetting people. All. The. Time. She told me about a night during the pandemic lockdowns when she was doing a jigsaw puzzle with her housemates. 'I noticed my internal thoughts about this process: "Am I doing too much of the puzzle? Am I doing too little of the puzzle? Did I start doing a section of the puzzle they wanted to do? Have I done all the easy parts of the puzzle and left them with the hard parts? Do they not like that I've bought this puzzle and it's too hard?

Have I been using the image of the box on the puzzle for too long and someone else wants to use it?" It's exhausting. It's taken so much time, money and therapy to get it to a manageable point, but it permeates my life in every aspect – in romantic relationships, at work and with friends.'

Within the dynamic her dad had created, Anna felt like she needed to always put him and his feelings first in order to be safe. This led to her putting other people's needs above her own in ways that weren't good for her. 'I rarely get frustrated or angry at people. It can be hard for me to recognise or ask for what I want. It used to be almost impossible for me to ask for what I want if I thought it would bother, hurt or upset another.'

Understanding the cause of these emotions led to great relief over time. Anna could finally begin to accept and forgive all her anxious traits and how they had made her life difficult. 'I remember a big moment for me in reaching acceptance and forgiveness was when my therapist explained that when you're a small child, your brain is unable to blame your parents for abuse, because that would weaken the relationship and leave you without the safety and care that they provide. Instead, it is really common in these situations for children to blame themselves.' She was able to understand that when she was a small child, these thinking and coping patterns were the best ways her brain could work out to keep her safe in an abusive environment.

Rosie Waterland, Australian author and podcaster, explains this in a different way: 'As a child, you have no choice but to rely on an abusive parent to survive – literally and emotionally. So you have to learn to ignore or block out the awful parts of them in order to get the good parts you so desperately need … Just because they can hurt you immensely doesn't mean they can't also offer moments of love that are almost impossible to find anywhere else. When you have an abusive parent, it's so understandable (and so normal) to crave the person who hurts you.'[10]

WHY AM I LIKE THIS?

Like Stephanie Foo, Anna hit a point in her thirties when she realised she could only do so much in terms of her relationship with her dad. 'I had poured so much time, energy, emotions and effort into trying to get our relationship into one that was manageable for me.' She had spent countless hours and thousands of dollars on therapy. She had attended courses on having family members with severe mental health issues, and had many open and frank conversations with the people in her life, including her father, trying to explain the basic boundaries she required to make things work. Anna was out there Doing The Work, and it still wasn't enough. 'My dad and I were in the best space we had ever been in, but he would still lash out in hurtful ways if I took reasonable actions to decide to prioritise my own needs.'

Anna now understood her dad would never really get it. And, more significantly, he lacked insight and remorse about his behaviour. 'I realised I couldn't see myself doing things like having a wedding or a baby, because I couldn't imagine being able to relax or enjoy them with him there. I knew he would have huge expectations over his time and presence in the life of any child I had and that I would prefer not to have a child than have to manage that. I didn't want my child to see me experiencing anxiety and shame, or see someone act abusively towards me. And even though I would have once said it was something I would never do, I clearly remember the day when I finally thought, *Maybe I want to go no contact*.'

The intense fear Anna felt when making the decision to cease contact with her dad exposed the layers of coercion and abuse she hadn't even realised were there. Even though she had moved house and her dad didn't know where she lived, she was scared when she sent him a letter requesting that they go no contact. 'I found myself programming my watch so I could dial 000 easily, not wanting to park my car on main streets and being too scared to go to the supermarket near the house

I previously lived in,' she said. 'It made me realise that Dad's previous references to suicide held a highly coercive underlying threat towards me that if I made a decision like this, he would not be able to control himself, or it would result in extreme emotions and behaviour.'

It took the better part of a year for Anna to work through her emotions and find the courage to put the no-contact measure in place. Even though most of her other family members were largely supportive, she could see the strain it put on their relationships and so she saw them a lot less. 'I know many would prefer that I change my decision, which makes me feel a lot of shame and guilt. It can feel quite isolating and lonely, and sometimes it feels like I don't have family at all. On Christmas, it reached the evening, and I still hadn't heard from anyone in my family and had to send out text messages. When I went to hospital last year, a few hours into sitting in ED, I realised there wasn't anyone from my family I would call.'

I could totally relate when Anna told me how she felt her estrangement was something she couldn't mention to colleagues or her partner's friends. How she had to pretend everything was normal, even though it wasn't. I thought about all the times I had been asked how my siblings were by people I knew, or asked if I have any siblings by complete strangers. It was easier to downplay the truth and say something like 'We're not close' as opposed to 'We have absolutely no relationship and I haven't seen them in more than six years.'

A few years ago, a quiz had been organised at a work development day. One of the questions was to name the employees with a twin. I was listed. When the answers were revealed, I would say about 99 per cent of my colleagues didn't know I had a twin and it was awkward having all of these people come up to me afterwards, wanting to hear more about her. I felt uncomfortable letting them know the reason they hadn't heard about her was because we didn't talk. I felt like I was making *them* feel uncomfortable even though I had come to terms with the situation myself. People are always shocked and can't understand why you wouldn't have a relationship with your twin – I mean, aren't all twins inseparable besties, like Mary-Kate and Ashley Olsen?

Anna and I agreed there is a huge stigma in making a decision to cut off a loved one and it might make you feel like you can't discuss your grief or be honest about the situation with many people. 'Even though people mean well, they often say hurtful things. There is often a general sentiment that you only get one set of parents and that reconciliation is the positive, noble, healing choice,' she said. So many people focus on reconciliation that they treat the concept of estrangement like it's just a bump in the road.

> **I WANT TO BE BETTER, ESPECIALLY IF I PLAN ON STARTING MY OWN FAMILY ONE DAY.**

Anna didn't necessarily believe that going no contact was the right choice, but it was the choice she had to make. 'There is no right choice. But I believe that by not discussing parent abuse and going no contact, we stop people from being able to explore if and the extent to which their parents were abusive, and what boundaries would be best for them to make the relationship as healthy as it could be, prevent future damage and allow healing.' Having that space to fully explore the effects of her father's abuse and work towards healing without him in the picture was crucial for Anna. 'It's allowed me to begin to take steps towards putting myself first. I'm beginning to address my intense shame and fear of making mistakes and upsetting people.'

As I leaned back into my chair and thanked Anna for trusting me with her story, she wanted to hear about my own family. I knew she would be surprised that I wasn't in contact with my siblings, especially my twin sister, who she had shared some classes with in high school. Naturally, given what she had been through, Anna expressed immediate empathy. We marvelled at how, despite spending so much time together in class and through debating, we had no idea about the adversity we had both experienced within the four walls of our respective homes, and that sixteen years after graduating high school, we were on the opposite side of the country, talking about it together.

Eventually I checked the time and realised it had been nearly five hours since we first sat down. I felt like we had at least another two hours in us, but it was pitch-black outside and Anna needed to get to her friend's house where she was staying, about thirty minutes away. We hugged and promised not to leave it so long between catch-ups next time.

I had a lot to take in from Anna's story. Growing up without a mother would have been hard enough, but to be raised in such a toxic, frightening and abusive environment by her father ... she deserved better, and no child deserves to be treated the way she was. While my heart ached for what she had endured, it was also bursting with pride. I was so proud of Anna. Not only her strength and self-awareness but also how determined she was to look at the past and work out how to heal, set boundaries and improve her relationships with the people she wanted in her life. It was bitter that we shared the experience of unfortunate family dynamics but, man, how sweet it was for us to reconnect after all this time and support each other.

My time with Anna got me thinking about a conversation I had had a few months earlier with someone else from my hometown, Ballarat podcaster Tess Griffin. Despite experiencing complex familial relationships, she was also determined to break the cycle, not just for herself but for her children. We knew each other through mutual friends and she agreed to tell her story for my podcast.

When Tess was three years old, her father, Aaron, took his own life. Aaron was only twenty-one and had grown up never knowing who his own father was. The year before Tess was born, he wrote a poem about the pain of feeling such a void in his life. Tess was eighteen when she learned the circumstances surrounding Aaron's death. 'That was a huge grievance in his life,' she told me from her home one night, where she held on to some of her father's letters and poems.[11] It wasn't until Tess became a parent herself that she started paying attention to the conversations around her speculating on who her grandfather could be. 'It just felt so unfair that I couldn't even say to my children, this is who your grandfather or your great-grandfather is.' Funnily enough, an adoption storyline in the TV series *This Is Us* first planted the seed for Tess to take an ancestry DNA test.

When Tess was thirty, she attended the funeral of one of the men she thought might have been her grandfather. 'I had no relationship with him but I just thought I'll go along and pay my respects because this must be the end of the line, I'm never going to know.' Instead, Tess received new information. 'At the funeral, I had all these different family members saying, "Oh no, he wasn't your grandfather." Some relatives said they believed it to be somebody who had come to Ballarat to study and boarded with my grandmother, which was a common thing to do in the '70s.'

FIGURING OUT THIRTY

That evening when Tess returned home, she started her online ancestry test. Within a week she received the kit (spit-in-a-tube kind of situation) and within a month she had the results. The email reached Tess one unsuspecting night after she'd put her kids to bed. Opening the email, Tess was greeted with a 93 per cent match being listed as a grandparent. His name was Barry. She flashed back to a childhood memory of the name. Tess instantly knew this must be him.

She sent a message introducing herself and shared her desire to explore how they could be related. Barry wrote back straight away and said while he didn't know of any Griffins, he was happy to hear more about Tess. With the help of her husband, Tess carefully constructed a reply that detailed her theory of Barry being her grandfather. She was hoping she might have a phone call with him. 'He wrote back saying that this was a shock and very upsetting and that he did not wish to continue the conversation. I was so upset,' Tess said. She went to work the next day and told her father-in-law what had happened. 'Oh, he's guilty as sin!' he exclaimed. 'He's not denying anything. He's just saying, "I don't want to deal with this."'

Tess was convinced she would never hear from Barry again, but two or three days later he emailed her. He had consulted his wife, who told him he couldn't leave Tess hanging. He was willing to hear more of what Tess had to say but was wary of her intentions. Tess understood this instinct. She had heard stories of people with ulterior motives. 'I was very conscious of letting him know we're really good people. Hard workers. We don't want anything from you, I've just always wanted to know, and my dad always wanted to know.'

Barry was the missing puzzle piece. He agreed to a phone call with Tess. 'He was just very upfront and open and said, "You know, I did have a casual thing with her. I was seventeen at the time." There were other young people living in the house and she was married with children – my dad's older siblings – so it was quite a bizarre situation.'

I jumped in. 'So, hang on. Your grandma was having an affair?'

'Yeah, she was sleeping with the boarders who were staying in her house.'

Well, that was some tea. I asked Tess if her grandmother was still alive and, if so, did they speak?

She was. 'I tried to make contact with her when I was on my journey after watching *This Is Us*, and I have seen her, but it's just really hard,' Tess answered. 'She's not a very upfront person. I did contact her when I found Barry that first night, and she just kept talking in circles. She never admitted anything and kind of acted like, "Oh, I don't know what you mean", like "That's impossible".'

It turned out that Barry was living in the house when Tess's dad was born. He was seventeen but never registered that the baby was his. For Barry, his way of life was going to TAFE, going to the pub, and that was that. 'He said to me that he left Ballarat and never thought about anyone from there ever again.' Naturally, to hear fifty years later that he'd had a son was a lot to digest.

The next weekend, following their phone call, Barry and his wife, Di, drove three and a half hours to meet Tess and her brother, Matt, for lunch. 'It was amazing,' Tess reflected. 'They both just made me feel super comfortable and it felt like we'd always known each other.'

Tess showed Barry and Di a bunch of photo albums and even read Barry the poem that her dad wrote about him. The next step was to introduce Tess and her brother to Barry and Di's three children, who were now discovering as adults that their dad had another son. 'Looking from the outside and on social media, they looked like this picture-perfect family, which they are, so I was a little bit nervous because I felt like I was going to blow it up or I'm going to be like, all right, here's the

> **ONE IN TWENTY-FIVE AUSTRALIAN ADULTS HAVE BEEN ESTRANGED FROM THEIR FAMILY AT SOME POINT IN THEIR LIVES.**

crazy people, here's the not-so-perfect part!' To Tess's relief, her newfound aunty and uncles were excited to embrace more relatives.

Tess couldn't speak more highly of her new grandmother in Barry's wife, Di. 'She has been so incredible,' Tess said, beaming. 'This all happened before they'd met, which was only a few years later, but the way that she has handled this ... She's so invested and she's embraced my kids as fully her own grandchildren. It's been so sweet.'

That's not to say there wasn't a deep sense of grief on both sides. For Barry, he went fifty years without knowing he had fathered a son who then passed away. For Tess, the older she gets, the more grief she feels. 'My daughter is almost the same age that I was when my dad died. To see the obsession that she has with Sam [her dad] and then if he were to just not be here anymore ... it's very real for me since I became a parent. It makes me really sad, but I think that's the grief that Barry and I both share and constantly talk about.'

But overall, Tess couldn't believe her luck: to not only find family after tragedy but also have that family want to *be* family. Tess and Barry even found common ground in their line of work, with Tess a podcaster and Barry a former radio announcer. Their birthdays are a day apart.

Delving into the past can be challenging, but as both Tess and Anna have shown me, it can also result in really positive things. And for both of them, it was about breaking the cycle to build a better future. For Anna, it was understanding that removing a parent can protect you, but it doesn't fix you. She has had to unlearn the anxiety and people-pleasing tendencies she formed in response to her dad's abuse to feel strong and sure within herself as a 33-year-old woman. For Tess, it was the determination to provide her children with the stability and unconditional love that she wished she had growing up. 'Even if you've had the perfect upbringing, there's always things you want to do differently, whether it's communication or your relationships with certain people in your family. But for me, there's been a lot of dysfunction still to this day. Family relationships are all over the place, but I just want my kids to know that it doesn't matter what they do or what happens or who says what. We are a unit. We stay the same and my love is the same.'

> **I HAD A STRONG DESIRE TO BREAK THE TRAUMA CYCLE.**

It was seven months after our argument that I told Dad about my conversation with my cousin. Ironically, it was at a winery, but not the same one from the Mother's Day when he'd shared his memory of the tank. I could tell Dad was being reserved when I told him about the dynamic between his twin sister and my cousin, so I reached for his hand and acknowledged his efforts to try to live a somewhat normal, functioning life after such an abusive upbringing. We both shed a tear as I expressed how I wanted to validate his trauma.

As the conversation with my dad unfolded, I couldn't help but feel a pang of longing for something more profound. Understanding Dad's trauma had not only forced a mirror upon myself, allowing me to change and grow and be in healthier relationships, but it also enabled me to look at the dynamics within my family with more empathy. I wanted him to do the same. I wanted my dad to acknowledge how his trauma had seeped into his role as a parent. It wasn't about pointing fingers or placing blame – I just wanted him to recognise and validate the impact his parenting had on me and my siblings, even though I now better understood the reasons behind his actions. But I didn't want to have to explicitly spell that out for him, and lunching at a winery definitely wasn't the time or place to do that.

Turns out, writing this book helped extend that dialogue between us. I was nervous to share my words with Dad. I even feared he wouldn't want to look at them. Five days after I asked him to read this chapter, I received a text message that felt quite profound. He said after reading it a number of times, he likened his own life to chapters – the first being painful, sad and out of his control. Ones he did not want to relive. He said he could have dealt with his issues and feelings better and not hurt other people in the next chapters of his life as an adult, as it wasn't his intention. 'At the time you think you are doing the right thing with the skill sets you have,' he wrote. 'In my final chapters, I hope to live with better understanding, love, tolerance and have a peaceful life. If writing your book is beneficial to your chapters of life and for you in the future, I'm comfortable with that. Love, Dad.'

Families are messy and complicated, and no one really knows what's going on under the surface unless you're in it – and even then, you might not have the full picture. It's only in my thirties that I have come to understand that my parents are more than just my parents. They are people, with a history and scars of their own.

One of Galit Atlas's mentors is known for saying, 'Research is me-search': 'Feelings are always the motivations for intellectual investigations, even as we rationalise the world around us,' she wrote.[12] I think the reason I have been so determined to understand why I am the way I am is because I want to anticipate my reactions in certain situations. I want to identify any patterns of behaviour that might hinder me. I want to be better, especially if I plan on starting my own family one day. And for me to even think about that, I need to take a look at the one I already have.

8 Things I Have Learned About Relationships
in my thirties

> **THERAPY CAN SERVE AS PREVENTATIVE CARE FOR YOUR MENTAL AND EMOTIONAL HEALTH. IT'S LIKE A CAR SERVICE, BUT FOR YOUR BRAIN!**

THERE IS NO RIGHT OR WRONG TIME TO SAY I LOVE YOU, TO MOVE IN TOGETHER OR TO GET ENGAGED

Many people in their thirties say this stuff happens faster than in your twenties, because there is less bullshit to navigate when you date with intention. With more life experience under the belt, you are surer of yourself and what you want, so when you find it, you lock it in. In the new relationship I found myself in at thirty-one, I said the L-word pretty soon after we met. I'm talking, like, within two months. It's just how I felt! We moved in together after nine months of being exclusive, but this was mostly circumstantial as both of our rental leases were coming to an end and we were spending so much time together anyway. As far as I'm concerned, there is no script for such milestones and it just comes down to what is going on in your own relationship, so don't compare or judge. As Dolly Alderton wrote in the bible, aka *Everything I Know About Love*: 'People should do it in the exact way that works for them, even if it doesn't make sense to people on the outside.'[1]

YOU DON'T HAVE TO BE IN A BAD RELATIONSHIP TO GO TO THERAPY!

Louder for those in the back! I wish more people realised that therapy is not just something you do when something is going wrong. Even if you are happy and with your dream person, therapy can still help you understand your partner's communication skills, improve how you resolve conflict and enhance self-awareness, which can deepen emotional intimacy. My psych and I deemed it 'behind the scenes' work. Just as you visit the doctor for regular check-ups to maintain your physical health, therapy can serve as preventative care for your mental and emotional health. It's like a car service, but for your brain!

Therapy can also help you ...

CHECK! YOUR! BAGGAGE!

Let's be real, we all carry a little baggage by the time we hit our thirties. For me, this has been the patterns and traumas from my previous relationships. I was the spitting image of Anxiety and her six suitcases when we first meet her in *Inside Out 2*. Thankfully, therapy continues to help me learn how to leave this out of my current relationship. I'm talking trust issues, self-sabotage tendencies, schemas, attachment styles, to name a few. Even redefining my belief system. By no means is it easy, but it has been a totally necessary practice. Check it before you wreck it!

MAINTAIN YOUR IDENTITY AND INDEPENDENCE
CC: CARRIE BRADSHAW!!

Yes, a relationship is an integral part of your life, but it does not and should not define your entire existence. When you lose your sense of self in the thick of romance, you'll grow needy. You'll probably lose some friends too. Pursuing fulfilment solely through a relationship can foster a sense of internal emptiness and you'll probably struggle if you break up. I know I did. Despite having such a public-facing brand for myself, I didn't know who I was without my ex, and as we saw time and time (and time) again with *Sex and the City* protagonist Carrie Bradshaw, she felt utterly lost without the king of being emotionally unavailable, Mr Big. Carrie had no problem rearranging her life at a moment's notice to fit Big's, whether it was ditching Miranda for a mediocre serving of veal in the form of a dinner date in season 2 or inviting him to her cabin getaway with Aidan (!!) in season 4. But he never did the same. Big made Carrie feel small, pun ~~not~~ intended. We give so much of ourselves to our lovers, but we also need to keep serving our own souls too.

'GOOD ON PAPER' DOESN'T ALWAYS MEAN 'GOOD FOR YOU'

We often tick boxes for potential partners based on factors such as education, career success, physical attractiveness and shared interests. However, these attributes sometimes only scratch the surface. It's crucial to delve deeper and evaluate whether the person – and relationship – will offer genuine fulfilment and compatibility. True connection transcends superficial traits and requires a deeper understanding of each other's values, emotions and dynamics.

I'M NOT SURE IF I BELIEVE IN 'THE ONE'

Despite the movies we watch and stories we read, life ain't a fairytale, folks. With more than eight billion people occupying the Earth right now, I don't think there is such a thing as 'The One'. Rather, I choose to recognise that there may be many 'Ones', or maybe 'The One' for a particular time in your life.

As I realised after The Big Break-Up, there were moments when I'd believed Mark was 'The One', but looking back, I recognise that this perception was probably influenced more by societal expectations than by true compatibility. We began our relationship in my mid-twenties and, over time, I convinced myself that he *should* be 'The One', as if it were a natural progression after my first youthful, less serious relationship. As noted by Katie Bishop for *BBC News*, research into hundreds of relationships found that having an expectation of finding a soulmate actually led to dysfunctional patterns of behaviour and even made you more likely to break up with your partner.[2] This is because people who believe in soulmates tend to have what is known as a 'destiny' mindset. Since they are holding out for the perfect person, they are more likely to doubt their relationship or view a bump in the road as a deal breaker.

I can see how people are able to reframe 'The One' as the one who they *choose* to be with for the rest of their life. But I feel that too many of us misinterpret 'The One' as this totally perfect person, when perfection is not something we should be striving for in a relationship. I am by no means telling you to settle, but relationships *should* be challenging to an extent. How do you grow and learn otherwise?

EXPECTATIONS – GET TO KNOW THEM AND GET A GRASP ON THEM

Esther Perel famously said that nowadays we turn to one person to provide what an entire village once did: a sense of grounding, meaning and continuity. 'Our expectations of our partners have never been so high. We still want everything the traditional family was meant to provide – security, children, property and respectability – but now we also want our partner to love us, to desire us, to be interested in us. We want to "marry our best friend", our confidant on all matters, someone to whom we should be able to tell everything. And, for that matter, they should not only be a stellar co-parent, they should also be a savvy co-decorator, a skilled sous-chef, a financial whiz, a motivated jogging partner and a devilishly funny gossip – depending on what we need that day. But why are we relying on one person to fill so many roles?'[3]

Reflecting on my own romantic relationships, I can see how I expected all of this from my ex. In my current relationship, with Oscar, I've been more aware of cultivating a balanced approach where we support and complement each other, while also acknowledging the importance of friendships and other sources of fulfilment. It's always going to be a work in progress, but I feel like I have achieved a much more grounded perspective and found greater contentment and harmony. Not only that, but the five-year age gap between us has helped me to recognise the importance of chilling out, enjoying the present moment and not getting caught up trying to predetermine anything. Of course, I'm with Oscar because I see a future for us, but my life doesn't depend on this relationship. I'm allowing our connection to unfold naturally and, slowly but surely, I'm learning to feel more secure within that.

AGE REALLY IS JUST A NUMBER!

So, let's talk about that five-year age gap! Not gonna lie, it had me a little hesitant at first, but then again, it was me who allowed 25-year-olds to pop up on my dating apps. And hey, thank god I did! After Oscar and I matched, a friend from primary school, Jess, messaged me. She sent a message screenshot of her husband, Max, asking her for any fun facts that he could pass on to his former teammate Oscar, who wanted to start our conversation with a personalised opening line. Turned out Oscar had sussed my Instagram for any mutual friends he could get some info from, which I found endearing. His messages were lengthy and considerate, and not only did he ask me on a date but he also scoped a place he thought would be my kind of vibe. I didn't have to do a damn thing except show up. And he nailed it – a quaint wine bar with a wall collection of vinyl records in Brunswick East. The rest is history.

I invited Oscar on my podcast to chat about our age gap, where he revealed it was something he didn't even think about, nor was it something we addressed until a few months into the relationship. Oscar shared that his age range on his dating profile settings had been set to include women no more than two years younger than him, and no more than five years older (I just scraped in lol). 'I'd rather see and meet people who are older. Personal preference!' he remarked.[4]

> **WITH MORE THAN EIGHT BILLION PEOPLE OCCUPYING THE EARTH RIGHT NOW, I DON'T THINK THERE IS SUCH A THING AS 'THE ONE'.**

Oscar and I both established that our current priorities lie in making inroads in our respective careers. 'We're both in similar situations in life even though we're not the same age,' he said. The only time Oscar has noticed our age gap is when it comes to alcohol ('Yeah, you can't drink') and when I 'get tired very easily'. Hey, lightweight nanna and proud of it! One of the most reassuring things for me is the fact that Oscar's brother, Tom, is a year younger than me and he is married with two kids. The concept of settling down is something Oscar and I have talked about and it isn't foreign or scary to him.

Featured on the same podcast episode as Oscar was Melissa Mason, who spoke about her experience dating a guy ten years her junior. If it wasn't for Paul Mescal being spotted around Sydney, Melissa would not have lowered her age range on the dating apps from twenty-seven to twenty-three. 'I just heard through people that he was on the apps. So I was like, you know what? I'm thirty-five, I'm fucking bored. I'm going to fuck Paul Mescal. That was my goal for the early stages of 2021.' At first, Melissa felt like it was quite a jump, but she quickly liked what she saw. 'I was like, god damn, there's some hot young dudes in the inner west! Maybe this is just gonna be me having some flings with some young guys and feeling really hot in the process.'

Instead of finding Paul Mescal, Melissa found her Tom, who, at twenty-five, was ten years her junior. At first, Melissa could not see how a 25-year-old man would ever want the kind of relationship she was looking for at thirty-five. 'I'm gonna bring up babies and this guy is going to run for the hills,' she said. 'But I think I just had preconceived ideas of what a 25-year-old man is going to think and feel about all of this really mature stuff. He said to me, "Why do you assume that's not something that I want?"' This response really threw Melissa, and it was one she didn't have an answer for. 'I think what I did with Tom was I just projected me at twenty-five on to him and went, well, there's no way you can be ready for this, because I wasn't at that age. But we don't all grow up the same way. All of our assumptions are very much rooted in either past experiences or our own experiences.'

Their age difference has only been really noticeable when random pop culture moments have come up in conversation, like the Sydney

Olympics. While Melissa has vivid memories of school excursions and a new train platform at Bondi Junction, Tom was only four years old at the time. For Melissa, it was a moment of 'Oh my god, now I feel really uncomfortable'.

My friend Ash feels the same about her new partner, also named Tom (would ya believe?!), who is seven years her junior. 'Initially, I felt really uncomfortable about the age difference and worried that people were going to judge me, but when you're with the person, you don't even think about it.'[5]

'The age gap has taught me that younger guys are actually more intuitive and tapped into their emotions. When I reflect on previous relationships, feelings were never discussed, but what I have noticed in Tom is that he is way more open to having conversations about what's bothering him or his mental health. He also checks in with me more, which has been really refreshing.'

The only times Ash has felt out of her depth is when spending time with some of Tom's friends, whose girlfriends are younger. But she said, 'I find it really reassuring that out of all these young people he could choose to be with, he picked me.'

Love transcends age, baby!

NO MATTER WHAT HAPPENS, I WILL BE FINE

Remember how I was driving back to Melbourne that Saturday morning after The Big Break-Up, belting out Miley's 'Midnight Sky' in the car courtesy of Georgia's 'delete men' playlist? A few songs later was a collaboration between Ariana Grande and Nicki Minaj that I had never heard before. Hearing Ari repeat how the light was coming to bring back everything the darkness stole became like an affirmation for me. A mantra. It reminded me that although it felt like my whole world was crumbling, I was going to be fine. It would take time, but things were going to get better. And they did.

As I alluded to earlier, if my current relationship was to end for any reason, I know deep inside that I will be okay. Perhaps not immediately, but eventually. I've weathered similar storms before, and each time I've emerged stronger. If my first relationship had never ended, I would never have pursued music presenting and have the career I have now. If my second relationship had never ended, I wouldn't be embarking on a new adventure on the other side of the country. And I don't think I would be writing this book.

Embracing this mindset isn't something we're born with, nor is it typically instilled in us during our formative years. It's a realisation we must come to on our own, a lesson learned through experience and self-discovery. This mindset is more than just a coping mechanism; it's an acknowledgement of resilience and the capacity for growth, and there's no expiry to that. Not in our thirties, not ever!

7
TO BABY OR NOT TO BABY

Content warning: this chapter discusses infant loss, infertility, miscarriage and abortion.

> YOU COULD SAY THAT MY FERTILITY IS MY ROMAN EMPIRE.

I fondly consider this book to be a big ol' word vomit of contemplations and feelings, so it goes without saying that this chapter is a bit of a power spew – which is fitting, given it's about babies. Or, as Nell Frizzell wrote in *The Panic Years*, the mother of all decisions.[1]

In *How to Endo*, I shared how, growing up, I'd wanted to become a mother at the age of twenty-four, a desire that stemmed from a primary school athletics carnival one year where I met my friend's grandma, who was celebrating her 45th birthday. I couldn't believe she was a nanna. She had bright coloured hair, fun jewellery and such an energetic presence that she felt more like a cool aunt than anything. It was at that point that I decided I would find a husband and have a child by twenty-four at the latest. Twenty-four sounded like a cool, young number, and my desire to be a cool mum was cemented well before Regina George's mother said it out loud. According to my calculations, twenty-four also meant that if my children had their own kids, I would be a cool, young grandma too.

However, with each lap of the sun, I realised that the decision to become a mother wasn't that straightforward. Mark and I had spoken about having children together and even discussed names, though we rarely reached an agreement, mind you. Looking back, it was me who had been initiating and driving this conversation. It was me who decided I would perhaps do two more years of my radio show before taking maternity leave, and that we would move into a larger space and I would become pregnant with baby numero uno at thirty-one, thirty-two at the latest. Mark never explicitly said that he didn't want or couldn't envisage children with me. But I'm not sure if he explicitly said that he *did* want them either.

When your five-year relationship breaks down six weeks before you turn thirty, you can't help but feel like a lost cause when it comes to fertility. I know this is utterly false and lowkey dramatic, but in the depths of heartbreak and rejection, it's hard to have any hope. It's hard not to freak out when you know that age is the single most important factor affecting your fertility. That in your early to mid-twenties, you have a 25 to 30 per cent chance of getting pregnant every month. That your fertility starts to slowly decline in your early thirties and a pregnancy beyond thirty-five has been considered geriatric (now referred to as 'advanced maternal age'). That by age forty, the chances of getting pregnant in any monthly cycle is around 5 per cent.[2]

It's also hard not to join Rachel Green in her shared New York apartment and calculate The Timeline. 'So I should probably have the first by the time I'm thirty-five,' she pondered from her dining table. 'So I don't have to get pregnant until I'm thirty-four ... But I do want to be married for a year before I get pregnant ... So I don't have to get married until I'm thirty-three ... But I'll need a year and a half to plan the wedding, and I'd like to know the guy for a year and a half before we get engaged, which means I need to meet the guy by the time I'm thirty ...'[3]

We assume that being in our thirties means having kids (expectation), when in reality the Australian birth rate hit a record low in 2020.[4] In fact, the ABS has predicted that at some time in the next decade, the number of couples without children will overtake the number of couples with children.⁵ KPMG have dubbed it a 'baby recession', with births across the country falling by 4.6 per cent year on year – the number of births in 2023 was the lowest since 2006. Yet we still can't seem to shake the societal pressure.⁶ As Jacinta Parsons noted in her book *A Question of Age*, the expectation to reveal whether you intend to use your body for its capacity to birth becomes greater as you get older. 'If you are a woman entering her thirties, regardless of your partner status, expect that question with an added head tilt to show a deep understanding of the pain you might be feeling.'⁷

In pop culture, let's consider the real Rachel Green: Jennifer Aniston. She was hounded for decades about her fertility. After divorcing Brad Pitt in 2005, Aniston was subjected to an overarching narrative that she 'refused' to have children and 'prioritised' her career. What strengthened this unfair portrayal of villain Jen and heartbroken, aspiring daddy Brad was that less than a year later, Pitt coupled up with Angelina Jolie, who he went on to share six children with. Not to mention that sixty-page (60!!) photo spread in *W* magazine titled 'Domestic bliss' featuring Pitt and Jolie as an early-1960s-style married couple with a brood of miniature blond Brads.

Jen, meanwhile, copped every trashy tabloid headline under the sun. 'Jen can't keep a man!', 'Pregnant and alone!', 'Pregnant and in hiding!', 'Jen's pain over Brad's new baby!' The number of results that appear when googling 'Jennifer Aniston pregnant' speaks to the sick, pronatalist obsession with a woman's womb, and it understandably took a toll on the actress. 'It was really hard,' Aniston told *Allure* in 2022. 'I was going through IVF, drinking Chinese teas, you name it. I was throwing everything at it.'⁸

Growing up, I never spent much time around babies. I was twenty-four when the first baby hit my hometown friendship group, but the first baby I really got to know was the firstborn of my ex-boyfriend's older sister, when I was twenty-eight. Despite being terrified to hold him in case he cried, I enjoyed watching him grow. It wasn't until we all stayed together down at the beach one New Year's that I realised just how time-consuming motherhood is. Gone were the spontaneous decisions to go out for lunch or to the beach, because every single day (and night) revolved around breastfeeding and naps. The walls in the Airbnb were particularly thin, so the baby's sleep schedule became all of ours. *This is all so … unappealing*, I remember thinking to myself. *Do I really want this?*

The second time I questioned my maternal desire was two years later when (ironically) I became a mum. A dog mum, that is. I was entering my sixth month of singledom and my mental health walks around Princes Park were not only a distraction from my heartbreak but also a good daily dose of socialisation. Not a word was exchanged with fellow walkers, but the simple act of having people pass by was all the comfort I needed. I loved looking around at the trees and up at the sky above. Each step felt like I was shedding the loneliness that clung to the walls of my quiet apartment, a sight I was getting pretty sick of by the fourth COVID-19 lockdown.

The best parts of these walks, aside from blasting Gretta Ray's debut album, were the dogs. I *lived* to see all the dogs. Each day I pondered getting my own. I called my mum, which probably wasn't the best idea because Debbie has a tendency to validate my decisions a little too much. But she knew I was in the pits. 'I think a dog would be really good for your mental health and anxiety,' she said to me one morning as I walked around Ikon Park.

'Yeah, but they're expensive and renting alone is expensive,' was my rebuttal, or rather, my attempt to be logical. 'And what if I want to go awa—'

"IT'S THIS PRONATALIST IDEOLOGY THAT PAINTS A PICTURE OF WOMEN WITHOUT CHILDREN AS DEVIANT, DAMAGED OR DERANGED."

'Oh we could look after it!' Mum practically leapt through the phone.

I was leaning towards getting a cavoodle because of Tillie, Mum and Dad's eight-year-old fur baby – the favourite child by a country mile. But Til and I were tight. I was back living at home when Mum and Dad got her. In fact, I influenced them to get her a couple of months after the unexpected, tragic death of their rescue terrier, Missy. They insisted that Missy would be their last pet, but I sent Mum photos of Jinkee, an Instagram-famous red toy poodle that could easily be mistaken for a piece of KFC fried chicken, and just like that, Tillie the apricot cavoodle came into our lives. I suppose Mum and I aren't the best influence on each other.

I had a few people ask me about adopting a rescue, but the process of finding a rescue small enough for my apartment in lockdown was more competitive than I thought. So Australia's most popular dog breed it was.

Her name was Daisy. Within a week, she was my world and I was hers. When I picked Daisy up, I felt so guilty about taking her away from her sisters and her mum. Hearing her sad little whimpers as we drove off made me question if I was doing the right thing. When we arrived home, the apartment was completely silent but the sound of my anxiety was deafening. My little black ball of fluff sniffed around, unsure of her new surroundings, of me. I watched her like a hawk. Every new pet owner will find this relatable, but I was utterly terrified she would die.

Within an hour of being in her new home, I had gained enough of Daisy's trust for her to come and sleep on my lap, my long-knit dress serving as a hammock of sorts. Sitting on the living room floorboards of my apartment, I burst into tears. *How am I going to do this?* I wondered, wiping my snotty nose with my sleeve as my little fur baby slept peacefully.

TO BABY OR NOT TO BABY

Everybody had told me how good the puppy phase was and to make the most of it, but can we also acknowledge how hard it is too? Holy shit. Nobody told me about the Puppy Blues, which is a big mix of overwhelm, stress and sometimes even regret that dog owners can feel after bringing a pup into their home. It sounds crazy – like what do you mean you're doubting this adorable, fluffy bundle of joy? But the reality of constant care, training challenges and the huge lifestyle shift can hit you like a tonne of bricks. And once we finally got out of lockdown, having to take care of her instilled some resentment in me. I know. I KNOW. I sound like the worst person alive. I love Dais but having to give myself a curfew to come home to check on her was a buzzkill at times. I would be lying if I said I enjoyed raising a puppy. The responsibility that comes with another living being depending entirely on *you* was something I had underestimated. Getting Daisy actually made me more anxious.

A 2022 Forbes Advisor survey of 2000 dog owners found that 54 per cent had regrets about getting a dog.[9] My friend Nathan got a black toy poodle, Leo, a week before I got Daisy. He told me that in the first two weeks, he and his partner thought it was 'the absolute fucking worst decision' they had ever made. 'The piss and shit everywhere, the crying, the sleepless nights. Should have just had a baby!' he joked.

As for me, getting Daisy made me realise I never wanted to raise a puppy on my own again. It also made me realise that I was far from ready to dedicate my entire self to a human child – a stark contrast to how I'd felt a year prior, awaiting my maternal future with the same eagerness as Daisy on a walk. Now, there was no strain on my lead. You would have had to have dragged me.

So, I considered freezing my eggs.

The first person I spoke to about egg freezing was my friend Ash, who you met earlier. Like me, Ash had a specific age in mind for starting a family – twenty-six. But while my maternal desire waned with age, Ash's only grew stronger. At thirty, Ash was divorced and not dating but after seeing an Instagram post about the AMH test, she decided to take matters into her own hands.

The AMH test is a blood test used to measure levels of the anti-mullerian hormone, a hormone produced by cells in the ovarian follicles. The level of AMH in the blood correlates with the number of these follicles and can give an estimate of the remaining egg supply. Generally, a higher level of AMH indicates a larger ovarian reserve, suggesting better fertility potential, while a lower level of AMH may indicate a diminished ovarian reserve, which could suggest reduced fertility or a higher likelihood of difficulty conceiving, especially as you age. The AMH test does not provide any insight surrounding the quality of those eggs, but it can serve as a starting point to exploring one's fertility.[10]

'The GP I saw was really hesitant to even explore it and give me a referral,' Ash told me.[11] 'She believed the test only prompts unnecessary stress and anxiety around fertility. Which I could understand, but at the same time, how else do you know? I practically had to plead my case with her.'

After explaining her divorce and deep desire to start her own family, the GP finally caved and Ash returned a month later to discuss the results. 'I remember having this sick feeling that I knew something was wrong. I just knew.' Turned out, Ash's gut instinct was right.

'I know I said not to stress or be anxious about the results,' the GP began, 'but yours are incredibly low for your age.'

Ash could feel the tears building but she held it together until she made it back to her car. She hadn't told anyone she was getting the test and called her mum in hysterics. 'There was a bit to catch her up on,' Ash said, laughing.

TO BABY OR NOT TO BABY

More blood tests and internal pelvic examinations indicated cysts on Ash's cervix and ovaries, as well as a low antral follicle count. Ash had the cysts on her cervix removed and underwent three cycles of IVF, took eighty-four needles, had three surgical procedures and came out with a small but worthwhile collection of eggs. Following this retrieval, Ash received an endometriosis diagnosis, experienced ovarian torsion (twisting of the ovary) resulting in tissue death and discovered a blocked fallopian tube. She was told that while not impossible, pregnancy was highly unlikely, with IVF being the best option moving forward. Two years on from our podcast recording, Ash is just happy that she backed herself. 'Imagine if I never got that AMH test,' she texted me.

Two days before my first date with Oscar, I drove to a fertility clinic in Fitzroy. It's funny to reflect on the casualness of our text exchange on that breezy Friday, Oscar unaware that I was investigating my fertility options, just as I didn't know it was his twenty-sixth birthday.

With my laptop, headphones and little USB microphone in tow, I was welcomed into Dr Fiona Cowell's office, which overlooked a traffic-dense Victoria Parade. Many people with endo can back me when I say that, sadly, it's not uncommon to encounter poor bedside manner from medical professionals, even when talking about something as personal as your reproductive potential. Speaking to Dr Cowell, however, felt like chatting to a trusted aunt or family friend. There was a lot of information to take in about the process of freezing eggs (did you know that the eggs don't expire, but it's recommended you use them before the age of fifty-three?!) and potential risks. We also went through my endometriosis surgery history. I agreed to an AMH test and an antral follicle count ultrasound.

A week later, Dr Cowell called to discuss the results of my AMH test. 'It's nine, which is on the lower end of what is considered normal for your age.' Based on the data that Melbourne Pathology use, it could be considered reduced ovarian reserve, which is basically when your ovaries have fewer eggs available for fertilisation than expected for your age, but she reassured me that there are many factors that influence a person's fertility and potential to conceive. We spoke again a few weeks later to discuss my ultrasound scan, which was much more promising. 'Look, it's all good!' Dr Cowell beamed down the phone line. The antral follicle count on each ovary was healthy and considered normal, and although the scan revealed a mild bowel adhesion, nothing was found in relation to deep, infiltrating endometriosis, which was music to my ears. I said I would consider egg freezing in the next twelve to twenty-four months, to which Dr Cowell had no objection. I also told her about my new relationship. Her response was classic aunty vibes. 'Well, make sure you're having safe sex!'

A wave of relief crashed over me. I could press pause and have a breather before jumping back into the race against my biological clock. I felt in control, knowing not only that egg freezing was an option but also that natural conception was still a possibility.

Chloe Fisher and her husband, Paul, never gave up on the idea of conceiving naturally, even through four years of trying, eight rounds of IVF, multiple surgeries and four miscarriages.

I met the couple back in 2018 when I gave Paul, a DJ better known as Fisher, his first triple j interview. His single 'Crowd Control' was going off on the text line so we knew we had to get him on my show. My producer, Celline, and I knew this guy was a loose unit so we were anxious as to how the interview would play out. But Fisher charmed our socks off! He did not stop expressing how humbled and grateful he was for the radio support and to be invited in for a chat. Accompanying him was Chloe. You could tell they were a solid couple. Chloe's profile began to build through her fashion and her lifestyle touring the world with her husband, but she really took off as a powerful voice on her podcast *Darling, Shine!*, where she and her co-host Ellidy Pullin opened up about grief and fertility.

Chloe joined me online from LA, where Paul was getting ready for his DJ set at Coachella, followed by a summer-long commute between Las Vegas and Ibiza for his nightclub residencies. The schedule sounded brutal, and amid all of this, Chloe and Paul were still trying for a baby. 'I've always wanted a baby my whole life,' Chloe told me. 'From as young as I can remember. I was always the one out of my girlfriend group – "Chloe's gonna be the first one to have a baby!" All I wanted was to be a mother.'[12]

Chloe first fell pregnant after their Bali wedding in February 2020, but seven weeks in, her doctor could not detect a heartbeat. The experience was not what she expected. 'You pretty much just get sent to the hospital. They give you a pamphlet and say if you need help, call this number.' Chloe returned to the hospital the next day for her dilation and curettage (D&C) procedure, where the cervix is gently opened and the remaining pregnancy tissue is removed. 'Just being pushed in there knowing that you're going in with your baby in your belly and then you're coming out empty – it was just the weirdest feeling.'

Chloe's mum had a miscarriage in between birthing her and her brother, but Chloe never thought it would be something she would have to endure herself. While miscarriage is common, occurring in around one in four pregnancies, Chloe found herself in the 1 to 2 per cent of women who experience recurrent miscarriages. Specifically, four miscarriages, with one of the pregnancies being twins.

Chloe's candidness about her miscarriages struck a chord with me, particularly because it was only the second conversation I'd had about it.

My first was on a girls' weekend trip only a few years prior where a friend revealed her experience with miscarriage. I had no idea what to ask her. I didn't know anyone who'd had one, or at least nobody had told me. Like most aspects of female reproductive health, we were raised to not discuss this kind of stuff, to whisper it behind closed doors. Endure in secrecy.

My conversation with Chloe was one of the heaviest interviews I had ever conducted, but despite the heartbreak, she held such a graceful demeanour. 'I'm actually grateful that I've been through it because I feel like I've completely changed as a person through this journey, and I think I'm a better person for it.'

It was the greatest gift to open Instagram one Christmas Day to see the Fishers at the top of my feed, announcing Chloe's pregnancy after conceiving naturally. It genuinely made my Christmas, and based on the 250,000 likes and more than 14,000 comments of congratulations, I don't think I was alone! Nine months later, she gave birth to a beautiful, healthy baby named Bobbi.

While motherhood had been a lifelong dream for Ash and Chloe, there are those who are confidently child-free. When I spoke to author and former Miss Universe Australia Maria Thattil after her 30th birthday, she said she recognised that living a public life meant external expectations would be imposed upon her as she entered this new decade. 'When I've shared that I don't know if I want to get married and I don't think I want kids, there's a lot of backlash towards that sort of thing.'[13] Especially when you consider Maria's own upbringing as a South-Asian Australian. Her parents migrated to Australia from India in the 1990s, and with her father being a Catholic priest, he and her mother held more conservative views when it came to family and relationships. But Maria decided to model what she wanted and how she wished people would receive her. 'I know that there are people within my community who think, like, that girl better settle down soon, and there are people who eye-roll because I've not had kids and done that sort of thing. But for me I'm going to really confidently live my choices. And that will help other people who are approaching their thirties to go, "You know what, stuff it. I'm going to do it my way and do what feels good for me."'

Upon entering her teenage years, adored Australian musician Holly Rankin, known as Jack River, wrote a list in her diary of all the things she wanted to do with her life. Record an album. Write a book. Make a movie. Sing to a million people. Work on a political campaign. Write a law that benefits people and the environment. A singer, a writer, a lawyer, Holly wanted to do it all – except be a mother.

I'm a big fangirl of Jack River. I was doing the mid-dawn shifts on triple j when she debuted her solo project in 2016. While I loved following her music journey, it was the personal content she shared on social media that really resonated with me; in particular, an episode of her podcast *To Rebel in the Times* that she recorded in 2020, interviewing her friend and fellow artist Kita Alexander on what it was like to be a mother in music.[14] I eagerly listened as they discussed how little space and support was carved out for women who wanted to embrace both caregiving and their creativity. Holly, who was twenty-eight at the time, and her partner hailed from small NSW towns, where it was common for young people to settle down and start families, but Holly wasn't sure this could be a possibility for herself.

But then a surprise came along: Maggie. 'I never imagined having a baby. It just wasn't something I ever thought about in my future,' she confessed on my podcast, a month before her album *Endless Summer* was released. 'I was all about career and doing stuff from a really young age but now that Maggie's here, I'm like, oh of course she's here!'[15]

After much deliberation with her partner, they decided to proceed with the pregnancy, which came at a busy time. In addition to being a full-time musician, Holly had also taken a demanding job in the 2022 federal election. Throw in a kind of sickness that was 'like eating raw eggs and being on a boat in the middle of the ocean', Raynaud's syndrome, which was reducing bloodflow in the nipples, and Maggie arriving ten days overdue after twenty-four hours of labour via C-section, it was a pretty hectic journey. The hours that followed, however? 'The most magical few hours of our lives,' Holly reflected.

Becoming a mother means not only birthing a tiny human but also birthing a new version of yourself, and I was curious to hear how Holly was navigating her identity as a mum, alongside her musical alias Jack River and also just Holly. 'I'll give you an interim report on how it's going, reporting in from identity crisis!' she joked. 'During the pregnancy, I really had mentally prepared to be washed away. Talking about thirty and everything that comes with it, I felt ready to be, like, control delete of who I am. Everyone says that's probably what mothers struggle with the most, grieving their old self and, interestingly, I felt excited to lose myself.'

What Holly found beauty in was seeing the world through Maggie's eyes, which has ultimately been a blessing for her artistry. 'My relationship to creativity felt a bit twisted and stale before motherhood,' she revealed. 'Now I have a million new emotions to speak to!'

However, she is easing back into the rhythm of the music industry with caution. 'A lot still needs to change. I think a lot about how record labels and music teams are in the space of selling emotion and that has a cost for the artist that the artist deals with alone.'

There are also the practical aspects. 'You need a lot of support going through pregnancy because you're going through an extreme life shift and your team need to, whether they know how to or not, ask about it, and they need to provide support. On the other side of having a baby you need extra support in how you tour, how you travel, who you take on tour, how that works financially and how your schedule might be different.'

So, where am I at with all of this? Well, for me to consider children means considering several things, the first being my endometriosis. If you don't know much about endometriosis, this is when tissue that is similar to the lining of the uterus grows outside of the uterus. Endometriosis can cause a lot of pain and inflammation and it can even stick organs together. Plus, up to 50 per cent of people with this chronic condition experience infertility.[16]

As I explained in *How to Endo*, experts believe there are two reasons for this. Firstly, the inflammatory nature of endometriosis can impair the function of both eggs and sperm, and prevent a suitable environment for egg fertilisation, embryo development and implantation.[17] Secondly, there's also a structural component because our anatomy can be distorted through scar tissue and adhesions as the disease progresses. This can potentially cause the blockage of fallopian tubes and affect the passage of sperm and eggs through the pelvis.[18]

There is also a third way in which endo can affect fertility, which is a bit more straightforward – painful sex. If sex hurts, you're usually less likely to do it.

So much is unknown when it comes to endometriosis and fertility. I won't know if it will affect my ability to conceive until I try, and I won't know how I will find the pain and discomfort of pregnancy until I am pregnant. I've heard from people who found their pregnancy to be quite easy in relation to their endo flare-ups and symptoms. They said that labour is nothing compared to a cyst bursting. But I've also heard from people who believed that their endometriosis made pregnancy much worse. More flare-ups, more pain. I've heard from people who found that some of their symptoms disappeared after having a child. I've also heard from people who said their symptoms got worse. That's probably my biggest fear: not being able to care for my child. I think about how debilitating the days leading up to my period are. I have to block them out on my calendar and limit my work commitments and socialising so I can have the peace and comfort of suffering in my own bed.

One thing for certain is that pregnancy does not cure endometriosis. Despite this, a 2023 research paper published by Australian endometriosis organisation EndoActive revealed that out of 3347 survey participants from sixty-four countries, more than half had been advised to fall pregnant or have a baby to manage or treat their endometriosis. Thirty-six per cent were told this would cure their endometriosis. Almost 90 per cent of patients were given this advice by a healthcare professional, such as a gynaecologist or GP.[19]

I've said it time and time again: the lack of education surrounding endometriosis, particularly among medical professionals, is a global issue. Such findings cement the need for investment in training of true endometriosis specialists, whose sole focus is to correctly excise the disease and provide correct guidance on pain and symptom management. Not only this, but as EndoActive co-founder Syl Freedman wrote for *The Guardian* in 2016, surely 'Let's get you well' should come before 'Let's get you pregnant'? 'The attention from health professionals seems to revolve entirely around fertility rather than the woman herself – as if she is purely a vessel for carrying children with no other aspirations.'[20]

This leads me to my next consideration: my career. I feel like I have so much more to achieve before I 'settle down' and because I work in a freelance capacity, a lot of my decision-making is based on a 'now or never' mentality. I want to seize every professional opportunity. Plus, freelancing means that I don't have any leave entitlements, nor are my finances consistent. Having a dog is expensive enough, alongside the general cost of living and soaring rental rates. I'm not the only one feeling the pinch – data from political research organisation RedBridge Group revealed that more than half of 18- to 24-year-olds are delaying starting a family due to the current cost of living pressures.[21] Not to mention things like childcare, or even if I did have to go down the IVF route, a single cycle can set you back more than $10,000.[22] I simply would not feel financially prepared if I were to fall pregnant. A 2019 study found the average family spends $7918 setting up for a new baby, and then $600 a month once they arrive – and that was before the post-pandemic cost of living increases.[23] According to *She's on the Money*, a woman's earnings drop by 55 per cent in the first five years of parenting.[24] These numbers are not cute to me.

> **EVEN THOUGH SOCIETY SANCTIFIES MOTHERHOOD, IT DOES LITTLE TO SUPPORT MOTHERS.**

Working in media, I am conscious that I may be considered 'less appealing' as a mother. Sounds cooked, but I'm afraid that shit still exists. Society is yet to rid itself of the underlying assumption that motherhood might compromise a woman's commitment to her career or that taking time off for maternity leave or childcare responsibilities can disrupt her work continuity and trajectory.

There's Oscar's career aspirations, too. His job as an AFL footballer currently has us living on the opposite side of the country from our entire family and friend network. It's a move that I have wholeheartedly supported (and will tell you more about later) but it has certainly delayed any plans to pop out a kid. I remember one night in 2021 (before I met Oscar), when I turned on the TV to watch *Footy Classified*. Journalist Caroline Wilson was discussing reports that Brisbane key player and then reigning Brownlow medallist Lachie Neale had dropped a 'bombshell, shock trade request' back to his previous club (which so happened to be Oscar's new team, Fremantle). The media release stated that Neale and his wife, Jules, were expecting their first child and weighing up where they would like to raise their family. 'He did not request a trade but has asked for more time to have further discussions with his wife and family,' it read.[25]

Neale is from South Australia and his wife is from Western Australia. A player of his calibre would be on some seriously tasty money and Neale was three years into a five-year deal, so sure, there is an argument for honouring one's contract, but family comes first. What about the sacrifices his wife has made? I was disgusted to hear the panel's commentary. Wilson regarded it as a 'terrible announcement' from Neale, saying that 'he's done the wrong thing'. Matthew Lloyd's response really irked me. 'It's just proven to me that players don't care anymore,' he said.[26]

Neale decided to stay in Brisbane, where his wife gave birth to a baby girl. I don't know the specifics behind their decision, but I found the entire discourse to be unnecessarily harsh and entitled. The media and fans spoke in a manner that disregarded the fact that beyond football, Lachie and Jules are human beings with personal needs. No matter who you are or what you do, it's perfectly valid to prioritise both your career and your family. They are not mutually exclusive.

When I question the appeal of having children, I'm not questioning that feeling of love and joy a mother has. I imagine it to be like nothing else in the world. Rather, I'm considering the labour that is involved in raising a child and what I would have to 'give up'. Because even though society sanctifies motherhood, it does little to support mothers.

This has been a topic close to the heart of Melbourne entrepreneur Phoebe Simmonds, who I met through a mutual friend at a music festival in 2019. At that time, Phoebe was single and living in a Fitzroy share house, her only baby being her CBD hairstyling boutique, The Blow. Fast-forward four years and Phoebe has launched another business, an online baby shop called The Memo, become a stepmum and birthed her first biological child. I spoke to her on my podcast shortly after seeing her Instagram post on International Women's Day, where Phoebe shared a photo of a book by Natalie Kon-Yu called *The Cost of Labour*. The caption read: 'When people ask me how it's all going, having a baby, businesses, adjusting to family rhythms and a "new role", I say, quite frankly, I don't think I'll ever come to terms with it. Particularly the inequality surrounding a woman's role as a caregiver, while balancing the pressures of paid work. This is less to do with my (wonderful) partner and more to do with the systemic misogyny and centuries of patriarchy dominating our social, legal, economic and healthcare systems that have a major impact on a woman's career, health and autonomy.'[27]

Kon-Yu's book articulated exactly how Phoebe felt, particularly this quote: 'It is not our kids' fault that childcare is expensive, or that women wait until they are secure in their jobs to have babies, or that men don't get adequate parental leave, or that the workforce has been casualised or that postnatal hospital care and education are inadequate. To complain about the cost and labour of having children in this particular culture results in being told not to have them then. It is reconfigured as an individual choice, rather than a social problem.'[28]

Phoebe and I spoke in depth about how the notion of caregiving essentially comes down to paid work versus unpaid work, and how society fails to value childcare as an occupation because it's never been valued in the home. She recognised that there was no quick fix. 'I don't think we're going to change major social, economic or political structures overnight. But I think the first point is communicating how we feel and acknowledging that there is inequity when it comes to conceiving, growing and raising a child.'[29]

Ten months following Phoebe's Instagram post, a group of famous dads including Hamish Blake, Simon Pryce (aka the Red Wiggle) and Australia's Local Hero of 2023, Amar Singh, rallied together alongside the Minderoo Foundation's Thrive By Five initiative and published 'Dads' Action Plan for the Early Years', in which they asked for a national strategy to support fathers to take an equal share of parenting. Their statement included requesting universal access to early childhood education and care, twelve weeks' paid paternity leave, better parenting and perinatal resources for dads, and incentives for men to become early childhood educators.[30] Achieving those goals would be a step in the right direction.

So what would I do if I were to fall pregnant right now? It's a question I struggle to answer, especially when I have friends like Ash, who is yearning to have children, as well as a loved one who recently delivered a twenty-week-old stillborn. I tried to describe this whiplash of emotions when I chatted with Madison Griffiths, who had an abortion at the age of twenty-seven and documented the experience in her acclaimed book, *Tissue*.[31]

TO BABY OR NOT TO BABY

Madison has been pro-choice ever since she was 'an arrogant teenager stepping foot into her arts degree at uni',[32] studying philosophy and criminology. 'I was always interested in women's issues but I had conveniently avoided it in terms of my own personal life. I was very privileged in the sense that no friend had ever come to me with an unwanted pregnancy and I myself had never encountered an unwanted pregnancy.'

Madison had a pretty strong intuition about how she would handle it if or when it came, which ended up being in the midst of the strict Melbourne lockdowns of 2021. 'I love talking about this in the context of your book because I did find a real generational complexity in the sense that I was in that late-twenties pocket wanting to date but with a curfew at 9 p.m., feeling perpetually grounded.' It was in those windows of freedom between lockdowns that Madison met her partner and became pregnant. 'It's interesting to think how we, as millennials, see being parents. I mean, I'm renting. I have nothing behind my name. I'm relying on a job seeker payment to maybe help me buy 3 grams of weed, you know? Like, how can I bring a baby into this world?'

Madison tells me about a friend who terminated a pregnancy in her early twenties and how different their experiences were. For her friend, people assumed that she was on her way to the abortion clinic. But for Madison, people were nervous. 'They didn't want to assume, which I actually found absurd,' she reflected. 'I was like, I'm a child! Assume that I'm getting an abortion, please, because you not assuming is making me crazy!'

This comment from Madison took me back to 2012 when Katy Perry spoke to the *Daily Mirror* about her maternal aspirations. 'I want to be a mother but now's not the right time. A baby can't have a baby, and I'm still a baby.'[33] Perry was twenty-eight at the time.

According to the Australian Institute of Health and Welfare, the average age of mothers has risen over time, from thirty in 2011 to thirty-one in 2021.[34] In 1975, the average age of women giving birth was twenty-five and that age has continued to rise with contraception becoming more widely available and women being granted greater access to tertiary education.[35] It's increasingly common for women to feel 'too young' to have children in their twenties as a result.

Despite being so pro-choice, the abortion was still traumatic for Madison. It came in a physical form, the pain of passing so much blood, which brought up feelings Madison had about the way women's pain is treated medically and, specifically, the dismissal she had previously experienced in her treatment of vaginismus. But it was also the grief and guilt, as Madison wrote in her book. 'Pregnancy was a betrayal to yourself and your future, abortion a betrayal to that life.' And the anger. 'It is not the mention of regret I find disagreeable; it's the word "decision" that leaves me irritated. As if this were ever my decision, to have life dissolve inside of me only to push it out, bloodied and hapless. No woman, no pregnant person, wants to make this decision.'[36]

I asked Madison if she still wanted children, which took her by surprise. 'I love that you asked me that because it's the big question that people are terrified to ask. You're the first person, even after doing media for *Tissue*.' She told me she doesn't think she's there. 'I think if I wanted kids, I'd want them more, if that makes sense.'[37]

It's a weird but somewhat common assumption that because you have had an abortion, it means you won't ever want children. Maybe it just wasn't right at that time. It also doesn't mean that you don't love children. Perhaps you just don't love them for yourself, and that's okay.

There are people in my life who would frown upon the decision to abort, and I feel like this goes back to the sense of entitlement that we have over women's bodies. But hey, my body, my choice. Women are encouraged to take control of our fertility from puberty, with some girls being prescribed the pill as early as age twelve. So why does this change when abortion enters the chat? Especially when you consider how common it is.

The *Australia and New Zealand Journal of Public Health* published an article stating that around one in six Australian women have had an abortion by their mid-thirties.[38] As Gina Rushton wrote for *The Guardian*, 'If we trust people with the decision to have children, we can trust them with the decision not to.'[39]

What I am experiencing – the Parenthood Dilemma – is the international title of Gina's book, *The Most Important Job in the World*.[40] When Gina was growing up, the women in her family were homemakers and she resented the notion that she too should confine her identity to the home because of her gender. So, she dedicated herself to a career in journalism. Through our laptop screens, Gina told me how she was raised on a kind of feminism that tended to degrade motherhood and the domestic sphere. 'It's kind of, like, you're gonna be a girlboss. You're gonna emancipate yourself through the office and your career is going to be the most important thing to you.'[41] It was anti-maternal and, as she wrote, calling for women to become 'more' than 'just' mothers.

Things took a turn for Gina in 2019 when she was rushed to hospital in an ambulance with severe abdominal pain. Emergency surgery revealed a large cyst had burst on her ovary. She was told the ovary was 'dead', which would affect her fertility, and just like that, Gina was forced to *really* consider her maternal desires. 'I was stuck because I really was like, *I definitely don't want kids*. But when someone's like, okay, the number of sites where you can produce an egg is about to halve, you do think, *Oh shit, do I actually want kids?*'[42]

Gina was surprised by how upset the experience of having her fertility threatened made her. 'I'm probably a bit more pissed off than the average person about how annoying it is that you have to even think about this stuff when you're not quite ready to.'[43]

From this, Gina's book was born, aiming to reject the notion that people 'just know' whether they want kids or not. 'Nothing so quickly confirms what you love and fear most about the world and yourself like the question of whether or not you want children.'[44]

I have many friends who are obsessed with their children and I love seeing how much they love being mothers, just as I know they love seeing my joy in the career I'm carving out for myself. But sometimes it is hard not to lean into the Mummy Binary, a concept that Ruby Warrington explored in *Women Without Kids*.[45] (Fun fact: Warrington initially wanted to call the book *Selfish C*nt*, but realised it probs wasn't the easiest sell.) It's this idea that mothers will be fulfilled by their decision to become mothers and will find themselves in their mothering. The non-mothers, on the other hand, are seen at best as deserving of our sympathy, or at worst as selfish, defective and destined to regret their decision.

Within the non-mother camp, there is another binary: the child-*less* people, those who are unable to have children; and the child-*free*, those who have made a conscious decision not to have children. The latter, Warrington wrote, were more likely to be painted in the least favourable light. That's the thing, growing up, it is instilled in us that our sole purpose is to have babies. That motherhood is our highest calling in this world. That motherhood is 'the path to her ultimate fulfillment', as Warrington said.[46]

This reminds me of my podcast conversation with Laura Henshaw, CEO of Kic, who attributed her maternal confusion to growing up fearing and trying to avoid pregnancy to then suddenly being faced with a deadline. The external pressure didn't help. 'We don't ask "Do you *want* to have children?" It's like, "*When* are you having children?", which automatically puts that assumption of "Well, you should be" and if not, it's a problem.'[47] A few months following our conversation, Laura published a piece in *Marie Claire Australia* titled 'Why I'm afraid to have a baby'. She wrote about how she feared that having a child would mean sacrificing the ability to prioritise herself during the very little free time she has. 'But then I feel guilty for being selfish – shouldn't I want to sacrifice those things to become a mother? Everyone tells me that you are never truly "ready" but I thought I would be closer to "ready" than this by now.'[48]

I found Laura's comment about being expected to want to make sacrifices to become a mother really interesting, because many women feel like they have to *make up* for not wanting to be a mother. That with all this supposed free time up their sleeves, women should make their lives big, busy and bustling to compensate for not having children. Because if not a mother, then what?

It's this pronatalist ideology that paints a picture of women without children as deviant, damaged or deranged. Think about the stories we were told as children and, specifically, who the villains were. From *The Little Mermaid*'s Ursula to the evil queen in *Snow White*, these fairytale schemers were more often than not childless women. If not an all-out villain, then we must either be 'ruthless' career women or 'weird' cat ladies. A life without having children doesn't necessitate being filled with fun, travel, money or career success unless, of course, you genuinely want those things. But it's also totally fine if your idea of a fulfilling and meaningful life is one that is chill, uncomplicated and, dare I say, average!

Rather than the Mummy Binary, Warrington instead proposed the Motherhood Spectrum – a way of recognising that any person, regardless of gender and biological sex, will have a desire or an experience of parenthood that is influenced by a multitude of factors, such as cultural background, health, finances, relationship status and life goals, that might shift throughout life. Warrington regarded this as a kinder, more compassionate and humane way of thinking about experiences of parenthood and non-parenthood. Some people sit on the affirmative yes side of becoming a mother and others sit on the affirmative no side. But there are also people in the middle, such as Miley Cyrus! In her June 2024 cover story with *W Magazine*, the singer-songwriter revealed that she is still unsure about her future plans when it comes to having a family. 'I'm thirty-one now, and I still don't know if I want kids or not,' Cyrus said. 'I feel like my fans kind of are my kids in some way. I've heard Dolly [Parton] say that too, because she didn't have kids.'[49]

As Gina said to me in our conversation, we have narrow ideas of what kind of people become mothers and what kind of people don't. But when we reconsider the fact that by 2030, families without children are expected to outnumber those with children for the first time,[50] having children may no longer be the norm at all.

And other ideas about parenthood are slowly broadening, with more queer people and couples becoming parents through adoption, IVF or surrogacy. Long before social norms, expectations or homophobia came into the picture, and long before he was pondering sexuality or gender, Sean Szeps wanted to be a mother more than anything. 'I loved my mum. I loved my grandmothers. I hoped in this fantasy land that I could have little nuggets running around and have a career and a husband and that's exactly what I have now. I'm not a mother, but hey, I am the primary parent and I am a father who mothers.'[51]

As a young boy, Sean quickly realised that women were the unsung heroes. 'I picked up on the fact that they were the ones getting everything done. But I also had a really great dad who praised my mum constantly. I had a father who acknowledged the amount of work she did and was constantly like, "We'd be nothing without you, where would we be without you, listen to your mother, we owe all this to your mother".'

Sean isn't sure if it has to do with gender or if it is more an observation of roles. 'No matter what your gender is, there are women who are not natural mothers and there are men who were born to be dads. Most of my life was spent watching this mother I had who was just such a good mum, a Mary Poppins in so many ways, and thinking, *I'm just going to acquire all those skills.*'

Sean described his journey to parenthood as a 'weird, sadistic rollercoaster ride'. His first job was babysitting, which came naturally given he had looked after many cousins growing up, and while he yearned to have his own kids, he didn't expect it to happen so soon. 'I would have preferred to have kids later,' Sean told me. 'My husband is ten years older than me and so he was approaching forty and I was approaching thirty when we had kids. He felt the clock ticking and said he didn't want to be at our kids' graduation in his sixties.'

Originally Sean had envisioned taking his career to the next level in his thirties and becoming a dad by the end of that decade, but he had to reimagine everything from scratch. A family member of Sean's donated their eggs and his husband, Josh, gave the sperm to create the embryo. Twins were born, and three months into their new chapter as a family unit, Josh got a job offer in Australia and they moved over from New York with babies in tow, where Sean swapped his title of advertising executive for stay-at-home-parent in a country he didn't know anything about. 'It was such an interesting start to that decade because it really humbled me. You had plans. You had a vision. And then in the blink of an eye, a decision is made and the plans and the vision shatter down. You rebuild.'

In his book *Not Like Other Dads*, Sean shared how he had felt disappointed by Sydney in comparison to his time in New York and LA, and how much the language surrounding diverse parenting was lacking. 'When I lived in LA, there was just an overriding expectation that there was the possibility someone was gay or lesbian, so people just constantly said partner. It was a constant stream of more accepting language that left me feeling more comfortable in outing myself and then I came to Sydney and it was almost like that script didn't exist. People were constantly like, "Where's your wife?"'[52]

Sean came to terms with the fact that it wasn't malicious and now feels fine correcting people, but that's not to say that it wasn't tiring. 'Of course this country has great examples of gay people and drag queens for literally decades. This country has been quite progressive in that case, but those people weren't having children. So the Australian community had decided. They are camp. They are fun. They party. They are a part of nightlife. It is art but they weren't people seen through the lens of parenthood really and so it felt like I was a forced advocate in a time where I wasn't emotionally prepared or capable of it because I was sad and depressed.'

You could say that my fertility is my Roman Empire. I think about it every damn day and go back and forth on how I'm feeling. Do I want to remain the main character in my life? Or do I want to step back into a supporting role until the kid leaves the nest? When my mum was my age, she had four children under the age of four. She was the primary caregiver but she also worked. I feel fortunate that she has never pressured me to follow in her maternal footsteps, but I would be lying if I said I don't melt at the thought of cradling a mini-me in my arms. Ugh, to baby or not to baby?!

It's still a big TBC from me. The decision to become a parent is not a once-off, 'Lock it in, Eddie' kind of decision. While I lack the desire to drop everything in my life right now for nappies and dummies, I may also become clucky as all hell in a year. What is important for me is knowing I can be trusted to make decisions about my body. Just like Ash when she insisted on the AMH test. Just like Madison, who chose to abort. *Not* like Treasurer Jim Chalmers, who in May 2024 publicly declared that he wanted to see an increase in the Australian birth rate, without giving much financial incentive in his budget announcement of the same year. My eyes could not have rolled further back into my head if I had tried. I spoke about this on *Today Extra*, asking for Jim to get back to us all once the government had improved policies regarding work and leave entitlements, caregiving incentives and childcare funding.[53] I also thought back to my conversation with Sean Szeps.

'Honestly, if our government stepped it up like other governments in other countries and said we're going to really support women who walk away from work, we're going to mandate strong financial support systems and praise, not judge, parents with children, we're going to figure out support systems, villages, community activities that make it easier to be parents and we're going to reward them somehow. Like if those things happen, maybe people would look at it as an option. It's kind of like being a teacher. It's like a thankless job that's underpaid. Why would any of the next generation want to become one instead of us going, "Wait a second. This is one of the most important jobs, let's pay them more. Let's figure out ways to support them better." So I don't blame young people who look at the options and go, "Why would I want to do those things?"'[54]

Preach. I deserve the space to figure out what I want and how I feel, as do you. And if I'm makin' babies or not, I'm doing it on my own terms.

i DO ...
need to talk about marriage

> CAN A WOMAN WHO'S FOUGHT FOR EQUALITY AND RESPECT, AGAINST SEXISM AND MISOGYNY, BECOME A BRIDE? OR DOES THAT MAKE THEM A WALKING CONTRADICTION?

The event was sold out and the Brunswick Ballroom was bustling with women, with very few men in sight – I saw no more than ten. As I scanned the room for a seat, the conversations echoing around me signalled that I wasn't the only one who'd rocked up alone. The chitchat was wholesome, with women asking each other what they did for work and what had enticed them to attend.

It was a crisp Sunday night in June 2023 and I was at 'Killing the Angel', a discussion on the topic of what it means to reject the burden of marriage and live purposefully alone.[1] The feminist writer Clementine Ford was moderating and I had previously interviewed two of the speakers, Jill Stark and Jacinta Parsons, on my own podcast. I was nervous about attending solo – and even more so as someone in a happy, heterosexual relationship. But despite living with a male partner, I felt the content was still relevant and important to me.

A kind woman towards the back of the room noticed my searching gaze and offered the bar stool next to her. She told me she was the only single person in her group of girlfriends and none of them had been interested in coming along with her. To my left sat two women in their forties. One was recently divorced, the other joining her for moral support. A minute or two later, Ford took to the stage, fairy lights softly glistening behind her.

Her opening address explained that the event title was a rebuttal to a poem titled 'The Angel in the House', by English poet Coventry Patmore, initially published in 1854, which celebrated the ideal of domesticity, portraying the poet's angelic wife as a model for all women in Victorian society.[2] The concept of the Angel in the House, Ford explained, required women to display unwavering devotion and submission to their husbands. This Angel symbolised passivity and powerlessness, characterised by qualities such as meekness, charm, grace, sympathy, self-sacrifice and, above all, purity. The poem was dissected and met with a collective cringe and a sea of heads nodded before me as Ford declared her desire to take down what this Angel represented, dropping iconic lines like, 'Men get to be fathers of the world, women just mothers of babies', and 'Motherhood first, marriage second, me last'.

Jill Stark was up next and shared how, at the age of forty-seven, she felt the societal expectation to have nightmares about reaching midlife without a husband or kids. Instead, her nightmares involved a man moving in, rearranging her belongings and bringing in ugly bro furniture. Stark revealed how often she is asked whether single life is lonely, when the loneliest she ever felt was during a loveless, toxic relationship. She questioned why society deemed it acceptable to inquire why someone is still single but never 'Why are you still married to that guy?'

After Stark was my former colleague Jacinta Parsons, who I affectionately dubbed my 'radio mom' after working together at the ABC. She provided a poignant reflection on living in solitude during her first year of being single following a 25-year marriage. Senior Lecturer Dr Yves Rees then gave a witty recount of being deemed 'the perfect woman' at twenty-seven, living with their partner for four years and ready to sail off into the heteronormative sunset, before cracks appeared and they realised they were transgender at age thirty. Last was gender equality commentator Karen Pickering, who delivered an emotional account of how partnership and family were modelled for her growing up, arguing that the way society treats single mothers is why so many people don't leave their marriages.

The ideas presented in 'Killing the Angel' were a far cry from my own childhood ideals, where I idolised *The Swan Princess* and wanted to marry Prince Derek. (What a spud, by the way – he was absolutely punching above his weight with Odette. Remember that iconic scene where Odette rejects Derek's marriage proposal because he can't think of any other reason to wed than the fact that Odette is beautiful?) Yet here I sat at thirty-two, ready to lift the veil on heterosexual marriage and figure out what's in it for me. Baby Bridget may have wanted to be a bride, but what about Bridget in her thirties?

While popular culture and broader societal norms instilled in me the idea that marriage is this wonderful, fulfilling institution that I should aspire to, there were no direct influences or pressures in my life pushing me in that direction. Mum's parents divorced when she was in primary school and I can't say I've ever witnessed my parents embody a particularly romantic or affectionate marriage, nor have they ever pressured me to settle down. One of my earliest memories involves gatecrashing Nanny's second wedding, to a man named George. My twin sister and I must have been around three or four years old when we squirmed out of our parents' arms mid-ceremony and dashed up to Nanny, who was standing at the altar. She kneeled to meet us at eye level and we asked her what she was doing – which was a fair question because George turned out to be a massive prick and they divorced shortly after. Yet somewhere along the way, between the ages of twenty-five and twenty-nine when I was in a serious relationship, I decided I wanted to get married.

Although nobody within my immediate friend circle in Melbourne was settling down, every time I opened Facebook or Instagram, I was met with an engagement post or wedding photo album from someone I knew back home in Ballarat. A number of my ex's friends were getting hitched, as was his older sister. Admittedly, the thought *How are they getting married before me?* crossed my mind more than once when it was a notorious high school bully or general douchebag.

> **'FIRST COMES LOVE, THEN COMES MARRIAGE, THEN COMES BABY IN A BABY CARRIAGE.' THAT WAS THE SCRIPT FOR LIFE, RIGHT?**

Suddenly, everything I did was marriage-minded. I actively looked up dresses, rings, flowers, cakes and table styling, bookmarking posts to an Instagram folder labelled with the ring emoji. I listened intently to the lyrics of songs that Mark and I both loved, wondering where they could fit in the ceremony. We weren't even engaged, for Christ's sake! But I found myself anticipating it, expecting it to unfold like clockwork, especially as thirty loomed. Just like the old rhyme: 'First comes love, then comes marriage, then comes baby in a baby carriage.' That was the script for life, right?

I DO... NEED TO TALK ABOUT MARRIAGE

Up until my thirties, I never questioned why I wanted something I didn't know much about. Sure, we grew up on weddings – Posh and Becks, Brad and Jen, not to mention the endless rom-coms centred around a bride! – but I had never stopped to think about what marriage actually meant or how it even began. I realised that I (like many others, I suspect) was fixated on the celebration, rather than the institution. All I was thinking about was The Big Day as opposed to All of the Days that Followed. This is where I give capitalism the side eye for hyper-valuing every aspect of weddings (Flowers! Doughnut walls! Random saxophone man!). Not to mention social media for creating the beast that is the highlight reel, consequently fuelling comparison culture. This is where I think the distinction between marriage and weddings becomes blurred. I truly believe some people enter into marriage without fully grasping that their decision is influenced more by societal norms and the ceremonial aspect, rather than a deep, heartfelt declaration of love.

Then again, marriage hasn't always been about love. If you were to google 'marriage', you would probably be met with a definition along the lines of 'the union of two people'. But as Elizabeth Gilbert wrote in her book *Committed: A Love Story*, marriage doesn't like to sit still long enough for anyone to capture its portrait very clearly. 'Marriage shifts. It changes over the centuries the way that Irish weather changes; constantly, surprisingly, swiftly.'[3]

Allow me to do a quick intro to Gilbert because perhaps, like me, you were also living under a rock and were late in realising that the major motion picture *Eat, Pray, Love*, starring Julia Roberts, is based on Gilbert's 2006 memoir of the same title. I discovered this upon reading her next book, *Committed*, which picks up with Gilbert and her partner (yes, the guy from Bali!) wanting to settle in the United States but facing the necessity of marriage due to immigration issues. Despite both of them having vowed never to marry again after their experiences with divorce, the couple are forced to reconsider returning to this institution, and Gilbert delves into her own apprehensions, doubts and – spoiler alert – eventual acceptance of the idea of marriage.

The book explores the history of marriage and examines its evolution from a practical and economic arrangement between families to a more romanticised, individualised institution. I was blown away to learn just how many different shapes and forms marriage has taken over the centuries, such as in China, where the definition of marriage once included a 'ghost marriage' between a living woman of rank and a dead man from a good family, in order to seal the bonds of unity between two clans. This union became a goal for many Chinese women in the nineteenth century who sought economic independence and autonomy. 'This brought her all the social status of marriage with none of the constraints or inconveniences of actual wifehood,' Gilbert explained. Love that for them. In modern revolutionary Iran, marriage was at one point treated as a deliberately temporary union. Young couples could request a special marriage permit called a 'sigheh' from a mullah. This permit, essentially a 24-hour 'marriage pass', allowed the male and female to be seen together in public safely or to legally have sex during that period. Even Ancient Rome recognised marriages between aristocratic males!

Numerous frameworks of marriage have existed, but one grim, persistent issue that has been difficult to shrug off is, of course, the patriarchy and, zooming in a little further, Christian beliefs that have exhibited patriarchal norms and structures. Now, I want to be respectful to people who have their own relationship with what they define as God. I also want to be transparent in sharing that I am an atheist. For that reason, you can probably see why I find it hard to ignore the extent to which Christianity has been used to justify and reinforce male dominance and control over women and their societal roles, especially within the context of marriage.

Just take a look at 1 Timothy 2:12, from the New Testament of the Bible, which states, 'I do not permit a woman to teach or to assume authority over a man; she must be quiet.'[4] *Shhhh!* Or how according to the Bible (Genesis 2:7), God made a dude named Adam and then he nicked a rib while Adam was asleep, and out of that rib made a woman to be a helper, who was later named Eve.[5] God appointed Adam as the head of the human race and Eve was there to serve. And I don't mean in a sassy way. She was basically at Adam's disposal. As Clementine Ford noted in her 2023 book *I Don't*, 'The biblical depiction of Woman as having been plucked out of Man's rib and therefore obliged forever more to live in deference to his authority isn't just a problematic footnote in an otherwise thumpingly good read – it's at the core of Judeo-Christian beliefs, which are consistently invoked by modern-day lawmakers as being integral to the "foundation of western civilisation".'[6]

Ford went on to say, 'I am a marriage abolitionist because I cannot in good conscience support an institution that has enslaved women sexually, reproductively, financially and domestically.' I can understand why Ford has no interest in marriage's salvation.

> ## MARRIAGE HASN'T ALWAYS BEEN ABOUT LOVE.

There is a question that has loomed over my own ponderings on marriage: can you be a feminist and still get married? Feminism, by my definition, is largely about choice and agency. But does that include the choice to wed? Can you not believe in The One but still get married? Can a woman who's fought for equality and respect, against sexism and misogyny, become a bride? Or does that make them a walking contradiction?

This question about feminism and marriage is pretty loaded, and one I couldn't answer alone, so I consulted some of my favourite female brains – the first being Hannah Ferguson, co-founder and CEO of Cheek Media Co. I wanted to talk to Hannah after reading her bestselling book *Bite Back*, which eloquently and fearlessly tackles social and political issues facing young women in modern Australia. For Hannah, it was about pondering that distinction between a marriage and celebrating love through the party of a wedding. 'You can be a feminist and still want to get married, but let's not pretend that getting married is a feminist act itself. I think most people want to get married not because of marriage itself, but because of the social pressure and belief that they desire it innately, when it's entirely because you want what your friends have done. It's like this phenomenon of mimicked desire, not true "want", if that makes sense.'[7]

Flex Mami, one of my favourite cultural commentators, thinks you can be a feminist and still marry on a technicality. 'If we can manage to be feminists under patriarchy, I think we can be a feminist and get married. However, I would argue that your cognitive dissonance would be the basis to justify [your decision], because traditional marriage customs are about subjugation to the man, which is not feminist. But you know, better the devil you know, et cetera, et cetera.'[8]

Gina Rushton, who you heard from when we talked babies, was

strong in her stance. 'Plenty of feminists are married! I think it's obviously got a gross history – women as property to be transferred between one man (father) to another man (husband) – but there doesn't have to be anything inherently anti-feminist in it in 2024.'[9]

What about the progressive women in my life who have chosen to marry? Jamila Rizvi, author, podcaster, writer and deputy managing director at Future Women, not only believed you could be a feminist and get married, but that you could also have a feminist marriage. 'When you're breaking down oppressive systems, like patriarchy, there are two pathways to doing so,' she said. 'You can metaphorically burn the whole thing to the ground, or you can re-form the structures it's created to be more equal. The fight for marriage equality was part of that reforming and, in my mind, having a feminist marriage can be too.' For Jamila and her husband, that looks like an ongoing conversation and negotiation about how they spend their time and labour. 'Equality in marriage is not a decision you make once. You have to actively practise it every day to avoid falling into the gender norms we've all been conditioned to follow.'[10]

As for Michelle Andrews, co-founder of Shameless Media, it never occurred to her that she couldn't be a feminist in her marriage. Mich told me via email how she fell in love with her now-husband at twenty-one and how they have grown into fully fledged adults side by side. 'He was raised by a feminist mother, as was I, so the concept that my dreams and priorities were of equal weight to his was never even a question. Almost a decade on, I co-own a business, and to ease the load, Mitch does the lion's share of housework (cleaning, grocery shopping, laundry) because I work longer hours than he does. The older I get, the more I realise how limiting it can be to make umbrella statements about what feminism is and isn't. A marriage is so personal. Every single one looks different. And sure, historically, the concept was steeped in patriarchy. But right now, in my life, my marriage certificate means: "I love you. We are a team. We are equals. And I have got your back."'[11]

In my research, I came across Dr Meagan Tyler, a professor of feminist theory in Melbourne, who told *ABC News* that 'just because you're a feminist and getting married, marriage doesn't become feminist'.[12] In her 2011 essay, 'Saying I don't: Moving beyond marriage', Tyler argued that 'opting out of marriage altogether will provide a quicker path to progress, as only the death of marriage can bring about the dawn of equality for all'.[13]

Despite both Ford's and Tyler's desire to abolish marriage, data indicates that the institution isn't going anywhere anytime soon. In 2022, the Australian Bureau of Statistics reported 127,161 marriages registered in Australia, the highest number on record. Of course, this followed two years of pandemic impact, with 78,987 marriages recorded in 2020 and 89,167 in 2021. Before 2022, the highest number of marriages was documented in 2012, totalling 123,243.[14]

We also need to consider the legalisation of same-sex marriage in Australia in 2017. In the following year, 58 per cent of same-sex marriages were between females, and as high as 66 per cent in Western Australia and 65 per cent in Tasmania.[15] According to ABS data, the predominant age range for lesbians to marry falls between twenty-five and thirty-five years old, which could be indicative of a desire to establish families within the framework of marriage. Conversely, gay men tend to marry at later stages of life, with almost 25 per cent tying the knot between the ages of fifty and fifty-nine.[16]

British feminist author Rachael Lennon walked down the aisle with her wife three years after same-sex marriages started to be legally practised in England and Wales. In her book, *Wedded Wife: A Feminist History of Marriage*, Lennon detailed how she 'did not spend a great

> **MY OWN MAJOR MARRIAGE ICKS INCLUDE TRADITIONAL VOWS AND PROMISING TO 'OBEY' MY HUSBAND – EW, I'M NOT A DOG!**

deal of time deeply interrogating' her motivations for marriage. 'Getting married provided an opportunity to commit to each other in a serious way,' she wrote.[17]

Not gonna lie, it was a bit of a headfuck to have two feminist books on marriage released within six months of each other, with Ford, the self-proclaimed 'hopeless romantic', wanting to abolish the institution, and the lesbian previously excluded from said institution believing you could have a feminist marriage. But it just goes to show how complex the history and discourse is. For Lennon, nothing about marriage was inevitable, natural or fated, nor did she believe that there was such a thing as a truly traditional marriage. 'History gives us licence to shake off customs where they pull us in a direction that we do not want to go. Thus marriage is, and always has been, what we choose to make of it.' Lennon believed, '[Feminism] is about questioning, about looking again. And again. Challenging the assumptions, defaults and expectations we have grown up with. Unpicking the partial versions of the past that we have inherited and imagining new and fairer futures.'

The varying stances extended to my podcast listeners. Alexandra from Langwarrin never thought she would get married. 'It always felt a bit icky and weird, and I didn't think as a gay woman that I could. Also, why would I need to get married?' Alexandra had always considered the institution to be ancient and ownership-oriented, but after the plebiscite and hearing other perspectives, mostly regarding unity and having the 'right' to get married, she started seeing things differently. 'I am lucky to be in a healthy relationship, we are engaged and we have a beautiful baby girl. Since having her, it's more about just tying us all together a little more and officially sharing surnames, which I guess is very surface level but is also a way of us being proud and being able to access the same ceremony as everyone else and celebrate with our nearest and dearest.'

I DO... NEED TO TALK ABOUT MARRIAGE

Lauren is thirty-one and from Melbourne, and while she hasn't discussed marriage with her current partner, she has been engaged twice before, to a man at age twenty-three and to a woman at the age of twenty-nine. 'Given my history you'd think I'd be against it, but I'm still for marriage!' she said. Despite the first engagement being due to heteronormative pressures, Lauren discovered that upon coming out, she still wanted the one and only to grow old with. 'Being married to them was part of that idea for me. It is hard to be a feminist and to believe such ideals as well given how they started but there's also the beauty in being able to redefine it. In my mind it's about the celebration and making it your own.'

Lily is thirty years old and in a same-sex relationship where she lives with her partner and wants to have children in the future. 'Overall, what's important to me is having a loving, grounded, secure and long-lasting relationship. But whether or not marriage is necessary is a big question on my mind,' she told me on Instagram. Lily thinks celebrating her and her partner's love with a big party would be magical, but grapples with the idea of legally binding vows. 'Particularly the ownership of a woman and emphasis on her purity. That creeps me out so much!' According to Lily, many of her friends are opting not to get married. Instead, they view milestones such as buying houses and having children as bigger signifiers of their everlasting commitment to each other. This is seen in the statistics too. Today, more than 80 per cent of couples already share a home before they marry.[18]

It seems that people are together for longer before marriage and really thinking about whether they want to take that next step. According to the Australian Bureau of Statistics, the average marriage age has increased to 32.5 years for males (from 32.1 years in 2021) and 30.9 years for females (from 30.5 years in 2021).[19] The world is vastly different to when my mum and dad got married, at the ages of twenty-four and twenty-six respectively. Mum reckons 'it's just what you did back then', but it goes deeper than that. Women faced numerous historical barriers such as limited access to education, career opportunities and financial independence. And, of course, there were the sexist attitudes and societal pressures regarding spinsterhood and the lack of an equivalent for men.

Unfortunately, this is still the case in a number of places around the world, and here's where I need to acknowledge the privilege I have in even being able to consider whether I want to get married. Women in many cultures are still being forced to marry, some still children themselves, and for many, divorce is not an option. I feel extremely lucky that I get to choose for myself whether to wed, and that my life literally does not depend on it.

So the question for me is one of want, not need. Do I *want* to get married? According to Elizabeth Gilbert, marriage becomes hard work once you have poured the entirety of your life's expectations for happiness into the hands of one mere person, a sentiment I believe applies to any committed romantic relationship.[20] So if marriage plays the same role in personal fulfilment and self-actualisation as being in a long-term relationship, and many of us in Western cultures don't actually need to get married, why take that step? What is the difference between being married and being in a long-term de facto relationship, also referred to as a domestic partnership? *Is* there a difference?

On the Australian Government website, three relationship types are listed. Firstly, there's legal marriage, which is the union of two people to the exclusion of all others, voluntarily entered into for life, solemnised by an authorised celebrant as prescribed within the *Marriage Act 1961*. Secondly, we have a registered relationship, which is also known as a 'civil union', 'civil partnership' or 'significant relationship'. They have

> **THE QUESTION FOR ME IS ONE OF WANT, NOT NEED. DO I *WANT* TO GET MARRIED?**

been registered under a law of an Australian state or territory as a prescribed kind of relationship, but they are currently not registrable in the Northern Territory or Western Australia. Thirdly, there is a de facto relationship, which is defined under the *Family Law Act 1975* as a relationship between two people (who are not legally married or related by family) who live together on a 'genuine domestic basis'.[21] According to the last census in 2021, over two million Australians were in a de facto relationship.[22]

For a lot of legal and financial stuff, married couples just need to flash their certificate or tick a box. It can be a lot harder for people in de facto relationships. And there are different definitions of what is considered a de facto relationship that are used for different purposes. Take Centrelink, for example, where a couple is considered to be in a de facto relationship from the moment they start living together. Under migration law, however, parties must be able to show that they have been living together for a period of twelve months or longer.[23]

The legislation goes on to outline further criteria to determine if two individuals qualify as 'a couple'. This includes things like the duration of the relationship, whether a sexual relationship exists, the presence of children, a shared residence, financial dependence, mutual commitment to a shared life, the relationship's reputation and public aspects, as well as the ownership, use and acquisition of shared assets by the individuals involved. How random is the reputation check – like, are they sussing people's Instagrams for that?!

Despite potential implications should shit hit the fan, de facto relationships continue to rise as a preferred dynamic. I think about Murray and Cathryn, a de facto couple who I met through my partner, Oscar. In 2013, Oscar's older brother Tom flew to the United States and was seated next to Murray and Cathryn. They were all headed for Las

I DO . . . NEED TO TALK ABOUT MARRIAGE

Vegas and ended up chatting for the entire fourteen-hour journey. Tom was to spend a few nights there by himself before meeting friends, so Murray and Cathryn passed on their number in case he wanted to hang out. They ended up having dinner, which led to cocktails and a rowdy night on the Strip. Now, Murray and Cathryn are like family. They look after Tom's kids, come to his and Oscar's football games, and we catch up for dinner. They're basically like our aunt and uncle.

Murray and Cathryn met at work in 1987 and became friends with common interests. Over the years, they both had other relationships (and marriages) that came and went. Eventually, their friendship developed into something more and they have been together ever since. 'We'd both been in marriages that didn't work, so we realised pretty early on that neither of us were keen to repeat the experience. Our families had accepted us as a long-term couple and that was enough validation for us,' they reflected during a weekend text message exchange.

When I asked why they chose not to marry, Murray and Cathryn's response was straightforward. 'What we have works, we figure why change it just to conform? Also, we've heard many times of people being happily together for years, they get married and then it all falls apart. Why take that risk? In our particular case, we are on top of the happiness ladder already. It doesn't get any better!'

Murray and Cathryn offered frank advice to those nearing thirty or navigating their thirties, feeling pressured to marry or fearing they're lagging behind: 'Follow your instincts. While marriage works well for many, it simply isn't the path for us at this moment.' They are one of the happiest couples I know.

One of the more obvious differences between marriage and a de facto/domestic relationship, however, is the d-word. While ending a de facto relationship is fairly straightforward, ending a marriage requires going through the divorce process ... which can get messy depending on the circumstances. The median age for divorce increased from 45.9 in 2021 to 46.7 in 2022 for males and from 43.0 to 43.7 for females[24] and I know quite a few women who divorced in their late twenties and early thirties. While divorce isn't always tragic, and is for many people the right decision, as Mandy Len Catron wrote for *The Atlantic*, the sentiment still prevails that marriage makes us happy and divorce leaves us lonely, and that never getting married at all is a fundamental failure of belonging.[25] But many women are pushing back against that idea.

Home cook and bestselling author Charlotte Ree met the man who would become her husband when she was nineteen. Ten years later, she filed for divorce and she cooked her way out of heartbreak, reclaiming her identity through food. 'I fully thought I'd be married and have a kid by twenty-eight, and now I am allowing myself to have hopes and dreams,'[26] she wrote for the *Sydney Morning Herald*. 'If it is meant to be, it will be.'

While some of her friends were bookmarking and circling photos of rings to leave out for their partners, my friend Ash didn't even think she wanted to get married. She was happy having a nice solid relationship. Becoming a mother was more important to Ash and she didn't feel like she needed to be married first in order to do that. 'It was never really on my radar,' she told me as we sat on her lounge room floor in her Ballarat rental one Sunday afternoon in 2022.[27] 'We were living in Geelong together and had just built a house. Things were going really well but I had stumbled across a receipt for a ring, so I knew it was coming.'

Ash was twenty-six when she got married. 'The wedding was beautiful. Everything was wonderful, but in hindsight, I was still very young.' A child bride, as Ilana from *Broad City* would say. Ash was also completely unsuspecting as to what would happen next.

'The first year into our marriage, we hit lots of bumps that I found quite unexpected. I found myself at twenty-seven, twenty-eight, single – having to completely redefine myself. I was studying as well at the time, so career-wise, I was doing really well and was really happy, but my relationship had completely fallen apart and I didn't know what to do with myself.'

Ash was officially divorced at the age of twenty-nine and she struggled with her value as a person due to her marital status. 'I knew there was writing on the wall with my relationship, but I was so ashamed and embarrassed to talk to anybody about it, even my closest friends. I didn't speak to my mum about it.'

Around the time Ash was getting divorced, many of her peers were getting engaged. She told me about a particularly low point when she attended her ten-year high school reunion. Having gone to a private girls' school in a regional area, Ash felt the pressure to have settled down, got married and had kids. 'I was in denial. I was still wearing my engagement and wedding ring, putting on this fake facade, that things were going really great. It was so devastating that I felt the need to do that in front of all these people. School reunions are such bullshit, everybody just stands around and are so judgey, asking each other what they're doing, how many kids they have, if they're married.'

Because she had met her ex at university and focused hard on her studies, she had never lived out the single uni girl experience. While people were sending her photos of their engagement rings and save-the-dates, Ash was planning a boozy, six-week escape overseas. 'I got divorced but I travelled to Europe for the first time, Bali with my family and finished it with a girls' trip to Sri Lanka. It was one of the best and worst years of my life.'

What made divorce difficult to grapple with for Ash was her age.

'You think of divorce, and you think of older people. You think of your parents who have been married for twenty years. For me, I felt that I hadn't accomplished what I set out to because I hadn't even been married for twelve months and it was coming to an end, and it ended in divorce. I'm somebody who likes to have answers, but I couldn't tell anybody what had gone wrong because I myself didn't even know. I do now and there was nothing that I could have done to change the outcome, but it was really hard to come to terms with.'

Content creator and author Helen Chik was twice divorced by the time she turned thirty. On my podcast, she said she couldn't be more grateful. 'They're the best decisions that I have made in my life, really!'[28] While Helen takes ownership of the part she played in both her divorces, she doesn't believe it should be a sad narrative. After all, they came about because she prioritised her happiness. 'I think when it comes to divorce, the shame really comes from what we think others are going to think of our choice. I think family and friends usually play a huge part. But at the end of the day, the way I saw it when I made both the decisions was that if I'm not happy and there is no way to salvage this relationship, I'm out. I'd much rather cut ties quickly than drag it on and waste my time, because you know it's not right and it's not going to be. You know it's not going to benefit anybody anymore to be in this marriage and stay unhappy, just so that you are the picture-perfect family from the outside. But really, you're miserable on the inside. Why bother?'

Helen co-parents her son with her second ex-husband. 'I think we get along much better now as separate entities. If we had stayed together, it just would not have worked. We would have been no better for it.' But she does understand why many parents choose to stay together for the kids. 'They don't want the kids to grow up in a broken family unit and, believe me, that came into play for my second separation. But I think it'll fuck up a child when they're growing up and seeing their parents fight every single day. It'll fuck up their minds way more than for you to just separate.'

In her article for the *Daily Star*, journalist and researcher Sushmita S. Preetha called out the need to normalise happy divorces, not unhappy marriages. 'We should, if not celebrate, at least appreciate the fact that, despite the taboo surrounding divorce, even in urban areas and among privileged classes, more and more women are now brave enough to decide what the best course of action for them and their children is, instead of suffering in silence to appease society.'[29]

Supermodel Emily Ratajkowski, who ended her three-year marriage due to her husband's alleged infidelity, was slammed for 'glamorising' divorce when she said that getting divorced before thirty was chic. She even remade her old engagement ring into two separate rings. I liked her explanation of why she did it: 'I loved the idea of a ring unabashedly representing the many lives a woman has lived.'[30] The model told *Vogue*, 'The rings represent my own personal evolution. I don't think a woman should be stripped of her diamonds just because she's losing a man.' Creating the rings was a fun project to work on 'amidst a hugely transitional period in my life' and 'the ring became symbolic to me – some kind of token or evidence of my life becoming my own again,' Ratajkowski said. 'Somehow, these rings feel like a reminder that I can make myself happy in ways I never imagined.'

Writing for *Mamamia*, Charlotte Ivan believed that entering into a marriage as a woman certainly does not make you any less of a feminist, but it would make complete sense to abstain from marriage on the grounds of feminism. To her, the only reason it would ever make sense to get married is financial. 'I don't see it as being romantic anymore. Getting married seems easy. Working towards a healthy, committed relationship with mutual respect and love, under stress and tragedy, seems hard.'[31] I take her point: surely being and staying in a committed long-term relationship is deserving of equal respect to marriage?

So if not to wed, then what? For writer Catherine Deveny and her partner, Anthony, it was a love party! The ceremony featured many markers of a typical wedding, but as Deveny wrote on her website: 'Bride? Groom? Wedding? Yes. Wife? Husband? Marriage? No.'[32] She explained, 'I was a 90 kilo, 47-year-old bride in a $260 dress on a bike. No Spanx, no fake tan, no dieting, no botox, no fillers, no gifts, no seating plan, no name changing, no marriage. There was a veil, flower girls, a ceremony, a certificate, rose petals, bubbles, confetti, a Love Parade with rainbow balloons, a sit-down dinner for 100, cake, exchanging of rings, speeches, vows and fairy lights.' Absent from the guest list, however, were God and the government, because according to Deveny, God and government have no place in people's hearts, relationships or bedrooms. 'Marriage was invented. Love wasn't. And love conquers all.'

Food writer and editor Sarah Norris loves love but the whole wedding thing turned her off the idea. 'In particular, the historical legal rights of women, plus (for many people) weddings are hijacked to please families, rather than being about love,' she told *Fashion Journal*.[33] But then Norris found the love of her life, Steve, and she wanted to tell everyone. The feeling was mutual, so in 2022 they held a 'Mutually Smitten Soiree'. A bus collected forty of their nearest and dearest and took them to a mystery location where the couple awaited, the opposite of a traditional wedding where guests wait for the bride. Instead of a wedding dress, Sarah wore a custom-made gold one-piece playsuit and cape. The occasion was marked with a short ceremony hosted by a celebrant who understood the assignment. 'No documents were signed and the government wasn't involved – just lots of heart-filled friends.'

> **WHILE I'M NOT OPPOSED TO SHINY THINGS, I'M NOT SURE THAT'S REASON ENOUGH TO SAY 'I DO'.**

My own major marriage icks include traditional vows and promising to 'obey' my husband – ew, I'm not a dog! I'm also not mad on the idea of walking down the aisle with my dad because, to me, the father 'giving away' the bride cements the idea of marriage as a property transaction from one man to another. I don't want to have to worry about feeling obliged to invite anyone I'm not 100 per cent keen on being there but feel like I have to out of politeness. Nor do I want to spend the whole day worried if the guests are enjoying themselves. I feel like people are overly critical of other people's weddings, too. From the choice of venue to the menu selection, attire and even the smallest details like table decorations – there's a tendency for some to offer unsolicited opinions and comparisons. It's as if every wedding becomes fair game for scrutiny, with some people feeling the need to impose their standards and preferences on to others' special days. It's like a bloody episode of *My Kitchen Rules*!

And then there's taking your husband's surname, which again stems from Western patriarchal culture. During the Middle Ages, while women did have recognised names, their identities were often closely tied to their marital status and frequently referenced in relation to their husbands in formal contexts. Around the turn of the fifteenth century, coverture emerged in England, a legal doctrine that subsumed a married woman's legal rights and obligations under those of her husband. You know what else a wife lost? Her ability to consent to sex. As Zoe Smith, PhD candidate for the Australian National University's School of History, wrote for *The Conversation*, in late nineteenth-century Australia, a husband could legally rape his wife.[34] Officially, he was still allowed to do so in some Australian jurisdictions until as late as 1994. NINETEEN. NINETY. FOUR.

There can be many reasons why women decide to take their husband's surname, such as to simplify administrative processes or to signal a new beginning. Some choose to hyphenate. If I decide to get married, one part of me wants to keep my surname due to my public-facing role in the media. The other part wants to get rid of my surname because it ties me to my dad's dad – I don't want to be a Hustwaite because of him.

I can't talk about marriage and not talk about the bling, but I find it interesting how men are not required to display their engagement physically, whereas women wear an engagement ring to symbolise their relationship status. According to the Gemological Institute of America, it was the Egyptian pharaohs who first used rings to represent eternity.[35] A circle has no beginning and no end, and reflects the shape of the sun and the moon, which the Egyptians worshipped. The engagement ring originated in Ancient Rome as a sign of ownership. It wasn't until 850 CE that the engagement ring was given an official meaning, with Pope Nicholas I declaring that this piece of jewellery represented a man's intent to marry. Diamond engagement rings didn't become popular until 1947 when De Beers, the British company that mines diamonds in South Africa, launched an advertising campaign. With the help of Hollywood stars and the slogan 'A diamond is forever', diamond engagement rings skyrocketed in popularity and forged the emotional belief that love could be just as enduring as the stone.

While I'm not opposed to shiny things, I'm not sure that's reason enough to say 'I do'. Not when in the eighteenth century, Mary Wollstonecraft published *A Vindication of the Rights of Woman*, in which she described marriage as a form of unpaid labour that stripped women of the few rights they had.[36] For many women, not much has changed. As Clementine Ford wrote, 'It's true that women are tired. But that's not because they were somehow tricked into working. Women are tired because they went out to work to alleviate the financial pressure weighing on men, but men did not reciprocate in the home to alleviate the domestic pressure inflicted on women.'[37]

Marriage has been built mostly to benefit men, and this even extends to health. Take the research from Japan's National Cancer Center, for example, which examined the medical records of half a million people in their fifties in Asia over the course of fifteen years.[38] In 2022, they determined that being married was associated with a 15 per cent overall lower risk of death from all causes compared to those who were unmarried (defined as people who were single, separated, divorced or widowed). They also found that married couples had a 20 per cent lower risk of dying from accidents, injuries and heart disease. Not only that, married men saw the biggest drops in mortality rates, with research pointing out that husbands were less likely to take risks, get into accidents or consume alcohol and drugs. The 'protective effect' of marriage, where a partner encourages their spouse to seek medical treatment, could be a contributing factor, as are better financial situations and healthier lifestyles. It was bad news for women, however, as further analysis of the data revealed that their mortality benefited less if they were married. Researchers said that this could be due to domestic labour not being equally divided in Asian marriages, thus putting more stress on women, which 'may counteract the health benefits of marriage'. The study suggested that unmarried women were more likely to have a job and have more money and access to better health.

In their own research conducted the same year, the University of Colorado found that married men were less likely to die from heart failure as they had someone close to them keeping tabs on their health.[39] The study did not identify this trend among married women, who were interpreted by experts as being more capable of looking after their health than their male counterparts. How about that?

It's a weird time to observe the current cultural landscape on marriage. While we're seeing Christianity's grip on marital traditions seemingly loosen over time – from 97 per cent of marriages being religiously conducted in 1902 to 81 per cent by civil celebrants in 2021 – we're also seeing 'Trad Wife' content absolutely poppin' off on TikTok and Instagram. I'm talking videos of subservient women embracing traditional gender roles and showcasing homemaking skills in aesthetically pleasing videos, growing their own food or, like Nara Smith, making cheese from scratch like it's the 1950s.

Rachael Lennon believed we can shape marriage for the next generation, 'retaining the traditions that serve us and forging new ones where it's time to let go of bad habits'.[41] For Elizabeth Gilbert, marriage will take any shape, adapt to any circumstances, in order to endure. 'And that is precisely because we seem to want it and need it,' she wrote.[42] 'Our longing for legally recognised private intimacy means that we will keep reforming and shaping this thing, generation after generation, in order to somehow make it our own.'

Contemplating whether I want to get married can often be misunderstood as questioning the depth of my commitment to my partner.

I DO... NEED TO TALK ABOUT MARRIAGE

However, my hesitation lies not in the love I feel for him, but rather in the implications and expectations tied to the institution of marriage itself. Feminism, to me – at least right now in my thirties – embodies the principles of change and choice. In the context of marriage, I hold on to the hope that we are redefining this institution to align with our values and beliefs while acknowledging its historical complexities. It's essential for us to confront the oppressive origins and dark history of marriage, just as we should acknowledge the injustices of Australia's colonial past. And it is our responsibility to continue shaping it into something that reflects love and equality. There is no one version of marriage – and never has been – just as there is no singular version of a relationship. Whether you choose to wed, be de facto, open or polyamorous, or live your best single life, the only 'I do' that matters is 'I do feel happy, respected and fulfilled'.

BODY BETTER

9

Content warning: this chapter discusses disordered eating and anorexia.

> LEARNING TO LOVE OUR BODIES, ESPECIALLY AS WOMEN, IS A LIFELONG JOURNEY.

I was six years old when I had my first procedure to enhance my appearance. I'm not sure if you would call it cosmetic exactly, but it was for external show as opposed to a medical reason: pinning back my ears. I don't know when I first noticed them but some kids at school started calling me Dumbo. Mum would later reveal that her brother said I looked like Yoda from *Star Wars*. Brutal, right?! She remembers me coming home and telling her that people were being mean about my ears, so she and Dad asked if I would like to get them pinned back. 'It was a mutual thing. We didn't want you to get bullied,' she reflected via text message.

I hated how my ears looked and was keen for the procedure. I remember sitting in the office of Dr Sheen on the blue examination bed, my legs dangling off the edge. I was quiet but excited. He complimented my glittery Spice Girls necklace and gently pressed my ears back to show me how they would look.

The procedure was called an otoplasty. The bandage wrapped around my head like a turban, which had to stay on for two weeks. It was a novelty at first, but by the end it got so itchy and sweaty that I was dying to take it off. I loved the time away from school and the plush toy of

Lulu from *Bananas in Pyjamas* that Mum bought me. I loved being able to stay in my pyjama pants and play fairy dress-ups at home. One day, I went in to school to visit my class and the kids gave me handmade 'Get well soon' cards in assorted colours. But when they all laughed and pointed at my bandaged head, my chest tightened and a lump formed in my throat. I thought that wouldn't happen anymore.

When I was eleven, my mum started WeightWatchers and she would track her food intake according to points. I remember her delight at cups of tea carrying zero points and a steamed dim sim only being one.

When I was twelve, I started high school and hated my Year 7 photos because my ears still pointed out. Not in the curved, floppy way like they used to; they were more pointed at the top. Elf ears. From then on, I always made sure my hair covered them. That same year, *America's Next Top Model* launched. I was obsessed and watched every episode of the first eight seasons as they dropped weekly. The show made me look at my body in a way I hadn't before. I used to want to be athletic-thin like Britney Spears but *America's Next Top Model* made me want to be stick-thin like the contestants.

When I was thirteen, I was already conscious of not having a flat stomach and resented the popularity of low-rise Face Off pants.

When I was fourteen, I hated my thick, wavy hair and begged my mum for a hair straightener. Almost every morning before school, I would insist on crouching down while my hair lay on the ironing board, the sizzling heat brushing against my ears as I urged Mum to iron it straight. A few of my friends brought their straighteners to school and we would use them covertly in the girls' toilets.

When I was fifteen, to my horror, I noticed cellulite and stretch marks forming on my inner thighs, hips and bum. I purchased Bio-Oil after seeing it advertised in *Dolly* magazine and applied it religiously.

Then I noticed fine facial hair on the outer corners of my upper lip, and I pleaded with Mum to let me get rid of it. I was terrified of being teased for having any trace of a moustache. She said I was too young for waxing and instead purchased an overbearingly scented bleaching cream.

When I was sixteen, I would skip class and catch the bus to one of the local solariums. Despite living in the cold, inland town of Ballarat, it was cool to look beachy and tanned. I used the introductory offer at Chokolat, but then another place called the Body Temple opened. I had mutual friends with the girl working there and she would sometimes only charge $8 for fifteen minutes in the solarium.

When I was seventeen, I would lie on my tummy on the floor for hours before going out, convinced that would help to flatten it.

When I was eighteen, I lost my virginity to my first serious boyfriend. I had planned it for the night of his birthday and basically starved myself in the week leading up to it, so that I would feel skinny enough naked. I also committed to the sharp and intense sensation of Brazilian waxing every four weeks.

When I was twenty-one, #cleaneating took over Instagram. My feed went from lomo-fi-filtered photos of cocktails to vibrant smoothie bowls, packets of SkinnyMe Tea, Sarah's Day, Freelee the Banana Girl and thin models posing in Triangl swimwear, showing off their thigh gaps. I couldn't afford SkinnyMe Tea but longed to look like one of the thin 'babes' they frequently posted. Instead of the 'leading detox tea and weight loss program', I opted for the local Asian grocer, where I would secretly stock up on a 'dieters' tea', extra strength, for a quarter of the price. I remember the potency surging from the rectangular box and the way it made my insides churn before I would shit my life away for the next couple of hours. I foolishly drank it before heading to my friend's house for a triple j Hottest 100 party, and about ninety minutes after my arrival, I felt my digestive system stressing the hell out. I had to be sneaky about my frequent and messy toilet trips, waiting until a big song came on that got everyone singing and dancing along before slipping away upstairs.

> **MILLENNIALS WERE RAISED IN AN ERA OF 'HEROIN-CHIC' FASHION, FAT-SHAMING TABLOIDS, CRASH DIETS AND KATE MOSS TELLING US THAT 'NOTHING TASTES AS GOOD AS SKINNY FEELS'.**

I was twenty-seven when I underwent my first endometriosis surgery. The night before, in the quiet of my Sydney share house bathroom, I stood before the mirror, lifting my shirt to confront the canvas of my untouched stomach. I contemplated the impending addition of four new scars and how they would make their presence known onto a surface I had long despised. I was scheduled to have the Mirena IUD inserted during the surgery, under the impression (which turned out to be incorrect) that it would help prevent further endometriosis growth.[1] While desperate for pain relief, I grappled with the fear of potential weight gain, a daunting side effect of the IUD.

Turning thirty, I'd love to tell you that I experienced a sudden shot of confidence about my body – people say you care less about how you look as you get older – but it hasn't been that simple. Being dumped prompted an exercise routine to help my mental health, but I also lowkey aspired to embody The Post-Break-Up Glow Up. I obsessed over closing the rings on my Apple Watch, and sometimes late at night, my watch would alert me that I was close to closing a circle so I would jump out of bed and start lunging in order to reach that daily goal.

I remember getting dressed for my 30th birthday party (yes, *that* night) and wondering why my boobs weren't bigger. You know how some girls can shove their phone and bank cards down their cleavage on nights out? That unfortunately was not me. If I lost weight, my boobs would be the first to go. If I gained weight, my boobs would be the last to receive. Dress shopping was awkward, as I couldn't quite fill out the top but my hips were too wide for the smaller sizes.

Learning to love our bodies, especially as women, is a lifelong journey, particularly considering what we have been exposed to growing up. Millennials were raised in an era of 'heroin-chic' fashion, fat-shaming tabloids, crash diets and Kate Moss telling us that 'nothing tastes as good as skinny feels'.[2] Those before us like to coin us as the snowflake generation but I don't think they fully grasp the war we were pushed into with our bodies. Because we weren't born with these insecurities. As Hannah Ferguson pointed out in her book *Bite Back*, industries have thrived on our insecurities and commodified our shame. 'We are expected to look this way to be accepted in society, but we are also expected to pay for it.'[3]

I'll never forget the whiplash of 2001 when Renée Zellweger gained thirty pounds to portray Bridget Jones, a character who constantly feels self-shame about her body and fears dying 'fat and alone' (despite being the same weight as the average British woman at the time[4]), before Zellweger dropped down to a size zero to appear as Roxie Hart in the film adaptation of *Chicago*. Or how after performing in Texas in 2009, Jessica Simpson was slaughtered in the tabloids for wearing figure-hugging denim jeans, with headlines like 'Jumbo Jessica' and suggestions that she had 'let it all go'. Speaking to *Glamour*, Simpson said the news coverage 'ruined the stage' for her. 'And the stage was my home. It broke my home.'[5]

In 2023, the Butterfly Foundation conducted research among twelve- to eighteen-year-olds to better understand what they thought and felt about their bodies, and what effect body dissatisfaction had on their lives. The survey found that nearly half (45%) of young people were dissatisfied with the way their body looked and nearly 70 per cent of young people said they had experienced appearance-related teasing, with 73 per cent of those respondents saying they'd experienced it at school.[6]

Born in 1995, Lucinda Price sits on the borderline of a generation divide. 'I kind of went through a stage where I was like, I'm so cuspy that I'll say gen Z but, actually, who am I kidding?' she told me as she finished her avocado on toast from her sunny Sydney bedroom.[7] 'Millennial through and through.'

Affectionately known as Froomes or Froomey, I first met the writer/presenter/comedian at G Flip's ARIA Awards afterparty. A classic case of two girlies coyly embracing each other with 'I know who you are, but we've never actually met'. Froomes yelled in my ear over the top of the music about how excited her friend Madison Griffiths was to be chatting to me about abortion. Fast-forward two months and I was in Froomes's DMs asking if I could pick her brain on body image. She had just submitted the first draft of her first non-fiction release, *All I Ever Wanted Was To Be Hot*, which explores how pop culture, the internet and modern beauty ideals intersect to influence our bodies and self-image, a topic she has candidly tackled in her popular newsletter, FROOMESWORLD. In 2022, she shared details of her disordered eating and anorexia to her 12,000 subscribers.[8]

While most millennials had body insecurities during high school, Froomes didn't start critiquing her body or considering changes until she turned twenty-one and took on the role of health and fitness editor at youth entertainment website *Pedestrian*. 'All through my teenage years, I didn't think much of it. Girls were pointing to a bulimic Lindsay Lohan and to Nicole Richie when she was self-destructive, and I remember looking at that as a young girl thinking, *Oh, I never want to look like that*.'[9] But that's not to say that Froomes didn't see the damage around her. 'I personally think it was worse before the internet because we had the magazines, which were actually fucking psychotic when you go back and look at them. You're like, how was this ever allowed?! It felt like there was no accountability for brands and magazines. Absolutely no diversity and body diversity.'

Things took a turn in Froomes's new career when she started writing articles on fitness trends and viral health content. 'I actually found all the wellness stuff hilarious and stupid,' she explained. 'But you take in as much of that stuff and it's like hypnosis. You think it's funny, you think it's stupid and then next minute you're totally subscribed to it.'

It was a 10-kilometre sponsored run for work that triggered the negative body thoughts for Froomes. As an asthmatic, a lot of training was required and Froomes took it as seriously as any other work assignment. 'Running became part of my job and I wanted to be really good at my job.' Consequently, she started losing weight. 'That was the inciting incident, turning it from diet culture to an eating disorder.'

Froomes told me she continued running for another two years but didn't let on about her physical changes in the content she was sharing online. 'I think in the back of my mind I knew that what I was doing wasn't sustainable so I would never post a bikini picture, or I wouldn't really post anything too revealing. Even though I was super proud of my body when I was underweight, I never posted it because I thought if I lose this, it's gonna be embarrassing. So I kind of kept that a little bit hidden.'

Behind the scenes, Froomes was miserably partaking in cycles of binge eating and acting like an asshole (her words!), with some of her friendships affected by her body obsession. In her newsletter, Froomes reflected on the day she hit a wall and couldn't go on any further. 'I was walking up the street towards my house, and putting my key in the door, I just burst into tears. I was so tired, physically in my body. I called my mum and cried and told her I couldn't cope.' Froomes saw a psychiatrist who said the word 'anorexic', which she considered simultaneously thrilling and terrifying. 'I wasn't at a weight that required hospitalisation, far from it, but my behaviours and my mood were enough to be diagnosed,' she wrote in her newsletter.[10]

The year 2020 was when things really started shifting for Froomes, who attributed a change in the right direction to her redundancy from Pedestrian and sessions with her psychologists. Now, as she approaches thirty, Froomes sees health in a completely different light. 'It's the ability to sit still and purely do healthy things when I feel like them. I'll go for a walk when the desire comes over me, but also the ability to not do those things and not feel bad and maintain equilibrium in my moods and my mental health is my number one priority.'[11]

Three years into this decade and I have noticed that some things do get better. Like most people I talk to, there are things I like and things I don't like about how I look. I've learned to embrace my endometriosis scars and now wear them like badges of bravery. I've come to like my stretch marks, especially how they stand out when I'm tanned. I'm pretty happy with my face and am comfortable being make-up free. But I grapple with the cellulite on my legs and I've tried Emsculpt on my stomach, hoping for a more toned look. I rarely feel the need to wear make-up but have skin-shamed myself for having periorificial dermatitis. I still hold on to clothes I used to fit in, in the hope I might wear them again one day. Although I thought my boobs would be bigger, the biggest perk of having no perks, so to speak, is that I can go braless basically all the time, without an eyebrow raised. Slay. Another thing I have realised is that every year I have wished to be thinner, and every year I have looked back on the previous and thought to myself, *Are you mad? You look GOOD.*

I'd be lying if I said that embarking on a new relationship at thirty-one with someone five years younger has not heightened my sensitivity about my physical appearance and body image. It's hard not to compare myself to girls that are Oscar's age, especially on Instagram.

I'd also be lying if I told you I haven't noticed that the cars have stopped honking. That I am no longer being asked for my ID at the bottle shop. That I felt embarrassed at American singer-songwriter Stephen Sanchez's disbelief that I was thirty-two when I hosted a music industry showcase he performed at. Super sweet guy, and I know he meant no malice in assuming I was younger, but it points to a wider perception of how people think someone looks beyond thirty.

People are constantly shocked when I tell them my age. They think I look much younger. While it's flattering, it's also a conflicting feeling, because what *should* I look like in my early thirties? We are so constantly bombarded with filtered or Photoshopped images, rom-com pairings of 50-year-old men with 25-year-old women, and 13-year-old runway models that we don't know what a woman in her thirties actually looks like anymore.

As Jacinta Parsons noted in her book *A Question of Age*, for much of our lives, the relentless objectification we have experienced has coerced

> I'VE LEARNED TO EMBRACE MY ENDOMETRIOSIS SCARS AND NOW WEAR THEM LIKE BADGES OF BRAVERY.

us into believing that we know what a woman should look like. She used the moment she realised she had 'tuck shop lady arms' as an example. 'They belonged to the bodies of the women, mostly mothers, who would don an apron and file into the school tuckshop to feed us. We laughed at their fat old arms that wobbled when they handed out our meat pies. And when it was summer and their arms were exposed and their breasts hung low, we prayed that our bodies would never betray us like this.'[12]

When Jacinta discovered the underside of her arm wobbled, she panicked. Externally, she laughed and 'felt a solidarity' with the women she had mercilessly mocked when she was a child. But with every disparaging remark she made and shared about her body, she knew she was playing a part in the mockery she had been taught to deal out to the bodies of older women since she was young. 'Through our giggles and jokes we reinforced a sense of shame about the changes that take place in these bodies. We are made to feel embarrassment about skin that is no longer snug around our muscles. We stop wearing clothing that might expose the sagging and wrinkly body underneath. And we laugh at the women who have no regard for hiding their upper arms.'

A research paper released in the December 2021 edition of the *Body Image* journal examined a six-year dataset involving more than 15,000 women spanning the ages of eighteen to ninety-four. The study revealed that 'body satisfaction improved across the lifespan in both men and women (though men consistently displayed higher levels of body satisfaction across their lifespan than women)'.[13] Speaking to the *Sydney Morning Herald* on these findings, accredited dietician Fiona Sutherland suggested that the results may coincide with increasing levels of self-compassion as we gain more life experience. 'Body confidence is not about changing our bodies. It's about changing the way we relate to our bodies.'[14]

While the body positivity and body neutral movements have gained strong traction, I can't help but feel like we have relapsed in some ways. Influencers are stick-thin again, girls in their early twenties are wearing bikini-tan lines as badges of honour. I saw one TikTok of two prominent Melbourne influencers: 'I'm a girl, of course I call in sick to work if the UVs are vibing.' Then there are the girls as young as twenty-two doing sponsored content for Baby Botox. The trend of having 'legging legs' or a 'clean girl aesthetic'. The Ozempic obsession, where people with diabetes are facing worldwide shortages because so many people are being prescribed this drug for weight loss, including those who are already considered to be a 'healthy' weight.

While grappling with my own perceptions of self-image, it's essential for me to recognise the privilege I possess in conversations surrounding body image. Throughout history, society's beauty standards have revolved around Eurocentric ideals, granting me certain advantages and protections. The portrayal of bodies in media, fashion and popular culture frequently reinforces these standards, marginalising individuals from diverse racial and ethnic backgrounds. Even the body positivity movement, while striving for inclusivity, has often centred on the experiences and narratives of white women. This spotlight has inadvertently overlooked the unique challenges and intersections faced by women of colour in navigating body image issues within oppressive systems of racism and colourism. I understand that my journey towards body acceptance is situated within a broader context of racial privilege and oppression. Someone who has helped me recognise this is body positivity activist April Hélène-Horton.

Known online as @thebodzilla, April joined me from her Sydney hotel room in the midst of the 2023 edition of Australian Fashion Week, her second year attending the event. 'The lobby bar is full of the chicest people I've ever seen,' she said, laughing as she logged on to our chat.[15] 'I felt so old in a room full of people dressed in such beautiful clothes and fashionable make-up, just moving with this most incredible grace and looking so youthful. I was like, my goodness, I cannot relate to that at all.'

April never felt like Fashion Week was for her. She didn't feel represented or welcome, but the 2022 edition took her by pleasant surprise. 'There were modelling agencies and apparel brands who got together to create The Curve Edit, a runway dedicated to plus-sized clothing and plus-size models and that felt really beautiful. It was super special and so many of my friends from the curve and plus-size community were there with me ... It was so incredible,' she told me. But this didn't happen again. She acknowledged that there are a lot of factors that might have contributed to that decision, but was disappointed, especially when she had come to expect a certain level of diversity from some brands. 'It was an unpleasant surprise to see that the opening day was full of very slim and small-sized models. I do think that's a concerning trend in fashion. The rise of the slim body as the ideal again is concerning for everyone.'

Prior to Fashion Week, April was making headlines for her appearance on *The Project*, where she participated in a roundtable discussion on what it meant to be healthy. Also on the roundtable was former *The Biggest Loser* trainer Michelle Bridges, who April admitted she was 'somewhat nervous' to see. 'I would genuinely say that the show *The Biggest Loser* was one of the most traumatic things that ever happened to me,' she revealed to Bridges.[16]

In the days leading up to my chat with April, I discovered that SkinnyMe Tea was still an active company selling detox teas, just slyly rebranded as SMT. I also saw that their founder was being regularly booked to deliver talks on the success of her business. It made me sick to see the narrative homing in on the fact that she started the business with only twenty bucks, with revenue growing to around $600,000 per month in the first six months of operation. Never mind making bank off impressionable and insecure young women or fostering a toxic diet culture – let's glorify the girlboss!

Around the same time, April shared an interesting post on her Instagram that looked at the link between diet culture, girlboss culture and anti-ageing. It was shared alongside the coverage surrounding 81-year-old Martha Stewart's recent cover shoot for *Sports Illustrated Swimsuit*. As April told me, 'Not only is there an interconnection, but the common denominator is a social phenomenon that leaves out people who are not thin, white, rich or from highly educated socioeconomic backgrounds and speak English as a first language.'[17]

April elaborated, 'I think that people who are older than forty are suddenly praised for looking like they're not what we think forty looks like ... While I applaud the idea that we could have someone on the front cover of a magazine who's eighty-one years old, that person is not celebrating their age. Martha Stewart's proud of being eighty-one because she thinks she doesn't look it ... She looks slim. She looks buxom. She looks unwrinkled. She's got big hair. She's got, you know, youthful-looking other attributes.' April went on to explain that most women can't achieve that. 'I think it's very clear when we celebrate Martha Stewart, like yassss queen, ageless queen, what we're signalling to older people in our lives is you look like you should be put out with the rubbish, because you're not hot like Martha Stewart.'

We can't seem to escape the pressure to enhance our image, with procedures becoming more accessible than ever. At shopping centres, laser clinics not only do hair removal but they also offer non-surgical procedures such as body sculpting and fat freezing. How does one reconcile the idea of this with feminism and body acceptance? While the availability of these procedures can be seen as a form of personal empowerment, allowing us to make choices about our bodies and appearance, it also reflects the pervasive influence of societal beauty ideals, which clearly prioritise thinness and youthfulness. This raises concerns for me about the pressure to conform to unrealistic standards and the perpetuation of body dissatisfaction among women. And with the commercialisation of beauty procedures, gender inequality becomes further entrenched as women are disproportionately targeted by advertising and social pressure to invest in such treatments.

On her podcast *It's a Lot*, Abbie Chatfield wrestled with a feminist dilemma. 'I understand that plastic surgery cannot be inherently feminist. I also understand that if I existed in a vacuum where I just lived without any mirrors, without any awareness of how I looked, I wouldn't want to get this done. I'm aware of that, right. This is all the feminist discourse that I have seen. But unfortunately, I don't live in a fucking vacuum. I live in a fucking Big Brother house where every **** is filming me from every fucking angle.'[18]

As Michelle Andrews from *Shameless* wrote in *The Space Between*, 'It seems particularly cruel that, after all their efforts to dodge the arrows, women are judged the second they give in to the pressure that encircles them, as if they are letting down the sisterhood when they wave their hands in the air and ask for a little respite. I don't want to feel shitty about myself considering cosmetic procedures or plastic surgery.'[19]

We're damned if we do and we're damned if we don't. Or we might not be – but who can predict when we'll be shamed or celebrated? Look at the amazing response to gorgeous Pamela Anderson fronting up to 2023 Paris Fashion Week completely make-up free. She was glowing – and so was the praise. More! Of! This!

I named this chapter 'Body Better' for a few reasons. Firstly, it's my favourite Maisie Peters song, composed in the aftermath of a break-up where Peters nitpicks every insecurity, right down to her image. The chorus resonates with so many people, myself included, but I also look at the song title as something to take moving forward, like the desire to treat my body better, to speak to my body better, to know that my body can better with age. Along with these lessons about accepting and loving my body, I also know that my body isn't the most important thing about me. I'm funny (sometimes). I'm driven and diligent. I'm a loving partner, friend and dog mum ... Beyond thirty, my bod is doing all right, and beyond this bod, I have a lot going for myself!

As Canadian writer and radio host Josie Balka said on TikTok: 'I promise you from the deepest part of my soul, you will be remembered for the way that you are, not the way that you look.'[20]

BODY IMAGE REMINDERS
I'm taking into my thirties

- If there is one external aspect of your body to focus on, it's your skin. Stay hydrated and wear sunscreen, damn it.
- Move for your mental health. Do it because it makes you feel good.
- Focus on and appreciate the things that your body CAN do, not how it looks. As Florence Given wrote in *Women Don't Owe You Pretty*, 'For too long we have internalised the belief that our bodies are things to be looked at – instead of lived in.'[1]
- I'm a different clothes size for EVERYTHING. Literally in every store and for every style of garment, my size is never the same. It's just a number, not a measurement of your worth. Take it with a grain of salt.
- Clothes are meant to fit us, not the other way around.
- Check yourself on how you view and comment not only on your own body but also the bodies of other people. We all have unlearning to do when it comes to fatphobia and body-shaming.
- Here's how you get a bikini body – you put a bikini on your body. Yep, EVERY body is a summer body! So throw on that bikini like it's nobody's business, because it literally is NOT their business!
- Everyone is too focused on their own perceived flaws to focus on yours.
- Not everything you see online is real – think filters, body angles and lighting! If any content is making you feel shit about your body, remember the power of the mute or unfollow button.
- Embrace that you are one of a kind. In turn, remember that you only have one body so please be KIND to it.

10
i QUiT

> **IS GIVING UP SOMETHING YOU WORKED SO HARD FOR PRETTY DAMN SCARY? ABSOLUTELY. BUT SOMETIMES IT'S WORTH THE RISK.**

'What's scarier, staying on for another year or leaving?'

This question was asked by my friend, DJ and former colleague KLP, and it made me realise I was done with my dream job. I was thirty-one and in my seventh year of presenting on Australia's national youth broadcaster, triple j. I loved being on the radio. Didn't I?

People would *kill* for this gig. I was being paid to listen to music and fangirl over my favourite artists every night with listeners right across the country, not to mention the fact I could wear whatever I wanted because, well, it was radio.

It was a far cry from my eleven-year-old dreams to be a WWE wrestler. No joke — if you flip through my Grade 6 graduation book, you'll see the declaration 'When I Grow Up, I Want To Be A ... WWE Wrestler' next to my grinning face. While other kids fantasised about putting out fires or twirling in ballet dresses, I wanted to be flipping off ropes, body slamming opponents and talking smack on a microphone in front of thousands of people.

Radio was also a stretch from my next career goal: dietetics. This came to me in Year 9, when teachers started telling us we needed to choose subjects that would help us get into university, as if that was the only option beyond high school. I was absolutely stumped as to what I wanted to do. However, a lightbulb moment struck one winter's night in Burleigh Heads where my family ventured for the school holidays. We had been watching *Super Size Me*, a documentary in which American filmmaker Morgan Spurlock ate nothing but McDonald's to explore its impact on his health. Obviously, scoffing endless burgers and nuggs required constant check-ins with health professionals, one being a dietitian. Her name was Bridget. I took that as a sign, or rather an 'eh, that'll do', and started looking up all the nutrition and dietetic university courses on offer.

I wasn't confident in my ability to obtain a high-enough ATAR score for the dedicated dietetic courses, but I did find a more realistic path in health sciences, to which I was offered a place and commenced after an eighteen-month deferral where I worked in retail. I was so excited to be a uni girly but quickly realised that the uni learning structure was not for me. I dropped out after three weeks.

While the wrestling ring and dietetics clinic weren't to be, my eventual dream office became the radio studio. I pursued music presenting at the age of twenty-one when I signed up for the Channel [V] Presenter Search in 2012. Channel [V] was an Australian subscription television music network that showcased the latest music videos and live performances, and offered exclusive access to festivals and major music events. It was known for being a little loose and it was also where the likes of Osher Günsberg and Yumi Stynes got their start in presenting. I would watch Channel [V] every day, and in Year 9 I won a competition in the newspaper to meet the presenters when they were in Ballarat for a special music event featuring Missy Higgins.

I was finishing up my diploma in visual merchandising, a course I decided to do from my time working in fashion retail, when Channel [V] announced the presenter search. This basically meant they were going to hire an average Joe off the street to join the presenting team. I had no prior presenting experience but I *loved* music and the channel, and I could speak pretty well in public due to my extensive high school debating background. The initial application required a video entry where you introduced yourself and explained why you were the perfect candidate, plus a written submission. Six thousand entries were received and narrowed down to two hundred – I was one of them!

The next round involved me heading to regional music festival Groovin the Moo in Bendigo, where I was required to do my first piece to camera, as if I was a presenter. It was a cold Saturday in May and I was dressed in peak 2012 fashion – striped leggings with a baggy long-sleeve shirt and a furry vest over the top, with a bunch of long layered necklaces and my hair in a high bun. What baffled me was that so many people applied without having even watched Channel [V]. I knew the station inside out and had watched so much of their festival coverage I knew exactly what they were looking for in the piece to camera. I nailed the cross, with one of the producers pulling me aside to tell me I'd done well.

The next task was to interview an artist from the line-up, which would also be my first time ever interviewing somebody. We were only given a couple of minutes' notice and a few sentences of their biography. Some contestants got to chat with Matt Corby and others had Melbourne duo Big Scary. As for me, I was allocated American rock artist Andrew W. K. His persona was very much loose party rock dude so I tried to lean into that energy and focus on fun banter, given I didn't know who he was. It was fine, but not as strong as my first piece.

The final task was a piece to camera with an actual Channel [V] presenter, Billy. He had won the last presenter search three years prior. We instantly bonded over hailing from regional Victoria (he, Bacchus

Marsh, and I, Ballarat) and the local bands who were doing well in the region. A few days later, Channel [V] aired a highlights package of what went down at the Bendigo auditions and Billy said I was his favourite, not only because I was a country girl but also because of my knowledge and passion for the station.

The group of two hundred was cut down to a top twenty – including me! – and we were flown to Sydney to participate in more challenges, including an impromptu on-camera album review of a record we only had two minutes to learn about. Mine was *Trouble*, the debut album by British electronic producer Totally Enormous Extinct Dinosaurs. I will never forget that this guy's real name is Orlando Higginbottom.

The top twenty was then narrowed down to a top four and you bet I was one of them. Not only that, I was the only woman. Our assignment was to conduct interviews from the red carpet of the ASTRA (Australian Subscription Television and Radio Association) Awards and before I knew it, I was in the top two. Our final task was to join the existing presenters on *The Riff*, a live music show that aired on Saturday mornings, and present a segment. I can't remember the specific brief but I was covering (read: mocking) Paris Hilton's DJ debut, and looking back, it was a cringey, misogynist segment that I'm not proud to have created.

At the end of the show, they announced the winner live on air. It wasn't me. I was obviously graceful and positive on air but once the cameras stopped rolling, I was devastated. I was quickly whisked out of the studios to the airport and flown straight back to Melbourne, where I continued on to Ballarat and got super drunk that night.

Growing up, I'd aspired to be like the hosts on Channel [V] but had never considered presenting to be something I could pursue. Creative, media-oriented roles weren't highlighted during high school, and growing up in a regional area, there was limited access to this stuff as work

I QUIT

experience. But coming second out of 6000 people in the presenter search made me realise that presenting *was* something I could do. For the next few years, I committed myself to writing (unpaid) for online publications, reviewing gigs and singles, and transcribing interviews with local and international acts. I volunteered at community radio while balancing minimum-wage jobs across the retail, hospitality and customer service sectors. Ya girl was raking in fuck-all money, but she was determined as hell to make it as a presenter.

Getting my foot in the door at triple j was just the beginning and I kinda have Twitter (now X) to thank for it. While attending an awards night for SYN, the community radio station I was volunteering at, I saw that a producer from triple j was presenting an award. The room was super crowded so I couldn't introduce myself in person, but I sent him a DM on Twitter, pretty much asking how I could get a presenting job. I didn't want to get my hopes up about receiving a reply but when I saw one come through, it was bloody hard to contain my excitement. Not only that, he invited me to come into the ABC for an in-person chat.

It was my first time stepping into a media organisation. I couldn't believe my eyes when I saw the massive radio studios and all the equipment. It was like a huge jungle gym compared to the modest toys I was used to in community radio. The producer asked if I could send him a demo of my presenting, which is basically an audio file of different talk breaks from my community radio show, and for the next few months, he provided feedback on each demo that I prepared. This was at the same time I was working as a travel agent, so it was quite the juggling act having a full-time job during the day and staying up late into the night at the community radio studios, while also leaving countless reviews for bands and artists on the triple j Unearthed website, where independent Australian acts could upload their music in the hopes of someone from triple j hearing it. The triple j Unearthed team took notice of my enthusiasm and added me to their group of 'superusers', and we even had special superhero-like icons next to our names to show that we were part of the Unearthed community. Essentially it meant that our reviews were the next best thing to receiving a review from an actual triple j employee.

I was then passed on to the station manager who, at the end of 2015, decided to put me on the roster as a casual presenter. I'd made it! I quit my travel agent gig and moved back home with my parents so I could make myself fully available whenever triple j needed me. From there, I had to work my way up from the gnarly mid-dawn roster, where I spent two years commuting between Ballarat and Melbourne to present on air from 1 a.m. to 6 a.m. It was beyond exhausting, especially when you throw in a three-hour return trip in the car. I'd often have to pull up at the servo in Rockbank or Ballan and recline my driver's seat for a snooze. But I couldn't get enough of it. Sure, my body clock was pretty cooked as a result, but I was having so much fun. I always received messages from people who said they could hear my smile leaping out through the speakers. One of my managers jokingly dubbed me her 'seagull' because I was ready to gobble up any fill-in shift like a delicious chippy.

Being offered the role of hosting *Good Nights* was completely unexpected. It came at the end of 2017 when one of my idols, Dom Alessio, announced he would be departing his Australian music show, *Home and Hosed*. I desperately wanted to take over but there was interest from a number of aspiring presenters, so management created an internal application process to keep it fair. Anyone who was keen to apply was required to record a demo as if they were hosting the show, alongside a written component with any segment ideas or visions they could propose for the program. I diligently completed the tasks alongside a long, desperate email direct to management outlining why I was the perfect person to take over from Dom.

A few days later, I was asked to take a FaceTime call with management who were based in Sydney.

'We're not going to give you *Home and Hosed*,' they said.

My heart sank. I had been so set on this program and I didn't know how my body could tolerate another year on the gruelling mid-dawn roster.

'Instead, we want you to host *Good Nights*.'

I couldn't believe what I was hearing. *Good Nights* was a weeknight slot from 6 p.m. to 9 p.m., focusing on new music from Australia and around the world. I had never been given the opportunity to fill in on *Good Nights* and I couldn't imagine the show existing without Linda Marigliano. My first reaction was distress. Where was Linda going? Management told me not to worry and that she had something else lined up; however, if I were to accept *Good Nights*, I would have to move to Sydney. Was I prepared to do that? They needed my decision by the morning.

Holy shit. I started crying. I knew Mark wouldn't want to move with me, because he had spent years building his clientele of guitar students in Victoria. The thought of long distance terrified me but there was no way I could pass up this opportunity. So off I went to Sydney and, as you read earlier, I found it pretty hard even though I loved the work itself. Beyond the long-distance relationship and my endometriosis, I was required to work alongside two alternating producers. One did the show with me on Mondays to Wednesdays and we were already friends, so it was really fun navigating this new experience together with fresh eyes and minds. The other producer did Thursdays and Fridays, and the dynamic took a bit more adjusting to; she had already produced this show for a number of years and was set in a particular way. I was pretty independent because we had fewer resources in the Melbourne studios and presenters did everything themselves. In the main studios in Sydney, there were always producers around to help.

When pitching segment ideas or artists to interview, there always seemed to be a reason from management that prevented an idea from coming to life. I was being told 'no' a lot and it felt like there was a lack of collaboration. Presenters often joked that it was like we were serving our ideas on a silver platter to editorial management or the social media team, who were sitting on their thrones. It felt rare to brainstorm together or for them to help you improve your ideas. One producer told me it was easier to ask for forgiveness than permission – that you were best to just go ahead with your content idea instead of pitching it first, because you would likely be told no.

Office politics aside, I was obsessed with the time I spent on air. I loved my listeners and the little community of music fans we had created. I loved receiving new song recommendations on the text line and chatting to people on the phone. Every listener felt like a friend – we spent every night hanging out! I could not get over the high that was introducing a new song on the radio for everyone to hear for the first time. Whether it was being handed a song to premiere or one I had found myself that I wanted to hype up, each talk break was an opportunity to validate the artist's work, their art form. My heart would soar when I saw the artists filming their reactions, sitting at home or in the car listening to their music on the radio. There was no better feeling.

Approaching the end of 2022, I was in contract negotiations. I was five years into hosting *Good Nights*, and although I loved being able to broadcast from Melbourne again, I was not feeling as enthused as I once had. I felt like I had hit a wall in terms of my professional progression.

I QUIT

There were no other programs I was interested in moving on to but I was yearning for new skills and opportunities. I thought I could achieve this by learning how to program music (scheduling what songs are played in a show) one day a week. I raised this with one of my managers in 2020, which she said she would look into but I never heard back. On another occasion, I brought it up with one of the music directors, who dismissively joked, 'What, just so you can play The 1975 all the time?'

I remember speaking to another presenter who had started at the station after me and was feeling a sense of grief in their role. They expressed how conflicting it was to grow up idolising a station and spending years finding a way in, only to feel such strong confines and limitations within those walls. It was extremely validating to hear that I wasn't alone in feeling isolated, but what a damn shame it was for another young presenter to feel this way. It seemed like there was a lack of trust in the ideas of on-air talent and I personally felt underutilised and like an afterthought for opportunities. Sometimes this was explicitly communicated to me when other programs, namely *Breakfast* or *Drive*, couldn't conduct an interview with an artist so I would be asked only because I was available, not because they deemed me the presenter best suited for it. I felt restless within a programming hierarchy, especially when I saw my skills being acknowledged externally. I was being offered a bunch of side gigs, like MCing festivals and DJing, all of which had to be approved by triple j and abide by the ABC editorial policy.

One example of this was when, in my first year of hosting *Good Nights*, MTV reached out about hosting the Australian version of iconic music show *TRL* (Total Request Live). 'We're looking for a new host that's cool, savvy and on trend. We think you'd be a great fit,' read the email. 'We're looking to pair two main hosts together to anchor the show as well as finding one roving reporter who will focus on the vox pops and stunt side of things. We'd be considering you as one of the main hosts and at this point it's looking like Ash London would be the second host.' Only one shoot day was required per week and although triple j did not have a TV show, they unfortunately considered this to be 'a pretty direct competitor'.

I also had some cool brands reach out to me to work on campaigns, but as per the editorial policy, we couldn't endorse that kind of stuff – even though the then chair of the ABC board was a Priceline ambassador. One year, Sportsgirl invited me to answer some questions on endometriosis for a blog post, which I was permitted to do but I was also told I couldn't accept their gift of an avocado-shaped heat bag. Yes, it was cute, but it wasn't just a random present. It was something that could actually help my pain. So yeah, I was a lil bit salty about that!

Back to the contract negotiations. I was offered two years, which had never happened before. Usually, we were offered twelve months at a time and wouldn't know until the end of October or November if we would be signed on for the following year. A two-year contract is something I would have eagerly signed at the start of my full-time presenting reign but, at this point, it felt like too huge of a commitment. I said I only wanted to sign for another twelve months and on the condition that my evening cab charge would be reinstated.

Okay, this might sound trivial but allow me to explain. Because I was on air late at night, I was provided with a cab charge to get home. I would take the train into work around midday and then get a cab home, paid for by triple j. This is pretty standard within the media and entertainment industry for those who work at night, especially if an organisation doesn't provide parking. In my fifth year of *Good Nights*, the cab charge was taken away because my show now finished earlier. But because my producer was taken away too, I was now working nights

> "AS SCARED AS I WAS TO LEAP INTO THE UNKNOWN, I WAS DETERMINED TO MAKE IT WORK. I KNEW I WAS FULLY RESPONSIBLE FOR MY SUCCESS AND, AS IT TURNED OUT, THE GRASS REALLY WAS GREENER."

alone and not actually finishing earlier due to the increased workload. I had security concerns because it meant I would be walking home alone in the dark. The ABC was a regular target for protests and angry individuals, even at night-time. There were a few times I had been ordered by security to wait inside the building until a situation de-escalated outside. My fears also stemmed from the fact that my older sister was brutally bashed and mugged in the city one night, and because I lived on the same street as Jill Meagher, a former ABC employee who was raped and murdered as she walked home from after-work drinks in Brunswick in 2012. Catching public transport alone in Melbourne at night is not something I have ever been particularly comfortable with.

I also had concerns regarding my chronic pain management. I had been legally prescribed medicinal cannabis for my endometriosis, but had to give it up (and consequently waste hundreds of dollars due to unused prescriptions expiring) in 2022 because I was driving to work every day. If I could get my cab charges reinstated, I could manage my pain better. I didn't want to come across as difficult, so I consulted the ABC talent manager before submitting my request.

The response I received from management was not what I expected. My request was rejected and I was asked if I was fit to work if I couldn't drive, which I took great offence to. From my perspective, I had proven over the course of my time at triple j that I was fit to work. This felt like the final straw.

I had annual leave planned for a week-long trip to Las Vegas for a music festival, so I used that time to ponder my next steps. On the way home, I opened an email from a producer at *The Project*, who wanted to discuss the possibility of me making an appearance on the show as a guest panellist. It felt like a sign. If I no longer worked nights at triple j, I could say yes to opportunities like this. I also received an email from a talent agency who was keen to chat about representing me. If I pursued freelance work, I would need a manager and here was a lead on that front.

A few days after returning from Vegas, I flew to Perth to host the triple j stage at WAMFest, a celebration of West Australian music where local artists and bands perform. There, I met up with a former colleague and confided in her that I was thinking about leaving. She validated my fears but assured me from her own experience leaving the station that the grass was greener.

I had a lot to consider. It had taken me six years of grind and hustle to land my own show. Was I ready to give up something I'd worked so long and hard for? Would I find another job that could top this? It's one thing to quit a job when a great opportunity comes up, but I didn't have anything to go to. I would be freelancing – working for myself.

After returning to Melbourne, I consulted my mum and Oscar. Mum leaned into the emotional side of it, saying I needed to do what would make me happiest. Oscar was supportive but came from a more logical perspective, encouraging me to speak with my accountant first before jumping the gun. I booked in to see my accountant to discuss the financial side of working in a freelance capacity. 'I'm surprised it's taken you so long,' he admitted. This is where he had envisioned my career heading.

As soon as I returned home from this appointment, I sent in my notice. I quit.

My decision was referred to a higher manager, who pleaded with me to stay, saying she would be happy to provide the cab charges I had asked for. But I had made peace with my decision and already emotionally signed off. I did, however, request an exit meeting so I could share my thoughts and feelings in case it could help change things.

While the contract negotiations left a bitter taste in my mouth (which I admit I still haven't quite let go of), I have some great memories and my final show was amazing, thanks to my colleagues. I felt so much love from the listeners and the artists that I'd played over the years. Between the messages, phone calls and emails, it honestly felt like the closest thing to attending your own funeral!

As scared as I was to leap into the unknown, I was determined to make it work. I knew I was fully responsible for my success and, as it turned out, the grass really was greener. I went on to have the best professional year of my life in 2023. Record labels wanted me to MC their events and interview their artists. Global brands like Garnier and Uniqlo wanted to work with me, with Garnier even taking me to the Great Barrier Reef and Tourism NT taking me to Darwin! I got to tick off a major bucket list item and not only attend the ARIA Awards, something I never got to do at triple j, but also host the official Red Carpet for Channel Nine and broadcast backstage for Stan Australia! I had my first taste of commercial breakfast television and became *The Today Show*'s Taylor Swift correspondent. I got my evenings back, which meant a) I could eat dinner at a normal time, and b) I could do fun things like attend movie and musical premieres! And, of course, I was given the opportunity to write this book.

All of this has made me reflect on the concept of a dream job. Does it really exist? Is it something we should even be striving for? To me, a dream job can feel as elusive as a soulmate. Just like within the context of relationships and love, I don't think there is 'The One' when it comes to work – we don't get just one dream job in our lives. A dream job isn't one specific position at one specific place. As we age, we gain life experience, which opens ourselves up to new interests and passions.

Similarly, just like with a partner, we can't expect or rely on a job to be our sole source of fulfilment. I acknowledge how hard this is when our identities are tied to our careers from the very beginning. From childhood, we are encouraged to imagine the ideal job, to take on large sums of student debt just to stand a chance in the workforce, and then to dedicate the bulk of our time, energy and ambition to our employers.

When we meet new people, the first question is usually, 'So what do you do?' How do we figure out how to separate who we are from what we do, especially in our digitally dense way of living when it is so hard to switch off? As Pandora Sykes wrote in her book *How Do We Know We're Doing It Right?*: 'Our professional and personal selves have become indecipherable; work has moved from an occupation to a status, so that for many people, work is no longer just *a* form of self-representation, but *the* form. If your work becomes your identity – I *am* a doctor, I *am* a writer – versus your occupation – I work *at* a bank, I work *on* a magazine – then the parameters are harder to draw.'[1]

In 2023, global hospitality group Accor surveyed 2000 workers and found that 46 per cent didn't believe 'dream' jobs existed, while 41 per cent said their ideal careers were not realistic goals. More than half (54%) of the respondents didn't think they'd ever be in their dream job or industry.[2]

One of my podcast listeners, Alana, believed a dream job was a mix of finding something you were good at, that paid well and that you were passionate about. Her conflict, however, was finding your dream job when you were young. 'I was twenty-seven when I got mine. Now as a 35-year-old, I'm thinking about moving on because I need a new challenge. But what will I ever find that is better than this?!'

Another listener, Louis, felt it all came down to perspective. When they were nine, their dream job was to be a radio presenter but fast-forward ten years and that isn't necessarily still the case. 'My dream job now is to really just be a lifelong learner. I love radio but I also love everything else around it – talking to people, learning stories, reporting, writing, interviewing. My dream job is to constantly be learning what it is to make life most meaningful to me.'

Some people don't have the luxury of aspiring to a dream job. Another listener, Sim, could only focus on working to live. 'I don't have an interest in climbing a career ladder, I just want to get by, pay rent and work flexibly with my chronic illness.'

Aaron reckoned there was such a thing as a dream industry, but not a dream job: 'It sounds like you want to be stuck in one spot forever.' Will, on the other hand, defined a dream job as one that allowed you to live your values and work to a common purpose.

> **TO ME, A DREAM JOB CAN FEEL AS ELUSIVE AS A SOULMATE.**

This just goes to show the multifaceted nature of career fulfilment. A key theme that emerged from these conversations is the idea that we change as we get older and what we want in our twenties might look very different to what we want in our thirties and beyond. But many people still seem to hold on to this idea that if you don't achieve your dream by age thirty, you're a failure. This is why I highkey hate seeing lists like 'Forbes 30 Under 30', which celebrate those who have made remarkable strides in the business world before the age of thirty-one. But as Arwa Mahdawi wrote for *The Guardian*, there is a deep problem with

I QUIT

'the vision of success that we've been sold and the fetishising of youth. 30 Under 30 isn't just a list, it's a mentality: a pressure to achieve great things before youth slips away from you.'[3]

Dearest reader, I need you to know that thirty is not a cut-off for career beginnings, nor do you need to feel that thirty is too late for career changes or endings. It's totally okay to experience major professional change at *any* time in your life.

I think of Australian singer-songwriter Amy Shark who, after hustling in the industry for a decade, released her breakthrough single 'Adore' when she was thirty. I think of former AFL footballer Jack Watts, who retired from the game at age twenty-nine and started a new decade of life free from the pressure and scrutiny of professional sport. I think of my friend Michelle Grace Hunder who, at the age of thirty-one, picked up a professional camera for the first time and went on to become one of Australia's most well-known and in-demand music photographers, touring the world and shooting the biggest gigs and festivals.[4] I think of fellow music presenter Ash London, who quit her prime-time radio gig at twenty-nine to move to Malapascua, a tiny tropical island in the Philippines. 'I felt like I just wanted to live and run away from all of this shit, which you can do at twenty-nine! So I told my boss I was quitting.'[5] Ash eventually returned home and landed an even better radio show than the one she was doing before, but so much of her current life would have not fallen into place had she not quit in the first place. 'For many years of my life and career, I just said yes, and I did what I was supposed to do, because I didn't want to let people down and I wanted people to like me. And of course, as a woman you think, well, if I leave this job then I'm not going to get another job. But I just had to learn to be okay with that.'

In your twenties, you're likely to have started to establish your true interests and gained some decent life experience that can help to determine what you want to get out of a job or career. This, is turn, can help you realise what success really means to you. On my podcast, I caught up with my high school friend Celia Gercovich, who went from overworking herself in the corporate world and her two side businesses (eyelash extensions and balloon installations) to building a career on TikTok with over 1.6 million followers.[6] For Celia, her idea of success has evolved from a corporate perspective of climbing a ladder, to valuing her worth and being in a position where she can actually do what she wants and create content. By doing so, she is earning more but doing less, which consequently allows for a greater work–life balance.

It has been estimated that you will spend one-third of your life at work – roughly 90,000 hours over your lifetime – so it's almost inevitable that your career will morph into a part of your identity. But don't lose sight of what else fulfils you! I was reminded of this when speaking to radio presenter Polly 'PJ' Harding, who in 2021 left her job as co-host of the very popular KIIS breakfast show in Melbourne. The previous year, PJ had celebrated her 30th birthday in lockdown, within the confines of her South Yarra apartment with her cat, Josephine. She was very career-focused at that point and doing long distance with her partner, who was back in her homeland of New Zealand. 'I was also kind of at this point where I started reassessing everything in my life and that's sort of what led to my decision to step away, some would say controversially, from this role that I was in,' she told me from her gorgeous farm property in New Zealand.[7] 'Because these world events were happening, I think everyone was forced to reassess what really mattered to them and their priorities. That's when I was like, oh my god, I think I really need to go home.'

In a job like PJ's, her decision to quit didn't just affect her. It affected her manager, her devoted Melbourne listeners, her radio team of producers and, of course, her co-host, Jase Hawkins. 'That was definitely the toughest part, feeling like you're letting a lot of people down,' she said. Fortunately, PJ and Jase were close enough that she could start a dialogue with him early on and plant that seed so it wouldn't be too much of a shock when it happened. 'We were having pretty open honest chats behind the scenes and being really transparent with one another and I think that really helped.'

The decision to leave her prime-time radio gig was bittersweet, but PJ is adamant that she made the right decision and was always wary of maintaining her own identity and protecting her mental health. 'I remember looking at people who had been in the industry for a long time who weren't the happiest. From quite a young age, maybe my mid-twenties, I knew I didn't want that to be me. I don't want my life to just be radio and then if I don't have radio, I've got nothing.'

I can relate to that. When I left triple j, I still loved radio, but I also didn't want my life to only be radio when there were so many other things to try, to learn, to explore.

There's a lot I'm still figuring out in my career. I don't have an exact vision as to what I see myself doing in five years but I imagine it will still be within a freelance capacity. I am in no rush to return to full-time radio, but it might be something I will do again some day. Perhaps a TV opportunity will pop up. Who knows! For now, I'm focusing on how to switch off and find a better balance in terms of how much of myself I share as 'content' – which is funny, given everything I have written for you! I'm an open book and I love sharing my experiences through writing, podcasting and random rants on Instagram because I truly love making people feel less alone. There's going to be at least one person out there who hears something I put out and thinks, *I needed to hear that* or *I feel seen*. But there can also be an expectation to overshare in the name of content, especially when *you* are your brand. I believe in having boundaries and I think it's important to keep some things just for myself.

Let me tell you the two most important pieces of advice I have received in the context of my career. One was during my pursuit to be on triple j – in fact, it was a few months before I was hired as a casual in 2015. It came from another female presenter who at the time was working for Triple M. She told me, 'If a door doesn't open, you fucking kick it down.' My interpretation was to not wait for opportunities to come my way – I needed to create them for myself.

Michelle Andrews and Zara McDonald are a golden example of creating opportunities. They were both working at *Mamamia* as journalists and pitched the idea of a podcast aimed at twenty-year-olds that covered 'fun, smart celebrity media'.[8] *Mamamia* liked the idea but weren't keen on Andrews and McDonald as hosts. The two friends knew there was a gap in the market for this content and wanted the podcast for themselves, so they took a leap of faith, quit their jobs at *Mamamia* and founded Shameless on zero budget. Fast-forward six years and Shameless is an EMPIRE, with two bestselling books, more than ten staff members, numerous podcast shows, 1.1 million followers across social media, plus one million unique listeners and 2.5 million podcast downloads a month.[9] If I sound obsessed with Shameless, it's because I (shamelessly – ha!) am. Andrews and McDonald didn't wait for someone to say yes to them. They made it happen by saying yes to themselves.

The other piece of advice came to me upon taking over *Good Nights*. Among all the congratulatory messages, I received one from DJ and former presenter Nina Las Vegas. 'Congrats! Now start thinking of what's next x.'

I remember reading this message and thinking, *Bloody hell, what do you mean? I just got this!* But it stuck with me and instilled a need to make sure I was forming an identity and purpose beyond my work at triple j. I knew working at a youth network, especially in an on-air capacity, came with an expiry date, so I wanted to minimise any potential identity crisis that might come when that day arrived. I became more vocal about my endometriosis and launched the *Figuring Out 30* podcast, both of which allowed people to see me talk about more than just music. Music presenting was a passion – still is! – but I wanted to show that I had more to offer. Any time I was approached by some of the newer presenters at triple j, I would pass on Nina's advice. Without it, I'm sure my transition into the freelancing world would have been much more difficult.

> **IT'S ALMOST INEVITABLE THAT YOUR CAREER WILL MORPH INTO A PART OF YOUR IDENTITY. BUT DON'T LOSE SIGHT OF WHAT ELSE FULFILS YOU!**

Is giving up something you worked so hard for pretty damn scary? Absolutely. But sometimes it's worth the risk. And there is no age limit to risk-taking, nor is there an age limit to having FUN. I know there is privilege in saying that life shouldn't be all work and no play, and this speaks to a bigger social issue concerning the cost of living, hustle and burnout culture. I think it speaks volumes that the World Health

Organization has deemed burnout as an occupational phenomenon,[10] with Dr Christine Sinsky from the American Medical Association commenting that the best response is fixing the *workplace*, not the worker.[11] Something needs to change so we can just *be* and not just *do*. I know I want more of that in my thirties. Even when I think back to being asked as a kid what I wanted to be when I grow up, it's clear how deeply our jobs are intertwined with our identities from an early age. Wouldn't it be refreshing if we could reframe that question and focus instead on the kind of person we want to become? Like being a good friend or someone who cares about the environment. Maybe in conversations with adults, instead of immediately asking about our occupations, we could inquire about what makes us happy or excited?

As driven as I am, I have come to realise in my thirties that I don't actually want my success to be solely measured by traditional career metrics. Nor do I want it at the expense of my wellbeing. Above all, I don't want to work more than I live. Even if I really love it, a job is something that I do, not who I am.

FAMOUS PEOPLE who made their career AFTER THIRTY

OPRAH WINFREY

The Oprah Winfrey Show launched in 1986, when Oprah was thirty-two.

KRISTEN WIIG

At age thirty-two, Kristen Wiig made her *Saturday Night Live* debut. After moving to Los Angeles in her early twenties, she spent nearly a decade working different jobs including waitress, graphic designer and florist. At age thirty-eight, Wiig starred in one of the most popular comedy films in modern times, *Bridesmaids*.

DEBBIE HARRY

Debbie Harry was thirty-one when her band Blondie released their debut album. Blondie didn't see worldwide success until their third album a couple of years later.

VERA WANG

The legendary fashion designer was a figure skater and journalist before designing her first dress at forty. The rest is history!

VIVIENNE WESTWOOD

Another iconic name in fashion, Vivienne Westwood was thirty when she quit teaching to fully pursue design.

JANE AUSTEN

The iconic author was thirty-six when her first novel, *Sense and Sensibility*, was published.

11

A NEW DIAGNOSIS
(or two)

> **RECEIVING A DIAGNOSIS OFTEN FEELS LIKE FINDING THE MISSING JIGSAW PIECE.**

There was a certain anticipation clouding over me as I eagerly weaved through the cars and bikes flowing on Sydney Road to my psychologist Lee's office. It was a cool Tuesday afternoon in spring and I was dying to talk to her. I don't usually get nervous for my sessions, but since our last appointment I had been grappling with a theory. A personal revelation that had the potential to reshape the way I understood myself. It was something I had been thinking about for a few months but had not yet verbalised to anyone in my close circle, not even Oscar.

I was seeing a lot of coverage on being diagnosed with ADHD later in life, particularly by women. From Em Rusciano addressing the National Press Club of Australia, to more than three million posts using the ADHD hashtag on TikTok, it seemed like everyone was talking about attention-deficit/hyperactivity disorder. I didn't know much about it and had always thought of it as something that kids dealt with, but according to the Australian Psychological Society, international studies have found that about 3 per cent of adults worldwide have been diagnosed with ADHD.[1] It is estimated that one in twenty Australians have ADHD, and in the past few years, there has been a significant increase in people seeking assessment, particularly adults.[2] My understanding of the symptoms was that they were external, like constantly making noise or talking over everybody. TikTok showed me otherwise.

I can't recall exactly when it happened, which seems fitting given that memory difficulties are a common symptom of ADHD, but I was a few months into the process of writing this book when the first video hit my 'For You' page. A friendly-looking British woman in a red knitted jumper with glasses and a nose ring stared back at me through the screen. Her name was Emma and she was sitting in her study, speaking into a podcast microphone about the signs of ADHD in women.[3] A gentle audio bed of classical music played in the background as she explained that women usually show up on the more inattentive side of the disorder, which can look like having no hobbies or losing interest in things very quickly. My ears pricked and my chest tightened when she mentioned a constant state of overwhelm and overthinking, which is usually due to the hyperactive side being in our brain rather than externalised by our bodies. *This is me*, I thought to myself.

Emma explained other signs, like how ADHD can show up as anxiety and depression, which is usually a by-product of undiagnosed ADHD and not having the right support or treatment. I eagerly nodded when she mentioned feeling a constant need for change, despite not knowing what that change entailed, and a need for your space to be organised and tidy so your brain can feel the same, but not knowing where to start or how to maintain this. My eyes wandered around my room looking at the various piles of clothes and belongings that had covered the floor for months. She said that the idea of starting a task, even if it was something you truly want to do, could be so overwhelming that just the feeling of being overwhelmed could easily burn you out. *This book*. Constantly feeling you are falling behind your peers but not vocalising it. *All of my maths and science classes in high school.* Only lasting three weeks at uni because of my inability to follow that kind of learning structure. Projecting an outward perception of being bubbly and happy-go-lucky but grappling with anxiety behind the scenes. *Me at triple j.*

I ticked off each of these in my head and bookmarked Emma's video. I also downloaded it to my camera roll to keep on stand-by. I rewatched the video another six times that day. It felt like Emma was speaking directly to me. This was something I really needed to think about – and talk about – with the people who knew me best.

Prior to my psych appointment, I had recorded a podcast episode with local drag queen Gabriella Labucci, who I knew from high school as just Cam. Since working our first jobs together at McDonald's in Ballarat, Cam has come out as gay and launched a blossoming career in drag, which has involved placing runner-up on season 3 of *RuPaul's Drag Race Down Under*. At thirty, he received an ADHD diagnosis.

For Cam, ADHD was never on his radar until some new friends came into his life and noticed a few quirks. They asked if he was familiar with the disorder, before making some recommendations for further reading. 'I was reading some articles and had never felt so personally attacked in my life,' Cam said as we sat across from each other at my dining table one afternoon, him in full drag after performing at a bottomless brunch in South Yarra.[4] He listed his main symptoms as restlessness and not being able to sit still, zoning in and out of conversations, a delayed processing of what people say, and struggling to stay organised and clean up after himself. The latter I found particularly funny, given how much the 'Clean As You Go' principle was drilled into our heads while working at McDonald's.

I felt my chest tighten, just like it did when I watched Emma's TikTok on ADHD, when Cam mentioned another symptom that he considered to be 'a big one' – rejection sensitivity dysphoria. Also known as RSD, this is basically when someone possesses an extreme emotional sensitivity to perceived criticism or rejection, and they can have a heightened emotional response like shame, sadness or humiliation. They can also display avoidant behaviours and go to great lengths to avoid situations or interactions that may result in criticism or rejection. Rejection sensitivity can also contribute to negative self-perception or negative self-image, with a potential strain on relationships and social interactions as a result.

> **I WASN'T READY TO BE BOTH NEURODIVERGENT AND CHRONICALLY ILL.**

Fortunately, Cam had someone in his life with ADHD who he could speak to and learn more from. He tried Ritalin, which is a brand name for the medication methylphenidate, a central nervous system stimulant used to treat the disorder. 'The best description for it is that there was fog in my brain, and it had just lifted,' he explained to me. Cam couldn't believe he was able to focus on just one thought and not have other random things swirling in his mind at the same time, like songs and awkward interactions with other people from five weeks ago. 'The thing is, I didn't know that wasn't the norm. I had no education around it. I had no point of reference to know that wasn't normal.'

Before he started exploring a diagnosis, Cam turned to marijuana in an attempt to slow down his thoughts. 'It was constant feelings of guilt, of obligation and that I'm letting people down. But I'm also burning myself out because I'm trying to people please.' His drag work started picking up so Cam made the decision to stop smoking weed and cigarettes and continue Ritalin. He described one breakthrough morning when he got up, made himself breakfast, ate the breakfast and cleaned up after himself. 'And I cried! I cried and cried and cried. Because not once in my thirty-one years of existence had I ever been able to do that. The dishes would just go in the sink and be a problem for another time.'

Cam mentioned TikTok and how the short, sharp video format helped him to understand his symptoms and pursue a formal diagnosis. He said it helped him move forward with his life. 'I just feel like I'm making up for lost time, to be honest.' He smiled. 'I'm pushing through and taking on the absolute most, especially with *Drag Race* wrapping up. I've got a lot of opportunity, so bring it on. I've got a lot of catching up to do because I locked myself in my room for literally ten years of my life, just hating myself.'

Maybe I could be living a better life too. I settled on Lee's couch, pondering when to throw my curveball into our conversation. Although I had been seeing her for over two years and she knew the depths of my thoughts and insecurities, I was worried Lee would consider my ADHD suspicions to be a lil delulu.

My eyes darted straight to the two bookshelves snugly positioned behind her chair, directly across from me. The books arranged there underwent a subtle rotation, each session revealing a fresh array of titles. I couldn't believe what greeted my eyes this time: *A Radical Guide for Women with ADHD: Embrace Neurodiversity, Live Boldly, and Break Through Barriers* by Sari Solden and Michelle Frank. I pointed and laughed in disbelief. 'Oh my god. I need to talk about that.'

Lee chuckled. 'Okay, what's on your mind?'

I explained how I'd seen Emma's TikTok and it had resonated with me, especially the constant state of overwhelm. How I wanted to cry when Cam introduced me to rejection sensitivity dysphoria. How I have felt paralysed by the constant stream of thoughts in my mind. How hard I have found it to manage my days as a freelancer and do simple tasks around the house. How much I related to Em Rusciano describing her exhaustion in her address to the National Press Club as 'a tiredness that crept into my bones and settled there. No amount of sleep or rest could rid me of it, and suddenly, completing the simplest of tasks became nearly impossible. It felt like my brain had been bleached of all its magic, and I felt completely overwhelmed by life.'[5]

Lee nodded empathetically. 'I'm so glad you brought this up.'

She said she had made a note to ask me about ADHD in our session a few weeks earlier when I was telling her how much trouble I was having writing this book. That the minute I woke up, my brain would go into overdrive about all the ideas I had, as if there were thirty Google tabs open in my head, but by the time I was ready to articulate them on paper, I couldn't because I was so strung up by it all. Based on our conversations and her behavioural observations, Lee said she could understand how these symptoms could be affecting me and that it would be worth exploring a diagnosis of ADHD.

I felt like a weight had lifted off my chest before a heavy feeling quickly returned. Sure, I was relieved that my speculation was being supported, but the thought of potentially having ADHD made me want to crawl up into a ball and sob. I wasn't ready for a new diagnosis.

Lee explained that we would need to do a screener, several questionnaires and answer some rating scale questions, emphasising the irony of how much these assessments rely on memory, which is not only challenging for individuals with ADHD but especially those seeking

A NEW DIAGNOSIS (OR TWO)

a diagnosis later in life. Being asked to provide collateral information that shows you have been dealing with symptoms since childhood is tricky when you no longer have school reports from two decades ago. Who keeps that shit? Some of these questions also relied on my parents' memory, and with me being one of four children, my confidence in their ability to answer was lacking, let's say. As senior lecturer and paediatrician Dr Alison Poulton suggested to *SBS News* in 2023, more accessible and inclusive assessment tools that ask adults about 'how their minds work, what actually happens, what are they having most difficulty with, why are they having difficulty and what happens to their attention', would make all of this *a lot* easier.[6]

One of the assessment tools was a twenty-page document called DIVA-5, short for Diagnostic Interview for ADHD in Adults, fifth edition. It is divided into three parts that are applied to both childhood and adulthood: criteria for attention deficit (A1), criteria for hyperactivity-impulsivity (A2) and the age of onset and impairment accounted for by ADHD symptoms. We actually had fun going through it, chuckling at questions that had my name written all over them. *Do you often find it difficult to organise tasks and activities? Are you often easily distracted by extraneous stimuli?* But there were also some that were met with a much quieter and sombre admission, like 'conflicts as a result of communication problems' and, well, literally everything under self-confidence/self-image:

- Uncertainty through negative comments of others. Tick.
- Negative self-image due to experiences of failure. Tick.
- Fear of failure in terms of starting new things. Tick.
- Excessive intense reaction to criticism. Tick.
- Perfectionism. Tick.
- Distressed by the symptoms of ADHD. Tick.

Lee calculated the rating score assessments and concluded that I sat more under the inattentive branch of ADHD. A million thoughts swirled through my mind. 'So, I definitely have it? Do I need to see anyone else?' I asked. My endometriosis diagnosis had been confirmed via laparoscopic surgery and a pathologist analysing the biopsy, meaning I had physical evidence. This is not to say I wanted a piece of my brain to be cut off and sent away, but I felt like I needed something more concrete. I didn't want people thinking I was jumping on the ADHD bandwagon – after all, some critics had labelled ADHD a 'trendy' diagnosis, which annoyed me, because I remember the anger I felt in 2020 when *Cosmopolitan* published a piece on endometriosis that opened with, 'It got popular the way a lot of things do: celebrities and social media.'[7] (Just so we are crystal clear, there is nothing to like or admire about a disease that embeds itself into your organs.) While Lee could help me implement cognitive-behavioural tools, a psychiatrist would be able to aid with further assessment. But based on the results of the diagnostic surveys, Lee said it would be incredibly unlikely for a psychiatrist to say that I didn't have ADHD.

A psychiatrist would also be able to prescribe medication. I had mixed feelings about meds. My reservations mainly stemmed from watching others in my life go through various medications for their mental health because, like with most things, it is a case of trial and error to figure out what works best. When they hit, great. But when they miss, they can *really* miss. I was scared that medication would end up doing more harm than good. Lee explained that immediate-release medications were available, which could provide relief for three to four hours and be used as I needed it, making me feel more at ease about exploring my treatment options.

Lee also told me that they considered women between the ages of seventeen and forty to be 'the lost generation' when it comes to obtaining

> I CAN'T HELP BUT THINK ABOUT WHY THESE THINGS COULD NOT HAVE BEEN RECOGNISED AND TREATED EARLIER.

an ADHD diagnosis. Why? Because we internalise. And testing has historically revolved around young, white males who, you guessed it, externalise their symptoms.

Before I knew it, my time was up. 'Think about who you want to start opening up to and sharing with that you are on this journey,' Lee said. I joked that it was like a soft launch, which made her chuckle before she turned serious again. My eyes had welled up throughout our session while Lee explained the ADHD symptoms in more depth, but the tears properly unleashed when she acknowledged how exhausting it must be for me to have to be dealing with both this and endometriosis, feeling like I am constantly trying to catch up with everyone else.

Receiving a diagnosis often feels like finding the missing jigsaw piece, especially as an adult, but I'd been there, done that with my endometriosis. Not to chuck a tantrum, but so much of me wanted to throw the whole bloody ADHD puzzle out. As journalist Matilda Boseley wrote in her book, *The Year I Met My Brain*, when you pursue a medical diagnosis, you are living in the wake of a life-changing revelation, with absolutely no clue what it means for you, your identity, your relationships or your future.

When I received my endometriosis diagnosis at twenty-seven, my initial reaction was more sweet than bitter. After twelve years of wondering why I had such debilitating pain and why it was so hard to get answers or anyone to believe me, I felt somewhat invincible when I woke up from surgery to hear that the disease was widespread across my pelvic region, bowel and pouch of Douglas. Emotionally invincible, that is. Physically, I was a fragile, bloody (and gassy) mess. But it was the ultimate validation and the way Matilda viewed her ADHD diagnosis at the age of twenty-three was much like how I had embraced my endo. 'Rather than being a dark omen of all the difficulties we may face in the future, for many of us who find out we have ADHD as an adult, it's amazing news.'[8]

Some of my followers felt the same enthusiasm. Dani messaged me on Instagram to share that she had just been diagnosed with ADHD at the age of thirty-three. 'It's really exciting to think about the power and possibility that comes with having more understanding and a roadmap as to how my brain works!' Vanessa shared a similar sentiment. 'It feels great to know I'm not a failure and my brain just works different.'

It is a kind of optimism I felt in relation to my endo journey. I was so eager to connect with other people that I dedicated a whole Instagram account to it, @endogram. I became a fierce and reliable advocate and willingly passed on my knowledge to others, in the hope that it wouldn't take them as long to get a diagnosis as it did for me. I can't begin to describe how rewarding it is to have people message or come up to me in public and tell me how much *How to Endo* has changed their lives.

But I have to be real in acknowledging that advocacy has also been exhausting and, at times, defeating. I have come to realise the political nature of the healthcare system and organisations that claim to represent their patient community, and I've spent a lot of time correcting publications that shared incorrect information about endo. The expectations of my audience has also been challenging: it got to the point where my inbox was flooded with messages, asking me to post about this and call out that. The more I did, the more people expected. I think people forgot that I was dealing with frequent pain and fatigue and that I had boundaries that deserved to be respected. I was chronically ill but also chronically online.

I didn't want to feel pressured to take on that kind of labour for ADHD, so in my session with Lee, I decided I would not talk about my ADHD publicly. I didn't want to make some sort of announcement post on my social media, nor did I want to speak about it on my podcast. I just wanted the chance to sit with it. Just me and my ADHD. Obviously, you're reading about it here, and that's because I have had time to process the idea. (Plus, the least it can do is help my word count!)

Returning home from my session with Lee, I was greeted by Oscar, who naturally wanted to know how it went. I kept it short. 'It was fine,' I said, brushing past him and making my way to the backyard. I was in full avoidant mode. I didn't know how to talk about this with him. I didn't know how I would bring it up with my parents. I had little hope for how they would understand this, given the common perception of it being something that little boys who can't sit still in school have, not grown women.

I wasn't ready to be both neurodivergent and chronically ill. While it is a privilege that I can afford to see my psychologist once or twice a month and that she is there to help me navigate my brain, ADHD hits different when you're already chronically ill. It has only been through exploring my neurodivergence that I have realised that, six years on, I am still wounded by my endometriosis diagnosis and the implications it has on my day-to-day life. The pain. The fatigue. And then to have ADHD tagging along for every decision and thought process. Let. A. Girl. Live!

I confided my feelings about my ADHD diagnosis to singer-songwriter Angie McMahon, who I'd invited to my house for a podcast chat about her new album, *Light, Dark, Light Again*. The record was her first in four years and one of the most highly anticipated releases of 2023. It was also a particularly personal release for Angie, capturing details of her Saturn return alongside the personal breakthroughs she had made during the end of her twenties. While arranging our interview with her publicist, I asked if Angie would agree to a separate chat about her ADHD that I could reflect on in this book. Despite having interviewed

A NEW DIAGNOSIS (OR TWO)

Angie before and being forty minutes deep into our conversation, I could feel my nerves resurfacing as we transitioned topics. She always radiates warm energy but I felt her demeanour soften even more, perhaps as a way of acknowledging my vulnerability.

ADHD was something Angie had briefly touched on in a few interviews for the new record, and it was in 2020 when she first started connecting the dots, during a whole year off touring. She likened it to my new job structure of freelancing. 'Nobody was determining how I spent my time, so it became quite obvious,' she told me, resting her head on her knees.[9] For Angie, her ADHD was a long process, despite knowing it existed within her family and believing she knew how it presented. 'But once I learned more about it, I came to realise how different it looked within.'

While Cam and I had found information mostly through TikTok, Angie turned to podcasts, some which featured other people with ADHD sharing their coping strategies. She said the knowledge gave her the language for why she felt so paralysed by her own negative self-talk. Angie shared my own imposter syndrome and fear of being seen as 'making it up', so it was important for her to embrace the tips she took from the podcasts. She started going on morning runs and eating protein for breakfast, as well as increasing her magnesium intake. Gathering the evidence for herself and seeing that these things were working helped give her the confidence to speak to others in her life. I also related to Angie's sense of grief. 'I just kept thinking, *Why did nobody tell me this before?* I had relationships breaking down where I was like, well, this wouldn't have happened if I had known this.'

It was important for Angie to implement a self-compassion practice and continue therapy. 'We have spent our whole lives, it turns out, having this thing in us, this neurotype, and then trying to talk ourselves through it. That becomes such a negative headspace, so I've had to do a lot of rewiring, the way that I talk to myself. That has been such a big part of it, more than medication. More than anything else.'

Angie became much gentler and nicer on the self-talk front, even if she felt like her productivity was lower. However, within a year of receiving her diagnosis, Angie was hit with another one. She told me she had started seeing a psychologist who specialised in ADHD and autism, and in their first session together, Angie was asked to start thinking about the fact that she might have autism. 'No one had ever said that to me before,' she said, 'and I was like, what? That was a bigger hit.'

For Angie, the stigma surrounding autism felt harder to accept than that surrounding ADHD. 'I had no idea what it was so I went to research and redefine it, which ended up becoming a beautiful thing. But in the first two days following that conversation, I fully shut down. I was so dark; I couldn't believe that nobody in my life ever told me I could be autistic.'

Angie now sees herself as a neurodivergent person and embraces that label. This helps her to rework her understanding of herself with a more compassionate lens. 'I think it's great for you to give yourself the space,' she told me when I shared how I planned to sit with my own ADHD revelation.

Around the same time that I spoke with Angie, Oscar and I discovered that we would be moving from Melbourne to Perth. As excited as I was about packing up and embracing the change of scenery, I was wary of how this could potentially delay my diagnostic process. I would have to find a new GP and I had no idea how many books would be open for new patients on the other side of the country. Thankfully, my new doctor was able to recommend a private psychiatry clinic that was taking new patients.

A NEW DIAGNOSIS (OR TWO)

As I scrolled through the list of psychiatrists for this clinic, BOOKS CLOSED was written next to each name but one. His said SIX MONTHS. Although the automated email advised it could take up to four weeks to receive a response, I opened my inbox six days later to find that my referral had been accepted and a $200 deposit would be required to secure my appointment. I swiftly made the payment and opened the pricing structure document they emailed across. An audible gasp escaped my mouth.

'Complex' ADHD Initial Consultation – Standard Fee = $1000
Medicare Rebate = $247.25
Gap Payment = $752.75
Initial Consultation = $750
Medicare Rebate = $247.25
Gap Payment = $502.75

My first appointment was scheduled for six months from my referral being accepted, but it didn't feel like too much of a drag, because I was already preoccupied with something else: another condition that had been simmering in the background. One I had been quietly aware of, for longer than my ADHD, but that I had been trying to push out of the picture, hoping it would go away.

Please welcome PMDD, or premenstrual dysphoric disorder, to the chat.

I'd always been aware of my mood leading up to my period, but in recent years, things began to intensify. I wasn't just sad. I wasn't just sensitive. I was anxious and overwhelmed, convinced my whole world was falling apart. I was aware it was happening but couldn't do anything to stop it. The lack of control over my emotions and my hormones almost felt like an out-of-body experience that left me feeling a deep, deep sense of helplessness. It was like a monthly existential crisis on steroids, where a dark cloud would loom over me in the days leading up to bleeding, sometimes even a week out. But then, as soon as my period started, the cloud would disappear out of sight. Like a light switch, things were bright again. I'd always been pretty good at masking my endometriosis pain, but PMDD was a different beast entirely.

A severe form of PMS, PMDD affects roughly 3 to 8 per cent of menstruators and can entail extreme mood swings, heightened emotional sensitivity and feelings of irritability or anger.[10] People may experience periods of depressed mood, marked by feelings of hopelessness, worthlessness or guilt, as well as heightened anxiety and tension. Other common symptoms include a diminished interest in usual activities, difficulty concentrating due to brain fog and overwhelming fatigue or excessive sleepiness. Appetite changes such as food cravings, overeating or binge eating may occur, alongside sleep disturbances like insomnia. Some physical symptoms can also be present such as breast tenderness, joint or muscle pain, bloating or weight gain, acne and headaches. According to *TIME* magazine, around a third of people with PMDD have attempted suicide and more than 70 per cent have regular suicidal ideation.[11]

To be diagnosed with PMDD, you must have five or more PMDD symptoms, including one mood-related symptom. When my doctor and I went through the list, I ticked them off left, right and centre.

I'd been determined to try to push through it but after asking for the experiences of my @endogram followers, I decided to give medication a go. My GP prescribed me 10 mg of escitalopram, which belongs to a class of antidepressants called selective serotonin reuptake inhibitors (SSRIs). It works by boosting levels of serotonin and I was to take one daily in the two weeks leading up to my period each month. I was warned that the side effects could be significant – things like insomnia, a dry mouth and an upset tummy – but that they would subside after the two weeks. Some

A NEW DIAGNOSIS (OR TWO)

people said their symptoms elevated for a bit before it got better. Others experienced no side effects whatsoever. Naturally, I hoped I would be in the latter camp.

I took my first dose on a Sunday morning after breakfast and was soon met with a wave of nausea crashing over my body. I felt heavy and foggy. Honestly, I felt like I had been drugged. Oscar and I had to cancel our dinner plans for that night. I shared my story on @endogram, and many people replied suggesting I take half a dose for the next day and to do it right before bed so I would hopefully sleep through the side effects. That was slightly better but still super intense. I couldn't focus or do any work, everything seemed hazy. I started panicking because I had TV commitments – and I also had this book to write! I didn't even think I could drive. There was just something in my gut telling me that this was not the right medication for me. So before I got too far deep, I stopped.

The period that followed absolutely sucked. I lost a whole afternoon of work to my PMDD after the most teeny-tiny conflict with Oscar blew up, where I misinterpreted him asking what I had done that morning as an attack on my productivity. I couldn't stop crying. While it's been a considerable strain on our relationship, we've identified the pattern of arguments that occur right before my period and we're working on how we can both be clearer and kinder during this time.

Another reason I stopped the escitalopram was because I wanted to see what the psychiatrist would say regarding medication for ADHD. I had a friend reach out who has both ADHD and PMDD, and she told me her medication for ADHD has actually alleviated her PMDD symptoms. Turns out there is some intricate interplay between the two conditions, specifically how hormones, neurotransmitters and genetic predispositions contribute to hormonal fluctuations that activate

> THERE WAS JUST SOMETHING IN MY GUT TELLING ME THAT THIS WAS NOT THE RIGHT MEDICATION FOR ME.

A NEW DIAGNOSIS (OR TWO)

PMDD symptoms and intensify ADHD.[12] In 2020, research from Vrije University in Amsterdam found a significantly higher prevalence of PMDD in women with ADHD than in the general population.[13] The study reported 45.5 per cent of women with ADHD having PMDD compared with 28.7 per cent in the general population. I was strangely relieved to hear of a potential connection between the two, because in some weird way my brain was telling me it could be a two bird, one stone kind of thing. Perhaps it was just a coping mechanism, but that comfort has helped me in how I have moved forward with these conditions.

By the time my psychiatrist appointment came around, I was fully dreading it. Mostly due to the fact that I had yucky period cramps and could not be bothered getting out of bed and driving into the Perth CBD. I also couldn't shake the image in my head of a cold, clinical figure in a white lab coat with a clipboard, ready to judge and dismiss me. Despite Lee's belief that I have ADHD, the imposter syndrome loomed large.

As it turned out, it was far less intimidating than I had imagined. The reception area was small and clean, with wooden finishes and plants lining a feature wall. I reckon the receptionist was in her twenties, with purple-tinted hair and Doc Martens. Soft '80s music played in the background before switching to Chappell Roan, which I suspected was the receptionist's own playlist. I felt at ease.

My psychiatrist appeared by the door, younger than expected – probably in his late thirties. He had short, curly hair with a single strand hanging in front of his forehead, and was dressed in a dark-green check suit. He greeted me with a big smile and directed me to his office, which had massive plush chairs. They looked comfortable enough for me to drop my life story for the next forty minutes.

He was extremely attentive, and then delivered his verdict. 'So today I'm going to diagnose you with ADHD.' My eyes starting welling. It wasn't like I was hearing this for the first time, but to have it confirmed by both a psychologist and a psychiatrist felt profound. I received a referral to see a cardiologist, who confirmed I had no heart issues and cleared me to start medication. I was prescribed Vyvanse to take daily, which would set me back a steep monthly cost of $99. However, I was informed that if my mum filled out a form verifying my childhood symptoms, I might be eligible for some sort of subsidised cost. The sting to my wallet was nothing in comparison to being told I couldn't drink my English breakfast tea for the first few days of taking my new medication, as caffeine can increase potential side effects like nausea and irritability. I mean, consider me already irritated!

So far I'm feeling hopeful about the medication, and I've realised how essential hope is to managing any kind of diagnosis. It's still early days in how I move forward with ADHD and PMDD but it has been interesting to see how these new diagnoses have helped me to recontextualise old ideas about myself. How I can better understand those times when I have felt sensitive and on edge, or where I have completely lost focus and struggled with my memory. It's also been interesting to reflect on how differently I have accepted all of this in my thirties as opposed to in my twenties. There's a deeper sense of grief I underestimated because, like with my twelve-year diagnosis journey with endometriosis, I can't help but think about why these things were not recognised and treated earlier. I can't help but think about how different my quality of life could have been. How kinder I could have been to myself. Yet I need to realise that my vulnerability in the context of my conditions does not make me weak.

It was only a few days after obtaining my medication script that British singer-songwriter Jessie J shared her diagnosis of ADHD and

A NEW DIAGNOSIS (OR TWO)

OCD. 'It's weird when you know you have been a little different and felt things differently your whole life, and finally one day when you least expect it, someone really explains why and you can't avoid it,' is how she described it, going on to say, 'I lowkey feel like it's a superpower as long as you look at it from the right perspective and have the right support and people around you that can navigate it with you.'[14]

I didn't want to talk about ADHD on my personal Instagram but the day before I started taking Vyvanse, I decided to jump on my @endogram stories and ask if any of my followers were on it. The replies came in thick and fast with people sharing their experiences and any tips they'd picked up along the way. I sat at the park down the road from home with Daisy in my lap and a big grin on my face as I went through them. I felt so lucky to have this platform – a place that started with educating and raising awareness about endometriosis but has, in turn, created a safe space for me to be vulnerable, ask questions and feel supported as I navigate my own health. And, best of all, decaffeinated tea recommendations!

ADHD, PMDD and me. It's ongoing, it's complicated, but as Jessie J said: 'Here's to getting to know yourself even more through life.'

12
FOR THE LOVE
and loss
OF FRIENDSHIP

> IF WE'RE CONSTANTLY CHANGING AND GROWING, SO ARE OUR FRIENDS.

Although heartbreak, family trauma and lockdowns were obvious low points around the time I turned thirty, one silver lining was a newfound appreciation for the friendships in my life. From the endless voice messages and mental health walks to surprise self-care packages and book exchanges, the collective effort from friends to reignite my spark was like witnessing a giant, shimmering rainbow emerge through a grey sky. The Big Break-Up had left me feeling like I was being pushed into a trust fall with no warning, yet there my friends were, a wonderfully chaotic and mismatched group of people reflecting different versions of myself – high school Bridge, retail worker Bridge, music industry Bridge, Ballarat Bridge, Melbourne Bridge, travel agent Bridge, endometriosis Bridge … just like all the Barbies! – together in position, ready to catch my defeated body and lift me up.

I think we have all been guilty of overlooking the enduring nature of friendships at some point in our lives, and often we fail to realise that while romantic relationships may ebb and flow, friendships remain a steadfast presence. And it's not just the life-affirming, ride-or-die mates who matter. Casual acquaintances can be equally valuable and nourishing. These connections really hit different in our thirties because it's a time when we tend to be in fewer situations of forced proximity or larger group settings like school, university, sports teams and even house parties. Because, if you think about it, most of our earliest connections were forged out of convenience. If your mum's friends had children then you would usually get together to play with them so the mums could hang out. Or you would be plonked with the other kids at the caravan park that your parents would take you to every summer.

This idea was echoed in my podcast conversation with human connection scientist and author Ali Walker, who highlighted that throughout different stages of human civilisation, connection has really been prepared for us. 'We lived in villages where you would know everybody else, and you would probably just end up being friends with the people around your age and your gender,' Ali explained to me from her home office in Sydney.[1] 'In a way, we are better off because we get to choose but, in another way, we actually need to be given the tools, skills and strategies to make friends because it's not actually part of our evolution. We are now evolving those skills because in the past it was just something that was pre-prepared, and that was the same with a lot of romantic relationships and arranged marriages.'

Ali likened the need to actively make connections with making the deliberate effort to exercise. 'Because we all worked in manual ways, our day involved a lot of incidental movements and exercise, so no one got to the end of the day and then said, "Wait, I have to go for a run or walk around the block!" That would have been ridiculous, up until thirty to forty years ago. So, in the same way, when offices and work moved to be sedentary, and people were sitting down a lot, we now have to make an effort to make friends and connect with other people because you can now work from home and go weeks without seeing anyone. This is a huge shift in our evolution.'

"IT'S ACTUALLY CRAZY HOW THE SINGLE TAP OF A BUTTON HAS NOW BECOME THE STANDARD MEASURE OF APPROVAL OR ACKNOWLEDGEMENT."

FIGURING OUT THIRTY

Convenience is still a cornerstone of adult friendship, especially when you consider the digitally dense world that we live in, but I see it as a double-edged sword. On one hand, the prominence of social media and messaging apps has made connection more immediate and accessible than ever. I love that my Scottish friend Amy, who I shared a student apartment with fourteen years ago, is only a WhatsApp message away, or that my friends with kids back home in Ballarat can still feel involved in my life as I share it on Instagram. I love how it has introduced me to new people, especially in the context of navigating my endometriosis. Technology keeps me connected in times of a chronic illness flare, when it is too painful or exhausting to make physical plans.

On the other hand, in revolutionising the way we communicate, the convenience and immediacy of social media have fostered a culture of fleeting, superficial and shallow interaction, particularly in the form of an emoji reaction to a story or liking and commenting on a post. It's actually crazy how the single tap of a button has now become the standard measure of approval or acknowledgement. I myself have been guilty of constantly refreshing a post to see how many likes it accumulates, not only prioritising the quantity of engagement over meaningful connection but also allowing such a simplistic action to affect my self-worth. Are these sorts of interactions forming the basis of actual friendship?

'All of us are thinking, *Well, I have all of this connection through text messages, WhatsApp, social media. It's at my fingertips! I have never communicated more with people my age therefore I must have a lot of friends,*' Ali said. 'But actually, you need to see texting, emailing and social media like eating a whole lot of sugar or processed food and expecting to feel nourished. It's not nourishing communication. Sure, it's functional and you need to see it for its function – like to let someone know that you're a few minutes away from catching up – but it's not actually nourishing us in terms of our needs for connection.'

Not only have we become obsessed with cultivating an idealised image of ourselves online, but we can also display exaggerated and performative portrayals of friendships through our highlight reels and curated posts. It's evident on Instagram and TikTok but, my fellow millennials, let's not pretend this is a new concept. We were pulling this shit on Myspace too! Remember the transactional nature of 'PC4PC' (pic comment for pic comment) requests? Or the hierarchical ranking of friends in our Top 8? Social media became a popularity contest and we got so focused on collecting friends and followers as if they were Pokémon that we failed to realise we didn't know how to *connect* beyond a request button.

On Facebook, I have 813 'friends' but I know there's no way I would consider them all actual friends. I'm not alone. In the early 1990s, evolutionary biologist Robin Dunbar proposed that human beings are only capable of maintaining stable relationships with a maximum of 150 people.[2] This has become known as Dunbar's number. According to Dunbar, we have five loved ones, ten close friends and between thirty-five and fifty friends within the 150 meaningful contacts in our social network (by meaningful, he means people you would stop to say hello to if you passed them in the street or in a cafe). Beyond that, we have 500 people who are social acquaintances and 1500 people we would recognise and know the names of.

Perhaps this fixation on quantity of friends throughout adolescence and even our twenties is why the 'splinter era' can come as such a shock. Apparently, many friendships enter this phase around the age of twenty-eight, which is kinda like a Saturn return for your friendships. During this time, you may find yourself diverging from friends as you navigate life at different paces or prioritise different goals. Some friends may be tying the knot, others purchasing their first homes, some relocating for career opportunities and some embracing parenthood, while others may feel adrift, unsure of their path, and sensing their friends moving ahead without them.

In her piece for *Mamamia*, Emily Vernem delved into how these splinters can manifest during significant life milestones, leading to subtle shifts in behaviour patterns among friends; for example, celebrating a work promotion may no longer prompt a call to your bestie, but instead to your partner.[3] Drinks with the girls might now feel like an obligation rather than a treat after a long day or week. Or bailing on this year's girls' trip to save for things like house renos or a wedding. I know for me, when I worked the graveyard radio shift, it was really hard to catch up with friends and that had an impact on some of my friendships. According to Vernem, these seemingly isolated incidents can accumulate, gradually altering the dynamics of friendships. Because up until that point, you've pretty much been progressing at the same pace. Stumbling through life *together*.

This reminded me of Dolly Alderton's bestselling memoir *Everything I Know About Love*. In the chapter 'Nothing Will Change', Dolly grappled with her bestie Farly's new romantic relationship and the gaps that appeared in their friendship as a result. 'You go from seeing your friend every weekend to once every six weekends. She becomes a baton and you're the one at the very end of the track. You get your go for, say, your birthday or a brunch, then you have to pass her back round to the boyfriend to start the long, boring rotation again,' Alderton wrote.[4] 'The love is still there, but the familiarity is not. Before you know it, you're not living life together anymore.' It's scary to feel like you are being left behind and it's scary to think that you'll never be in the same place as your friends again.

FOR THE LOVE AND LOSS OF FRIENDSHIP

When I consider how this might have played out in my own life, I can see how my career has been a factor in the splintering of some of my friendships. While pursuing music presenting, I was so committed to the grind and hustle of getting my name out there that I lost touch with a number of people. I can also see how my chronic illness and ADHD have affected my friendships, because I have had to bail on plans when I am in pain or might not be in the mood to see people – this was especially hard during the diagnosis journey when I didn't even have concrete answers for myself.

When I asked my podcast listeners to share the biggest cause of change to their friendships in their thirties, an overwhelming majority responded with one word: kids. Emily said, 'Some of my friends have definitely got lost in their kid bubble and I have found myself walking away from catch-ups feeling like we only spoke about their children and, sadly, that interest and curiosity is not reciprocated. I can understand that parenting is hard and consuming, but it feels very disheartening and invalidating to hang out with a friend and not feel like your child-free life is important too!'

Grace had experienced more-positive change. 'It's made our hangouts much more lowkey, relaxing, affordable and intimate. I'm so happy to go to a friend's place for morning tea and playtime with the kids, or join them on a picnic. There is also usually an end time due to kids' routines, which I am totally here for. A two-hour window is more than enough time to catch up. Sure, it can take more forward planning, but I feel like our time together is much more genuine. I love seeing my friends in that stage of their lives because they seem so happy and fulfilled.'

Good or bad, change can be hard. As Liz explained, 'My best friend is pregnant and I have just realised that I am mourning our friendship of just us two. I know we will always be best friends, but I am worried she will replace me with her new "mummy" friends. I feel selfish and like my feelings aren't valid – I feel like I shouldn't be feeling this way at all. But I can't help it. Obviously I'm happy for her, but I'm also upset.'

It can be difficult on the other side too – when you're the first one to have kids. Tim said, 'My mates were all still living the party/pub/music scene life and I had to knuckle down for full-time dad commitments. I very quickly struggled to relate to them, their interests and priorities. I wanted to be able to, but I couldn't. Likewise, they seemed to lose interest in me and my priorities. Some of them drifted back much later when they had kids of their own, but never to the level or intensity of the friendship we had before I became a father.'

> **SOME FRIENDSHIPS SURVIVE THE SPLINTER ERA AND SOME DON'T.**

Samantha felt similarly. 'The hardest part for me is conversation, because until you have a baby, you don't know very much about them aside from the basics. So when you catch up with your childless friends, they don't really know how to have a conversation with you because they just seem to ask about basic baby stuff. I actually don't want to talk about my kids at all, because I have my mothers' group and other friends with kids to do that with. I just want to be able to talk about the stuff we used to talk about before I was pregnant. It's like, can we go back to random shit talking, please!'

FOR THE LOVE AND LOSS OF FRIENDSHIP

While I have close, sustaining friendships (the oldest stemming from the age of five – hi, Katie!), I do not have a singular best friend. There is no Thelma to my Louise, or Romy to my Michele. When I asked my followers on Instagram if they had a singular best friend, out of 2022 respondents, 54 per cent answered yes, while 46 per cent responded no. I was surprised to see how evenly split the responses were. For a long time, I had interpreted me not having a best friend as some sort of personal failing, or an indictment of me as a person, but these results made me realise that there's nothing wrong with *not* having a best friend.

Again, I can't help but liken the concept of a best friend to the concept of 'The One'. I don't believe it's particularly fair or realistic to expect someone to be *everything* for you. To be the best is to exceed all others and I think it's too much pressure to expect one person to be the best at being your friend. As Dunbar said, we typically have around five loved ones in our most intimate circle, meaning these people are all pretty important. How do we pick one person from this five to place on our special 'best friend' pedestal? Instead, we might turn to different people for different things. It's natural for people to move in and out of the different phases of our lives. After all, if we're constantly changing and growing, so are our friends. As Reema Hindi wrote in *InStyle*, when it comes to thinking about the friends in our lives, they should be a constellation, rather than a single person being our sun and moon.[5]

I don't believe in confining myself to one soulmate, but neither am I anchored in a tight-knit crew. I'm talking about the ones we see on *Sex and the City*, *The Sisterhood of the Traveling Pants*, *Pretty Little Liars* or *The Cheetah Girls*. Don't get me wrong, I love these girl gangs, but I've also felt alienated by them. As much of a Swiftie as I am, I did not vibe with the flaunting of Tay's squad during her 1989 era. The exclusivity of being an 'It girl' means you can only be part of it if you're deemed hot or cool enough. I was a floater in high school, with friends spanning different groups, and I spent each lunchtime with different people. I found it fun and fulfilling to get to know a range of personalities and what they brought out in me.

Interestingly, research commissioned by Bumble's friend-finding mode, Bumble For Friends, revealed that millennials are seeking new friendships more than any other generation but are struggling to get out of platonic relationships that no longer serve them.[6] Of millennial respondents, 73 per cent wanted to find new friends, but nearly one in two (43%) respondents agreed that they were stuck in outdated friendships. The data suggested a reason for this: while a majority (65%) of respondents met their friends in college, 78 per cent shared that they were a different person now that they were out in the adult workforce.

Some friendships survive the splinter era, and some don't. After all, friendships need to evolve to reflect the changes and growth we experience, especially as we navigate the complexities of adulthood. During my podcast interview with clinical neuropsychologist Dr Hannah Korrel, she likened friendships to a solar system, where your connection with a friend is akin to a planet orbiting within that system. 'You are going to orbit close with another person (another planet) and you're going to align because those factors in your life are similar,' she told me.[7]

But what happens when you no longer align with your people? Though it's not uncommon for there to be turnover in our friend groups throughout our life, drifting away from a friend can still be difficult, whether you both acknowledge it or not. Sometimes it feels right and you can celebrate each other's new paths while mourning what once was, while other times it's a gut-wrenching ending akin to a romantic break-up. As Gyan Yankovich wrote in her book *Just Friends*, for us to understand how much happiness our friendships can bring to our lives,

FOR THE LOVE AND LOSS OF FRIENDSHIP

we also need to appreciate how painful it can be for them to come to an end.[8] And if there's one thing that we don't talk about enough, it's the grief of a friend-split.

My first friendship breakdown happened a few months into Year 7 and, of course, it took place in the most millennial way possible: on MSN. Each day after school, my siblings and I would rush home to take turns on the clunky desktop computer in my brother's room, connecting the screeching dial-up internet and logging on to the instant messaging platform that was basically the source of all teen joy and angst.

I would almost bet money that Taylor Swift's love for planting Easter eggs was born from being on MSN or AOL. We know she loved her Myspace, so as if Tay wasn't just as unhinged and calculated as we all were in using song lyrics, emoticons (the OG emojis) and mystery initials in our MSN names, as a way of inviting others to crack the code on how we were feeling and who we were -talking- to. Icon behaviour. Alongside lurking for crushes, and repeatedly appearing 'online' and 'offline' just so our crush would receive a notification and hopefully initiate a conversation, MSN was mostly used to chat with the people we literally just spent six hours at school with. I remember logging on one night after dinner and joining a group chat with a few other girls from class. Everything about the conversation seemed normal until a message from Sara popped up.

'Bridget, I'm surprised you're even talking to me after what you said to Clara.'

Sara abruptly left the chat and I was left stunned. I had *no* idea what she was talking about. My heart racing, I opened a separate chat with Sara and asked her what was going on. I stared at the bottom of the chat screen, desperately waiting for 'Sara is typing …' to appear. Nothing. I sent a few more messages but didn't want to spam her out of fear that she would block me. Sara finally responded, claiming I had called her annoying behind her back. WTF?! I had never said anything bad about Sara. I thought she was the coolest girl and wanted nothing more than to be her friend. Someone had made this up and I didn't know why.

With no 'g2g' in sight, Sara logged off and ignored me at school for a good few months. I asked my other friends about it but they said they didn't know either, so being a people pleaser I didn't push anyone for more info. I was already feeling insecure from the transition into high school, yearning for acceptance among my new peers. Facing my first high school friendship conflict, especially one that had been initiated through a screen and stemmed from something I never even said, was disorienting. Amid the confusion and isolation was a sense of shame I had never felt before. I was doing so well in the classroom and getting good grades, but socially I felt like a total failure.

Sara and I ended up in different social circles and she eventually started talking to me again. She probably doesn't remember this even happening and if I saw her now, we would stop and have a nice conversation. But there was never an official resolution or follow-up about what had transpired between us and, sadly, that seems to be the norm for a lot of friendships. Even as adults, when you think we would have our shit together, we can be just as poorly equipped to address conflict as in our peak bitchfest teenage days.

I've always hated confrontation and more recent friendship fallouts reflect that. In my thirties, lines have been crossed between professional and personal relationships and friends have taken advantage of my influence as a music presenter to serve their career. I have had friends lose my trust due to how they speak about others and I've had friends ditch catch-ups because they had 'cooler' things to attend. I wanted to avoid a splinter era with a friend who I made every effort to include when I first started seeing Oscar, only for them to fail in reciprocating and instead blatantly exclude me from their own new chapters. I've also seen where I have distanced myself, fostering a slow and unspoken fizzle where the voice memos and phone calls stop, the responses to text messages take longer and the eventual unfollowing of each other across social media ensues.

There is grief and an awkwardness to a friendship breakdown, just as there is to a romantic break-up. Especially when you have so many mutual mates. The slow and silent fade-out often means that mutuals don't even know that there has been a fallout – I know I have found myself simply nodding and smiling when someone mentions a former friend who just like that, went from being like a sister to a total stranger.

We often say that friends are chosen family but we must remember that friendships, just like familial bonds, are not exempt from complexity or conflict. I once read an advice column on *The Cut* that described friendships as fraught playgrounds for our insecurities and that our approach to them tends to reveal the things we're afraid of, the things we want the most and the things we think we don't have or can't give to ourselves – and I think that means some splits are inevitable.[9]

While I'm only a couple of years into my thirties, this decade has already imparted invaluable lessons about friendship unlike any other period in my life. It's a time when many of us understandably get caught up in the pressures and uncertainty of things like fertility, love and careers, but we cannot neglect the constant thread that is our friendships – both the existing ones we cherish and all the new potential connections that await. My friends help me make sense of life, and often I need them to help me escape it too! Whether that's through laughing, crying, gossiping, eating, drinking, walking or dancing – my friends provide a sanctuary for authenticity and vulnerability.

> **FOR THERE HAVE BEEN LESSONS IN ALL FRIENDSHIPS – THE TRUE AND TOXIC, THE TEMPORARY AND TIMELESS.**

FOR THE LOVE AND LOSS OF FRIENDSHIP

If you're wanting to make new friends as an adult though – something that's been on my mind as I establish my life in a new city – it's not always easy. Meeting new acquaintances, sure – I'll say hi to people at the footy or the dog park – but researchers say it takes upwards of fifty hours of quality shared contact for a familiar face to become an actual friend.[10]

Building new connections in the context of adult commitments and problems isn't easy but, at the same time, we inevitably become more intentional about who we choose to spend our time and energy on. One thing that stuck from my chat with Ali Walker was how she likened her pursuit for new friendships to the dating scene. 'I always have my friend radar on because I'm an extrovert and I love people. I know that I'll probably be making new friends in my eighties! I will always be making new friends because I love people. When I find someone in life who matches me in either frequency or intensity, I have this mindset of openness to that, like oh this is fun. Where could this go? You have to think of yourself as that you're always dating. You're always looking for friends. You're always open, your light's always on.'[11]

You might be wondering what Ali meant by frequency and intensity. In her book, *Click or Clash*, Ali outlined these as two connection types.[12] Frequency is how often you like to connect and how often you like to be in the company of other people. Intensity is about how you bond and is measured by emotional energy, tone and topics of conversation. By understanding your connection type, you can start to understand what kind of traits you are drawn to in a friend, as well as your own boundaries – essentially, what you can offer as a friend and what you expect from your own friendships.

When I spoke to Gyan Yankovich, she asserted that as a society, we're obsessed with wanting to find the right friends and making sure we're not around toxic people, but there isn't that much self-reflection where we are asking ourselves, 'Why would people want to be friends with *me*? How can I make myself a better friend and someone who people will be more drawn to?' 'Too often we fixate on why we can't meet any new people, but I think sometimes we also need to look at what *we* are doing,' she told me.[13] Similarly to Ali, she believed we should be making ourselves a more attractive friend in the same way we try to make ourselves a more attractive date. 'I feel like there's so much of that introspection, especially for women, of asking ourselves how can we attract a date and what are we putting out there to attract what we want,' she said. 'It works the same way with friendship. We don't tend to think about that because we expect friendship to be really easy.'

It's not the first time I've thought about the link between friendship and dating – after all, numerous dating apps now have a friend mode where you can connect on a platonic level with people in your area.

Take Jessie Wright, for example, who I read about on *ABC News*. Just before the arrival of COVID-19 in 2020, Jessie relocated from South Australia to Melbourne with her then-partner. However, during that initial year of lockdown, their relationship ended, leading Jessie to the realisation that most of her social circle in her new city revolved around that partnership. Determined to cultivate her own network, she made it a New Year's resolution to initiate friendships by sharing a meal with a stranger once a week for a year. Yep, potential for fifty-two friends! Jessie went viral on TikTok for documenting her experience, helping to normalise an all-too-common desire to date for mates. Her resolution taught her how important it is to have diverse connections in her life. 'I don't want my whole world to fall apart if one person isn't in it.'[14]

Dating to pursue romantic relationships is completely the norm, so what's stopping us from doing the same for potential friendships? We're aware of the detrimental health effects of loneliness, but why is it that we often fear loneliness within the context of romantic relationships when the foundation of love is always friendship?

My friends were the beating heart of my 30th birthday and it was their love that shone brighter than any candle or sparkler. It is friendship that has made me hopeful about this decade and it is friendship that serves as my compass as I continue to navigate my way through it. For there have been lessons in all friendships – the true and toxic, the temporary and timeless. With that, I want to be more intentional and appreciative. Thankful for the people I am already lucky enough to call my friends, those who have just recently enriched my life and those yet to leave a special mark.

Finally, I want to say that the most essential best friend you will ever have is yourself. Ultimately, everything circles back to you. The longest and most enduring relationship you'll experience is the one with yourself – you are with yourself every second of every day. The least you can do is be nice to yourself!

THIRTIES: *A vibe check*

ASH LONDON

'It's nothing to be scared of and your life is going to be infinitely better. You're on the right path.'[1]

MICHELLE GRACE HUNDER

'Your thirties are the best, just stepping into your own power and your own confidence. I honestly just think it keeps getting better! It's definitely not over.'[2]

HELEN CHIK

'I was terrified when I was turning thirty and was in a bit of a rut but after I actually hit thirty, I realised that my life is great. I have loved every moment of being in my thirties. We have way more freedom and a better understanding of ourselves than what we had in our twenties. The best is yet to come!'[4]

JACINTA PARSONS

'Trust yourself and know that every step you take is a really cool one. You will find your way somehow. It's a really exciting time, hardcore but exciting!'[5]

POLLY 'PJ' HARDING

'It just keeps getting better. Everyone likes to talk about their twenties as the glory days and all that freedom but I think you get freedom when you start to really know who you are as you get older and the more shit you go through, that's just priming you to be the best version of yourself. Don't be afraid to take it on!'[3]

THIRTIES: A VIBE CHECK

LAURA HENSHAW

'Let go of any expectations that you or the world place as to what you should be or where you should be when you are thirty because it is different for everyone. We have our whole life to do things!'[6]

APRIL HÉLÈNE-HORTON

'When you turn thirty, people really start to see you as an adult ... but you're not in it alone. There are always going to be people around you who respect you and see you for who you are. Your thirties can be the best years of your life! It's a banger, honestly. When I was twenty-nine, I was already telling people that I was thirty because I could see that something good was on the horizon. Don't worry, it doesn't feel older ... just in the mornings when your knees go click.'[7]

SEAN SZEPS

'Highly recommend, this is the most exciting decade of my life so far. Ageing is beautiful, learning more about yourself is fab, stepping into your power with money, relationships, having learned and lived. With age comes wisdom, as long as you're doing the work.'[9]

GABRIELLA LABUCCI

'I'm in the best position of my life – mentally, physically, financially, emotionally, everything. I'm fucking tired but it's a different kind of tired. Previously I was tired because I was locking myself away and doing nothing with my life and spiralling. Now I am exhausted because she's working hard!'[10]

CHARLOTTE REE

'I would never go back to my twenties! I am so excited to meet my future self. If I could tell my "turning thirty" self where I would be now, it is so great. All I want to do is find joy and I'll stuff up along the way but I'll have fun while I'm doing it.'[8]

13

THIRTY-THREE

> I CAN CONFIDENTLY AND GENUINELY SAY I HAVE LET GO OF WHAT I BELIEVED MY LIFE *SHOULD* BE LOOKING LIKE BY NOW.

I started this final chapter on my 33rd birthday (10 April, shout out to my Ariessss). The day unofficially commenced at 3.16 a.m. with Daisy's damp nose gently but persistently poking my chin, telling me it was time to go outside for 'toilet'. I had been on overnight duty for the past week as I'm much quicker and quieter than Oscar. A tall man on crutches navigating the dark is like a baby giraffe learning to walk. He was out like a light on painkillers anyway.

Daisy took her sweet-ass time out the back so I decided to head to the bathroom myself. I returned to the living area but my food demon insisted on a detour to the fridge where a box of Cadbury Favourites awaited alongside a block of Whittaker's Hokey Pokey Chocolate. They were a small gift from Oscar, delivered by one of his teammates the night before. It had been a week since Oscar had major surgery on his knee that included the repair of his ACL. A more positive result than a full ACL reconstruction, which was speculated about, given how freakish the hyperextension of his left knee was. It had happened during the third quarter of round one versus Brisbane at Optus Stadium a few weeks prior and was one of the most disgusting injuries I have ever seen. It was Oscar's first AFL game in two years, after major back surgery and being delisted by Carlton at the end of 2022. Oscar spent the following year playing for Williamstown in the state competition, known as the Victorian Football League (VFL). He wanted to get back into the AFL but didn't get his hopes up. Then the Fremantle Football Club called with a two-year contract, which slightly dampened the blow of the injury, given he'd be on the sidelines for at least sixteen weeks. At least he has the last few rounds and all of next year to get back out there and play.

Anyway, it was my birthday so I was going to eat a mini Cherry Ripe at 3 a.m. if I wanted to. Under the glow of the microwave clock, I tried to quietly tear the sticker on the top of the box. I was as careful as I would be if I were playing a game of Operation. Of course, it took unplucking every single chocolate bar out of the box and holding it against the microwave light to check the wrapper before I found my first Cherry Ripe right at the very bottom. I shooed Daisy back into the bedroom. I couldn't be bothered gathering up all the discarded chocolates and instead left them scattered across the kitchen bench. I would tell Oscar that I did this the night before as he was jumping into bed.

As I pulled myself under the doona, I felt a damp puddle underneath my left thigh. Daisy had licked the absolute shit out of the fitted sheet, so much so that it had gone through to the mattress protector. I had no choice but to wake Oscar so we could change the sheets. He was dazed but not fazed as he hobbled around, helping me pull each corner of the linen across the mattress. He made a toilet trip of his own before turning on the kitchen light for a glass of water. Shit. I peered around the corner to find him staring at the chocolate crime scene, amused. He believed me when I said I did it at bedtime and broke out into a grin. 'Happy birthday, darling!'

It was 3.29 a.m. by the time we got back into bed. My phone lit up at 3.52 a.m. with my first birthday message notification. It was from my

THIRTY-THREE

friend Karla. It would have been 5.52 a.m. for her on the East Coast. *She's up early for a run*, I suspected. I thought back to when I turned twenty and how I used to obsessively count how many people would write on my Facebook wall for my birthday, the quality of my day riding on how many posts I received. So cringe.

Oscar's alarm went off at 4.45 a.m. for no apparent reason. He was just as confused as me. I woke again at 6.42 a.m. A broken night of sleep but I was in good spirits. I would be spending my birthday flying to Melbourne, my sixth trip back to the East Coast since moving to Perth four months ago. It was for a work trip, to attend a rooftop bar launch and post about it on my Instagram. The fee was equivalent to what I would have received for working *six weeks* at triple j. What. Is. My. Life?

Moving to Western Australia was certainly not on the bingo card for 2024 but the beauty of my freelancing career is that I can work basically anywhere. So when Oscar got the call from the Fremantle Football Club for a two-year AFL contract, there was no hesitation about me joining him. The timing was perfect and I've always wanted to live somewhere warmer. I actually asked Oscar as we came out of the last Melbourne winter if a sunnier relocation could be possible for us one day. And funnily enough, at the start of that winter, I spoke about the concept of relocating for love on the podcast with my friend Alisha Aitken-Radburn, who packed up her life and moved from Sydney to Perth for her now-husband, Glenn. Little did I know that I would be doing the same thing six months later.

For an interstate move, it all went pretty seamlessly, with our belongings packed up and freighted across the Nullarbor, and Daisy taking her first ever flight like a boss. We secured a rental in a peaceful street with friendly neighbours in East Fremantle, the south-east tip of the Swan River just a few blocks away. The beach a mere four-minute drive with crystal clear water, the sand so fine and soft. Plus, free parking! Who has free parking at the beach?! Sunset dips and acai bowls aplenty, the Western Australian summer really hit different. Our only complaint was the supermarket not opening until 11 a.m. on Sundays. But everything else – *mwah*, chef's kiss. No notes. After moving house five times in the past three years, I felt settled. *Finally.*

Until my manager texted. The opportunity to apply for a high-profile entertainment role on national television had emerged. Real dream-job kinda shit. The catch? Moving to Sydney. Again.

A new potential crossroads had dawned and suddenly I was reacquainted with that persistent lump in throat, tightness in chest feeling. This kind of gig carried opportunities and experiences that would do absolute wonders for my presenting career. I had vowed to never live in Sydney again after 2018, but this job would have been the only exception. I was so torn. There was every chance that I wouldn't land the gig anyway, but I felt like I owed it to the twelve years of hustle and grind I had done in the media and music industry to put my hand up and have a crack. If I decided not to apply or if I did turn it down, I would forever be looking on at whoever did get it and bitterly thinking, *That could have been me. I could have done that better.*

The mere act of applying meant that I had to consider what getting the job would mean for other aspects of my life. Like my relationship with Oscar. Our two-year anniversary was approaching. He wouldn't be able to move to Sydney with me; he'd just locked this deal with Fremantle. We'd just got here! Our only choice would have been long distance, something we would both be willing to try, but the idea instilled a familiar anxiety within me. I thought back to how frustrating long distance was with my ex. How much effort I made, coordinating our calendars and pausing my savings goals to spend my pay on flights.

> **WE NEED TO STOP VIEWING EVERYTHING IN LIFE AS A RACE, WE NEED TO STOP STRIVING FOR HAPPILY EVER AFTER AT A CERTAIN AGE AND WE NEED TO STOP USING THIRTY AS THE SUPPOSED DEADLINE.**

Oscar is a much more diligent partner but Sydney to Perth is *much* further than Sydney to Melbourne.

Taking on the demands of this job would also delay any plans I had to conceive. I'm not ready to have a baby but at thirty-three, I was still thinking about my biological clock. I found myself referring back to our old friend, The Timeline. Let's say I got the job and fully focused on it for the first two or three years. It might not be until I'm thirty-six when I feel like I'm ready for children, but my egg quality would be starting to decline by then. Should I go ahead and freeze my eggs now? And where would I do it – Perth, Sydney or Melbourne? Maybe this job will make me not want to have kids. Who bloody knows!

I could hear it faintly at the back of my head – the older you get, the higher the stakes. Damn it, Helen Gurley Brown.[1] Here was proof that I couldn't 'have it all'. I thought about the Four Burner Theory, specifically how I wanted to ignore it and set the whole kitchen alight. *Why should I have to turn down the heat on family and my personal life if I want to crank the burner on my career?* I thought to myself. *Why can't I have my cake and eat it too?*

Part of me didn't want to 'have it all' anyway because it actually meant 'doing it all'. Part of me just wanted to ~trust the process~. If I got the job, I would move to Sydney and we would take it from there. If I didn't get the job, I would continue my new chapter in Western Australia. Everything happens for a reason, right? Everything could be worse!

As it turned out, I didn't get the job. And I was totally fine. In fact, I was relieved. I could continue getting to know my new home state and build this new chapter with Oscar and Daisy. I could even book in some holiday time (helloooo, Italy and Greece!). Just like so many things that have happened in my thirties so far, from the chaos and confusion, I gained clarity.

THIRTY-THREE

That's not to say that I've figured everything out. I mean, heck, even beyond career and fertility, I'm still wondering what I want to do with my savings. Or more importantly, how to tan my back and curl my hair properly. Is there a difference between hand wash and body wash? What about regular white vinegar and 'cleaning' vinegar?

My podcast community makes me feel less alone. Amy tells me that she's still figuring out if she even likes her job or if she needs to change careers. Lauren says she's still working out how to flip an omelette without scrambling it. Aleisha doesn't know if she wants kids or not. Belle is wondering how to manage her budget. For Maja, it's figuring out how to love herself. Grace is wondering whether to sacrifice her lifestyle and move far away from the city so she can afford to buy a house. Sean is figuring out how to relax. Renea is deliberating how to stop people pleasing and start articulating what she wants. Mads wants to work out her bra size.

At the very least, I can confidently and genuinely say I have let go of what I believed my life *should* be looking like by now. I deserve a life I love – we all do. And nobody can provide that but me. But I don't think I would have realised that had I not gone through everything I have gone through these past few years. You know in job interviews how the company asks where you see yourself in five years? I used to always make sure I had this question down pat, but perhaps for the first time in my life, I don't think I can answer it. Because if my thirties have shown me anything so far, it's that *anything* can happen.

It has only been in my recent psych sessions that I have taken a moment to think about the beliefs and principles that I consider important in the way I live and work. How my values influence the ways in which I respond to situations and make decisions within relationships and in times of uncertainty. We started doing this by laying out a deck of eighty-five cards on the floor, each representing a value. Wealth, health, friendship, security, romance. All that kind of stuff. I had to sort them into three categories: not important, important and very important. Then I narrowed the very important down to just ten. When I left the session, I could only remember two: fun and inner peace.

> **I DESERVE A LIFE I LOVE – WE ALL DO. AND NOBODY CAN PROVIDE THAT BUT ME.**

I already mentioned the importance of fun when talking about careers, but man, in this whole whirlwind of adulthood and societal pressures, I feel there is no greater need than to chase and savour those moments of laughter and playfulness and spontaneity. I think back to enduring six lockdowns in Melbourne during the COVID-19 pandemic. There was so much time to sit and reflect on what I had made of my life thus far and what I wanted to do once we were free and safe. All I could think about was all the travel I had done in my twenties. All the places I got to see, the cultures I got to experience first-hand. How I couldn't wait to get out there and do it again. I want to go to adult dance classes. I want to get better at snorkelling. I want to spend my days off driving along the West Coast of Australia. I want to expand my cooking skills. That feeling of adventure and possibility feels more alive than ever.

Inner peace holds a distinct resonance in the tumultuous landscape of my thirties and knowing that I am capable of making decisions that

THIRTY-THREE

best serve me and my growth. That I can survive the curveballs that life throws at me. And that it is okay if something doesn't work out, whether that be a break-up, friend-split or job rejection.

'Fun' and 'inner peace' aren't just about fleeting moments of happiness or tranquillity; they're a deliberate choice to prioritise my wellbeing and honour the values that bring depth and meaning to my life.

I hope the stories and reflections in this book have helped in reminding you that age is more than just a number and why we need to reject it as a measure of how worthy we are. That it is important we resist the urgency and fear that marketing agencies, the media and the patriarchy create in order to sell products and services such as fertility consultations and the idea of aspirational living. Age is not and should not be used as a tool to play upon our insecurities for someone else's gain. Not to be Captain Cringe but sometimes it really is about the journey, not the destination. Instead of being so focused on that end goal, we need to enjoy the pitstops and learn from the bumps. We need to stop viewing everything in life as a race, we need to stop striving for happily ever after by a certain age and we need to stop using thirty as the supposed deadline. What's the fun in having everything figured out by then anyway? Boring! I will be forever figuring things out so I may as well make sure I'm having fun in the process.

As you close this book, I hope you feel like you can flip the narrative and let age work for you, rather than you working against it. Lean in to the chaos, confusion and clarity. Fall into it! You might be pleasantly surprised to see who and what's there to catch you.

Age is a privilege. And to age is to live. Not everyone gets to do that.

ACKNOWLEDGEMENTS

It is a truth universally acknowledged that when I enter author mode, I am a terrible person. I am stressed, grumpy, unreliable. I am unhinged, as per my favourite Maisie Peters lyric. I am also eternally grateful to so many people for sticking by me throughout this process.

Firstly, I would like to acknowledge the traditional custodians of the lands on which I have had the privilege of writing and living – the Wurundjeri people of the Kulin Nation and the Whadjuk people of the Walyalup area. I would also like to pay respect to the Wurundjeri and Whadjuk Elders, past and present, and extend this respect to Aboriginal and Torres Strait Islander people from other communities who are reading this book.

To my psychologist, Lee. You once told me that my year of turning thirty could be turned into a movie, but I reckon a book is just as good. I know I pay you, but you're obviously doing something right if I'm still coming back after nearly four years! Thank you for being so approachable, compassionate, trusting and insightful.

I would like to extend a huge thank you to the team at Penguin Random House Australia, particularly my editing penguins Isabelle Yates and Amanda Martin. Thank you for believing that I had something of value to say on this decade of life and for helping me get those ideas on paper. Your flexibility, empathy and encouragement have meant so much. Huge thanks to Camha and Madi, Heidi and Kaelee – I feel so lucky to have worked with you all!

Thank you to George Saad for an absolute slay cover design. I love your work.

ACKNOWLEDGEMENTS

To my manager, Kate, thank you for unknowingly signing up as additional therapist throughout this time. I appreciate you putting up with my angsty teen huffing and puffing!

To my partner, Oscar, I am so grateful for your patience, hugs and all the food you cooked when I was glued to my laptop. Thank you for showing love and remaining calm in my chaos. To Mum and Dad, sorry for going MIA again and thank you for supporting my endeavours.

To my friends for always hyping me up, you know who you are. A special thanks to Ashy for always being a voice memo away and being so generous with your own experiences for me to share with everyone.

To my podcast guests, listeners and online followers who generously shared their personal stories with me, your contributions have enriched this project immeasurably. I could not have done this without you.

ENDNOTES

Introduction
1. Winick, G. [director], *Suddenly 30* [film], Sony Pictures Releasing, 2004.

Suddenly (and Unsoberly) Thirty
1. Lees, P., 'From the archive: Emma Watson on transcending child stardom', *British Vogue*, 15 April 2022.
2. Gerwig, G. [director], *Barbie* [film], Warner Bros. Pictures, 2023.
3. McDonald, Z., & Andrews, M., *The Space Between: Chaos. Questions. Magic. Welcome to your twenties*, Penguin Books, Sydney: NSW, 2020.
4. Frizzell, N., *The Panic Years*, Transworld Publishers Ltd, London: UK, 2022.
5. Schwartz, B., *The Paradox of Choice: Why more is less*, revised edition, HarperCollins, New York: US, 2016.
6. Sedaris, D., 'Laugh, Kookaburra', *The New Yorker*, 17 August 2009.
7. Hughes, S., 'Helen Gurley Brown: How to have it all', *The Guardian*, 15 August 2012.
8. Schneider, K., 'The pandemic skip', *The Cut*, 14 September 2023.
9. Ibid.
10. Hustwaite, B., 'Queer parenting with Sean Szeps', *Figuring Out 30* [podcast], season 3, episode 1, 29 August 2023.

The Big Break-Up
1. Foster Blake, Z., *Break-up Boss*, Penguin Books, Sydney: NSW, 2018.
2. Dawson, B., 'Fear of starting over – the unhappy couples afraid of breaking up', *Cosmopolitan*, 23 January 2024; cosmopolitan.com/uk/love-sex/relationships/a46459835/fear-of-starting-over-unhappy-couples-afraid-of-breaking-up/.
3. Australian Bureau of Statistics, 'Estimating homelessness: Census', released 22 March 2023; abs.gov.au/statistics/people/housing/estimating-homelessness-census/latest-release.

ENDNOTES

4. Mercy Foundation, 'Older women and homelessness', n.d.; mercyfoundation.com.au/our-focus/ending-homelessness/older-women-and-homelessness.
5. Ree, C., *Heartbake: A bittersweet memoir*, Allen & Unwin, Crows Nest: NSW, 2023.
6. Hustwaite, B., 'Dating, divorce and desserts with Charlotte Ree', *Figuring Out 30* [podcast], season 2, episode 25, 18 July 2023.

Bridge's Unsolicited Pep Talk on Heartbreak
1. Foster Blake, Z., *Break-up Boss*, Penguin Books, Sydney: NSW, 2018.
2. Van Cuylenburg, H., Shelton, R., & van Cuylenburg, J., 'Chrissie Swan', *The Imperfects* [podcast], season 5, episode 1, 6 March 2023.
3. Hustwaite, B., 'Rethinking my relationship with alcohol', *Figuring Out 30* [podcast], season 2, episode 14, 2 May 2023.
4. St Vincent's Hospital Heart Health, 'Takotsubo Cardiomyopathy', n.d.; svhhearthealth.com.au/conditions/takotsubo-cardiomyopathy.
5. Patrick King, M., 'Take Me Out to the Ballgame', *Sex and the City* [television series], season 2, episode 1, 13 June 1999.

Saturn Return
1. Wills, S., *Of Gold and Dust: A memoir of a creative life*, Allen & Unwin, Crows Nest: NSW, 2021.
2. World Music Awards, 'Adele's *25* is the world's best-selling album of 2015', 23 January 2016; worldmusicawards.com/index.php/news/adeles-25-worlds-best-selling-album-2015/.
3. DeSantis, R., 'Adele announces new album "30", calling it her "ride or die" during her life's "most turbulent period"', *People*, 13 October 2021.
4. Aguirre, A., 'Adele on the other side', *Vogue*, 7 October 2021.
5. Hustwaite, B., 'Saturn return with Natasha Weber', *Figuring Out 30* [podcast], season 1, episode 2, 25 April 2022.
6. Hocking, J., personal communication with author [Instagram], 8 August 2023.
7. Hustwaite, B., 'Saturn return with Natasha Weber', *Figuring Out 30* [podcast], season 1, episode 2, 25 April 2022.

ENDNOTES

8. Odyssey, D., 'The ultimate guide to surviving your Saturn return', *Nylon*, 29 July 2021.
9. Allied Market Research, 'Astrology market research, 2031', January 2023; alliedmarketresearch.com/astrology-market-A31779.
10. Tovey, A., 'Is it your Saturn return or just, you know, life?', *Sydney Morning Herald*, 29 June 2023.

Saturn in Song
1. Au-Nhien Nguyen, G., 'Angie McMahon: *Light, dark, light again* review – delicate album packs an emotional punch', *The Guardian*, 27 October 2023.

Things I Have Learned About Being Single in My Thirties
1. Gulla, E., 'A brief history of the word "spinster" and how it's still used today', *Cosmopolitan*, 15 February 2020; cosmopolitan.com/uk/love-sex/relationships/a30868873/spinster/.
2. Taylor, J., '"It gets into your bones": The unique loneliness of coronavirus lockdown when you live alone', *The Guardian*, 3 September 2020.
3. Connolly, M., 'Wellness defined: The ultimate guide to health and happiness', *Everyday Health*, 12 January 2018.
4. Purvis, J., 'Tinder: Women get many more matches, but it's quantity, not quality', *Sydney Morning Herald*, 15 February 2017.
5. Knee, C. R., Nanayakkara, A., Vietor, N. A., Neighbors, C., & Patrick, H., 'Implicit theories of relationships: Who cares if romantic partners are less than ideal?' *Personality and Social Psychology Bulletin*, vol. 27, no. 7, 2001, pp. 808–19. doi.org/10.1177/0146167201277004.

Why Am I Like This?
1. Atlas, G., *Emotional Inheritance: A therapist, her patients, and the legacy of trauma*, Little, Brown Spark, New York: US, 2022.
2. Schetzer, A., 'Are you estranged from your family? It's more common than you think', *SBS Voices*, 15 August 2017.
3. Orth, T., 'All on the family: Ties, proximity, and estrangement', *YouGov*, 21 December 2022.

ENDNOTES

4. Schetzer, A., 'Are you estranged from your family? It's more common than you think', *SBS Voices*, 15 August 2017.
5. McCurdy, J., *I'm Glad My Mom Died*, Simon & Schuster, New York: US, 2022.
6. Schetzer, A., 'Are you estranged from your family? It's more common than you think', *SBS Voices*, 15 August 2017.
7. Foo, S., *What My Bones Know: Memoir of healing from complex trauma*, Ballantine Books, New York: US, 2022.
8. Hill, J., *See What You Made Me Do: Power, control and domestic abuse*, Black Inc., Melbourne: Vic, 2019.
9. University College London, 'Maltreated children show same pattern of brain activity as combat soldiers', *ScienceDaily*, 5 December 2011; sciencedaily.com/releases/2011/12/111205140406.htm.
10. Waterland, R., 'Part of me hoped, many times, that my mum would die. Last week, she did', *Sydney Morning Herald*, 22 February 2024.
11. Hustwaite, B., 'Finding family at 31 ft. Tess Griffin', *Figuring Out 30* [podcast], season 2, episode 23, 4 July 2023.
12. Atlas, G., *Emotional Inheritance: A therapist, her patients, and the legacy of trauma*, Little, Brown Spark, New York: US, 2022.

Things I Have Learned About Relationships in My Thirties

1. Alderton, D., *Everything I Know About Love*, Penguin Books, London: UK, 2019.
2. Bishop, K., 'Why people still believe in the "soulmate myth"', *BBC News*, 15 February 2022.
3. Perel, E., *Mating in Captivity: Reconciling the erotic and the domestic*, HarperCollins, New York: US, 2006.
4. Hustwaite, B., 'My first cougar Valentine's Day', *Figuring Out 30* [podcast], season 2, episode 3, 14 February 2023.
5. Hustwaite, B., 'Divorce, lockdown and IVF – a candid chat with a bestie', *Figuring Out 30* [podcast], season 1, episode 5, 16 May 2022.

ENDNOTES

To Baby or Not to Baby
1. Frizzell, N., *The Panic Years*, Transworld Publishers Ltd, London: UK, 2022.
2. Better Health Channel, 'Age and fertility' [fact sheet], n.d.; betterhealth.vic.gov.au/health/conditionsandtreatments/age-and-fertility.
3. Weiss, B. [director], 'The One Where They All Turn Thirty', *Friends* [television series], season 7, episode 14, 13 June 1999.
4. Australian Bureau of Statistics, 'Australian fertility rate hits record low' [media release], 8 December 2021; abs.gov.au/media-centre/media-releases/australian-fertility-rate-hits-record-low.
5. Australian Bureau of Statistics, 'ABS shows changes on International Families Day' [media release], 15 May 2017; abs.gov.au/ausstats/abs%40.nsf/mediareleasesbyCatalogue/5E4BABA5BD22D73DCA2581210009D3D8.
6. KPMG Australia, 'The baby recession continues as births drop to lowest level in almost two decades' [media release], 24 July 2024; kpmg.com/au/en/home/media/press-releases/2024/07/baby-recession-continues-as-births-drop.html.
7. Parsons, J., *A Question of Age*, HarperCollins, Sydney: NSW, 2022.
8. Siegel, E., 'Jennifer Aniston opens up about IVF and fertility struggles', *Allure*, 9 November 2022.
9. Megna, M., '54% of dog owners have regrets about getting a dog', *Forbes*, 25 January 2024.
10. IVF Australia, 'Anti Mullerian Hormone (AMH) Test & Ovarian Reserve' [fact sheet], n.d.; ivf.com.au/planning-for-pregnancy/female-fertility/ovarian-reserve-amh-test.
11. Hustwaite, B., 'Divorce, lockdown and IVF – a candid chat with a bestie', *Figuring Out 30* [podcast], season 1, episode 5, 16 May 2022.
12. Hustwaite, B., 'Miscarriage awareness with Chloe Fisher', *Figuring Out 30* [podcast], season 2, episode 12, 19 April 2023.
13. Hustwaite, B., 'Two pans on a pod! Chatting sexuality with Maria Thattil', *Figuring Out 30* [podcast], season 2, episode 4, 19 April 2023.
14. River, J., 'Sounds of change – Kita Alexander', *To Rebel in the Times* [podcast], season 1, episode 3, 15 July 2020.

ENDNOTES

15. Hustwaite, B., 'Jack River's endless summer and call to the music industry', *Figuring Out 30* [podcast], season 2, episode 15, 10 May 2023.
16. American Society for Reproductive Medicine, 'What is endometriosis?', *ReproductiveFacts.org*, 2016; reproductivefacts.org/news-and-publications/fact-sheets-and-infographics/endometriosis-does-it-cause-infertility.
17. Endometriosis Australia, 'Endometriosis and infertility' factsheet, 2024, endometriosisaustralia.org/wp-content/uploads/2024/05/Endometriosis-Infertility_FINAL-w-QR-Code.pdf.
18. IVF Australia, 'How does endometriosis affect fertility', ivf.com.au/planning-for-pregnancy/female-fertility/endometriosis.
19. Freedman, S., 'Patients told to get pregnant to treat endometriosis', *EndoActive*, 11 December 2023.
20. Freedman, S., 'With endometriosis, shouldn't "let's get you well" come before "let's get you pregnant"?', *The Guardian*, 19 February 2016.
21. Gordon, O., & Roberts, G., 'More than half of young Australians are putting off having children. What does that mean for future growth?', *ABC News*, 4 June 2024.
22. Walker, S., 'How much does having a baby cost? Here's what you should know', *Sydney Morning Herald*, 1 March 2023.
23. Westpac, 'What are the costs of having a baby?', May 2021; westpac.com.au/help/lifemoments/setting-up-life/having-a-baby/cost-of-a-baby/.
24. She's on the Money, 'The rise of DINKs' [Instagram post], 23 April 2024.
25. 'Lachie Neale yet to request AFL trade as he weighs up future with Brisbane Lions', *ABC News*, 6 September 2021.
26. Footy on Nine, 'Panel reacts to Lachie Neale's shock trade request – Footy Classified' [YouTube video], 7 September 2021.
27. Simmonds, P., 'The cost of labour' [Instagram post], 8 March 2023.
28. Kon-Yu, N., *The Cost of Labour: How we are all trapped by the politics of pregnancy and parenting*, Affirm Press, South Melbourne: Vic, 2022.
29. Hustwaite, B., 'The price of motherhood with Phoebe Simmonds', *Figuring Out 30* [podcast], season 2, episode 10, 5 April 2023.
30. Thrive By Five, 'Dads' Action Plan for the Early Years', January 2024.
31. Griffiths, M., *Tissue*, Ultimo Press, Ultimo: NSW, 2023.
32. Griffiths, M., interview with author [unpublished], 22 January 2024.

ENDNOTES

33. Brinsford, J., 'Katy Perry hits out at the "popular misconceptions of being a full-time mum"', *Mirror*, 25 September 2020.
34. Australian Institute of Health and Welfare, 'Australia's mothers and babies', 13 December 2023; aihw.gov.au/reports/mothers-babies/australias-mothers-babies/contents/overview-and-demographics/maternal-age.
35. Australian Bureau of Statistics, 'Australian women having fewer children and later in life' [media release], 18 October 2023; abs.gov.au/media-centre/media-releases/australian-women-having-fewer-children-and-later-life.
36. Griffiths, M., interview with author [unpublished], 22 January 2024.
37. Ibid.
38. Australian Longitudinal Study on Women's Health (Women's Health Australia), 'One in six Australian women in their 30s have had an abortion – and we're starting to understand why', n.d.; alswh.org.au/resources/one-in-six-australian-women-have-had-an-abortion/.
39. Rushton, G., 'Mothers, of course, have abortions. And it's their time to accept they are experts in their own lives', *The Guardian*, 9 December 2023.
40. Rushton, G., *The Most Important Job in the World*, Pan Macmillan, Sydney: NSW, 2022.
41. Rushton, G., personal communication with author [Instagram], 20 February 2024.
42. Rushton, G., interview with author [unpublished], 12 December 2023.
43. Ibid.
44. Ibid.
45. Warrington, R., *Women Without Kids: The revolutionary rise of an unsung sisterhood*, Sounds True, Colorado: US, 2023.
46. Ibid.
47. Hustwaite, B., 'Lessons in taking care with Laura Henshaw', *Figuring Out 30* [podcast], season 2, episode 16, 17 May 2023.
48. Henshaw, L., 'Why I'm afraid to have a baby', *Marie Claire*, 3 October 2023.
49. Walsh, L., 'Miley Cyrus opened up about why she's unsure about having kids', *InStyle*, 3 June 2024.

50. Australian Institute of Family Studies, 'Australian family facts and figures released on World Statistics Day' [media release], October 2015; aifs.gov.au/media/australian-family-facts-and-figures-released-world-statistics-day.
51. Hustwaite, B., 'Queer parenting with Sean Szeps', *Figuring Out 30* [podcast], season 3, episode 1, 29 August 2023.
52. Szeps, S., *Not Like Other Dads*, HarperCollins, Sydney: NSW, 2023.
53. Hustwaite, B., appearance on *Today Extra*, 10 May 2024.
54. Hustwaite, B., 'Queer parenting with Sean Szeps', *Figuring Out 30* [podcast], season 3, episode 1, 29 August 2023.

I Do ... Need to Talk About Marriage

1. Ford, C. [host], *Killing the Angel with Clementine Ford* [event], Brunswick Ballroom, Melbourne, 25 June 2023.
2. Patmore, C., *The Angel in the House*, Macmillan & Co, London: UK, first published in 1854.
3. Gilbert, E., *Committed: A love story*, Penguin Putnam Inc, New York: US, 2011.
4. Holy Bible, 1 Timothy 2:12, NIV, *Bible Gateway*.
5. Holy Bible, Genesis 2:7, NIV, *Bible Gateway*.
6. Ford, C., *I Don't*, Allen & Unwin, Crows Nest: NSW, 2023.
7. Ferguson, H., personal communication with author [Instagram], 20 February 2024.
8. Flex Mami, personal communication with author [Instagram], 20 February 2024.
9. Rushton, G., personal communication with author [Instagram], 20 February 2024.
10. Rizvi, J., personal communication with author [email], 17 March 2024.
11. Andrews, M., personal communication with author [email], 25 March 2024.
12. Ziwica, K., 'There's a case to be made for feminist marriage – and here's why', *ABC News*, 27 September 2019.
13. Tyler, M., *Freedom Fallacy*, Connor Court Publishing, Brisbane: QLD, 2015.

ENDNOTES

14. Australian Bureau of Statistics, 'Marriages and divorces, Australia', released 1 December 2023; abs.gov.au/statistics/people/people-and-communities/marriages-and-divorces-australia/2022.
15. Agius, K., 'Gay marriage data shows more women are tying the knot', *ABC News*, 29 November 2019.
16. Australian Institute of Family Studies, 'Marriages in Australia', March 2023; aifs.gov.au/research/facts-and-figures/marriages-australia-2023.
17. Lennon, R., *Wedded Wife: A feminist history of marriage*, Aurum Press Ltd, London: UK, 2023.
18. Australian Institute of Family Studies, 'Marriages in Australia', March 2023; aifs.gov.au/research/facts-and-figures/marriages-australia-2023.
19. Ibid.
20. Gilbert, E., *Committed: A love story*, Penguin Putnam Inc, New York: US, 2011.
21. Australian Government, 'Guides to social policy law', May 2023; guides.dss.gov.au/social-security-guide/2/2/5/10#defacto.
22. Australian Bureau of Statistics, 'Household and families: Census', released 28 June 2022; abs.gov.au/statistics/people/people-and-communities/household-and-families-census/2021.
23. Acacia Immigration Australia, 'Proving a de facto relationship' [fact sheet], n.d.; acacia-au.com/de-facto-relationships-for-partner-visas.php.
24. Australian Bureau of Statistics, 'Marriages and divorces, Australia', released 1 December 2023; abs.gov.au/statistics/people/people-and-communities/marriages-and-divorces-australia/2022.
25. Len Catron, M., 'What you lose when you gain a spouse', *The Atlantic*, 2 July 2019.
26. Rocca, J., 'Charlotte Ree: "I met my partner on Tinder at 30. He picked up my heart and healed it"', *Sydney Morning Herald*, 23 July 2023.
27. Hustwaite, B., 'Divorce, lockdown and IVF – a candid chat with a bestie', *Figuring Out 30* [podcast], season 1, episode 5, 16 May 2022.
28. Hustwaite, B., 'Dating after divorce with Helen Chik', *Figuring Out 30* [podcast], season 2, episode 5, 28 February 2023.

29. Preetha, S. S., 'Normalise happy divorces, not unhappy marriages', *Daily Star*, 24 May 2022.
30. Allaire, C., 'Emily Ratajkowski repurposed her engagement ring into "divorce rings"', *Vogue*, 19 March 2024.
31. Ivan, C., '"I always thought I'd get married. But I've come to realise marriage is inherently anti-feminist"', *Mamamia*, 26 January 2021.
32. Deveny, C., 'Love party day. No God. No government. No marriage. Just Love', *Catherine Deveny* [blog], n.d.; catherinedeveny.com/the-love-party-day/.
33. Holgate, E., '7 Australian creatives share their non-traditional weddings', *Fashion Journal*, 25 January 2023.
34. Smith, Z., 'Friday essay: "A prisoner on the rack" – how 19th-century Australian women wrote about marital rape', *The Conversation*, 22 March 2024.
35. Gemological Institute of America, 'The origin of wedding rings: Ancient tradition or marketing invention?', n.d.; 4cs.gia.edu/en-us/blog/origin-of-wedding-rings/.
36. Wollstonecraft, M., *A Vindication of the Rights of Woman*, printed for J. Johnson, London: UK, first published in 1792.
37. Ford, C., *I Don't*, Allen & Unwin, Crows Nest: NSW, 2023.
38. Wilford, D., 'Married men live longer; married women, not so much: Study', *Toronto Sun*, 25 June 2022.
39. Sauer, R., 'Never-married men diagnosed with heart failure have increased risk of death', *University of Colorado School of Medicine*, 19 April 2019.
40. Australian Bureau of Statistics, 'Marriages and divorces, Australia', released 10 November 2022; abs.gov.au/statistics/people/people-and-communities/marriages-and-divorces-australia/2021.
41. Lennon, R., *Wedded Wife: A feminist history of marriage*, Aurum Press Ltd, London: UK, 2023.
42. Gilbert, E., *Committed: A love story*, Penguin Putnam Inc, New York: US, 2011.

ENDNOTES

Body Better

1. Center for Endometriosis Care, 'Endometriosis: A complex disease', 2024; centerforendo.com/endometriosis-understanding-a-complex-disease.
2. Costello, B., 'Kate Moss: The waif that roared', *Women's Wear Daily*, 13 November 2009.
3. Ferguson, H., *Bite Back: Feminism, media, politics, and our power to change it all*, Affirm Press, South Melbourne: Vic, 2023.
4. Hind, K., 'Bridget Jones film to "play down" her obsession with losing weight – as new sequel is thought to be first time Renee Zellweger is not putting on pounds to play iconic role', *Daily Mail*, 28 April 2024; dailymail.co.uk/tvshowbiz/article-13357833/Bridget-Jones-film-losing-weight-Renee-Zellweger.html.
5. Barry, S., 'Jessica Simpson: "I was addicted to being wanted"', *Glamour*, 4 February 2020.
6. Butterfly Foundation, 'More than 90% of young people in Australia have some concern about their body image', 29 May 2023; butterfly.org.au/news/more-than-90-of-young-people-in-australia-have-some-concern-about-their-body-image/.
7. Froomes, interview with author [unpublished], 18 January 2024.
8. Froomes, 'We need to talk about tuna', FROOMESWORLD, Substack, 12 January 2022; froomes.substack.com/p/-we-need-to-talk-about-tuna.
9. Froomes, interview with author [unpublished], 18 January 2024.
10. Froomes, 'We need to talk about tuna', FROOMESWORLD, Substack, 12 January 2022; froomes.substack.com/p/-we-need-to-talk-about-tuna.
11. Froomes, interview with author [unpublished], 18 January 2024.
12. Parsons, J., *A Question of Age*, HarperCollins, Sydney: NSW, 2022.
13. Hockey, A., Milojev, P., Sibley, G. S., Donovan, C. L., & Barlow, F. K., 'Body image across the adult lifespan: A longitudinal investigation of developmental and cohort effects', *Body Image*, vol. 39, 2021, pp. 114–24. doi: 10.1016/j.bodyim.2021.06.007.
14. Lewin, E., 'Why body confidence actually grows with age', *Sydney Morning Herald*, 29 October 2021.
15. Hustwaite, B., 'The Bodzilla: I am not here to pay bills and stay thin!', *Figuring Out 30* [podcast], season 2, episode 17, 24 May 2023.

16. Hélène-Horton, A., appearance on *The Project*, 10 May 2023.
17. Hustwaite, B., 'The Bodzilla: I am not here to pay bills and stay thin!', *Figuring Out 30* [podcast], season 2, episode 17, 24 May 2023.
18. Chatfield, A., 'SOLO: A feminist dilemma and Gypsy Rose', *It's a Lot* [podcast], 16 January 2024.
19. McDonald, Z., & Andrews, M., *The Space Between: Chaos. Questions. Magic. Welcome to your twenties*, Penguin Books, Sydney: NSW, 2020.
20. Josiebalka, video, *TikTok*, 29 December 2023; https://vt.tiktok.com/ZSYusBToJ/.

Body Image Reminders I'm Taking Into My Thirties
1. Given, F., *Women Don't Owe You Pretty: The record-breaking best-selling book every woman needs*, Octopus Publishing Group, London: UK, 2020.

I Quit
1. Sykes, P., *How Do We Know That We're Doing It Right? Essays on modern life*, Cornerstone, London: UK, 2020.
2. Accor, 'New careers study from Accor reveals perception of dream jobs, careers in hospitality and the key motivators for the British workforce', *H Trends*, 14 March 2023; htrends.com/trends-detail-sid-125361.html.
3. Mahdawi, A., '30 under 30-year sentences: why so many of Forbes' young heroes face jail', *The Guardian*, 7 April 2023.
4. Hustwaite, B., 'Turning failure into success with Michelle Grace Hunder', *Figuring Out 30* [podcast], season 1, episode 7, 31 May 2022.
5. Hustwaite, B., 'The power of saying no with Ash London', *Figuring Out 30* [podcast], season 1, episode 3, 3 May 2022.
6. Hustwaite, B., 'Making a living on TikTok with Celia Gercovich', *Figuring Out 30* [podcast], season 2, episode 19, 6 June 2023.
7. Hustwaite, B., 'Identity beyond work with Polly "PJ" Harding', *Figuring Out 30* [podcast], season 2, episode 2, 7 February 2023.
8. Waters, C., '"You're not going to be everyone's cup of tea": The perils of podcast success', *Sydney Morning Herald*, 29 October 2022.

ENDNOTES

9. Shameless Media, 'What is Shameless Media?', n.d.; shamelessmediaco.com/about.
10. World Health Organization, 'Burn-out an "occupational phenomenon": International Classification of Diseases' [departmental update], 28 May 2019.
11. Berg, S., 'WHO adds burnout to ICD-11. What it means for physicians', *AMA*, 23 July 2019.

A New Diagnosis (or Two)

1. Australian Psychological Society, 'ADHD in adults', n.d.; psychology.org.au/for-the-public/psychology-topics/adhd-in-adults.
2. Blackwood, F., 'What is it like to have ADHD as an adult? Australians share their highs and lows', *ABC News*, 23 October 2023.
3. Mindovermatterwithemma, video, *TikTok*, 20 September 2023; https://vt.tiktok.com/ZSYupoNHP/.
4. Hustwaite, B., 'Gabriella Labucci is 31 and couldn't be happier', *Figuring Out 30* [podcast], season 3, episode 5, 26 September 2023.
5. Rusciano, E., 'Address to the National Press Club of Australia', National Press Club of Australia; npc.org.au/speaker/2022/1003-em-rusciano.
6. Hall, A., 'Jennifer had to "battle" to get an ADHD diagnosis. This is why it's so difficult as an adult', *SBS News*, 6 November 2023.
7. Grant, R., 'This was supposed to be endo's big moment. What happened?', *Cosmopolitan*, 18 February 2020.
8. Boseley, M., *The Year I Met My Brain: A travel companion for adults who have just found out they have ADHD*, Penguin Books, Sydney: NSW, 2023.
9. McMahon, A., interview with author [unpublished], October 2023.
10. Henderson, M., '"Like someone flicked a switch": the premenstrual disorder that upturns women's lives', *The Guardian*, 15 September 2019.
11. Gupta, S., 'The menstrual mood disorder you've never heard about', *TIME*, 4 April 2024.
12. ADDitude Magazine, 'Exploring the PMDD-ADHD link: How to recognize and treat PMDD (with Dara Abraham, D.O.)', YouTube, 21 May 2024; youtube.com/watch?v=rl34TGcbu7k.

13. Dorani, F., Bijlenga, D., Beekman, A. T. F., van Someren, E. J. W., & Kooij, S., 'Prevalence of hormone-related mood disorder symptoms in women with ADHD', *Journal of Psychiatric Research*, vol. 133, 2021, pp. 10–15. doi.org/10.1016/j.jpsychires.2020.12.005.
14. Kaufman, G., 'Jessie J opens up about ADHD/OCD diagnosis: "I have always been honest in the journey I'm going through"', *Billboard*, 22 July 2024.

For the Love and Loss of Friendship
1. Hustwaite, B., 'How to make new friends in your 20s/30s', *Figuring Out 30* [podcast], season 2, episode 21, 20 June 2023.
2. BBC, 'Dunbar's number: Why we can only maintain 150 relationships', 9 October 2019.
3. Vernem, E., 'There's an exact age your friendships will go through a "splinter era". Here's how to survive it', *Mamamia*, 22 March 2024.
4. Alderton, D., *Everything I Know About Love*, Penguin Books, London: UK, 2019.
5. Hindi, R., 'The end of the "best friend" era', *InStyle Australia*; instyleaustralia.com.au/culture/the-end-of-the-best-friend-era/.
6. Bumble, 'Bumble For Friends data shows importance of new friendships, including those made online, to combat loneliness', n.d.; bumble.com/en-au/the-buzz/bumble-for-friends-bff-data-friendship-loneliness-online.
7. Hustwaite, B., 'Navigating friendsplits with Dr Hannah Korrel', *Figuring Out 30* [podcast], season 2, episode 20, 13 June 2023.
8. Yankovich, G., *Just Friends*, Ultimo Press, Ultimo: NSW, 2024.
9. Brammer, J. P., 'Hola Papi: "I'm jealous of my best friend's other friends"', *The Cut*, 12 January 2024.
10. Hronis, A., 'Why do we find making new friends so hard as adults?', *The Conversation*, 21 January 2022.
11. Hustwaite, B., 'How to make new friends in your 20s/30s', *Figuring Out 30* [podcast], season 2, episode 21, 20 June 2023.
12. Walker, A., *Click or Clash?*, Penguin Books, Sydney: NSW, 2023.
13. Yankovich, G., interview with author [unpublished], 17 January 2024.
14. Macdonald, M., 'The creative ways adults are making new friends and combating loneliness', *ABC News*, 15 October 2023.

ENDNOTES

Thirties: A vibe check
1. Hustwaite, B., 'The power of saying no with Ash London', *Figuring Out 30* [podcast], season 1, episode 3, 3 May 2022.
2. Hustwaite, B., 'Turning failure into success with Michelle Grace Hunder', *Figuring Out 30* [podcast], season 1, episode 7, 31 May 2022.
3. Hustwaite, B., 'Identity beyond work with Polly "PJ" Harding', *Figuring Out 30* [podcast], season 2, episode 2, 7 February 2023.
4. Hustwaite, B., 'Dating after divorce with Helen Chik', *Figuring Out 30* [podcast], season 2, episode 5, 28 February 2023.
5. Hustwaite, B., 'A Question of Age with Jacinta Parsons', *Figuring Out 30* [podcast], season 2, episode 7, 14 March 2023.
6. Hustwaite, B., 'Lessons in taking care with Laura Henshaw', *Figuring Out 30* [podcast], season 2, episode 16, 17 May 2023.
7. Hustwaite, B., 'The Bodzilla: I am not here to pay bills and stay thin!', *Figuring Out 30* [podcast], season 2, episode 17, 24 May 2023.
8. Hustwaite, B., 'Dating, divorce and desserts with Charlotte Ree', *Figuring Out 30* [podcast], season 2, episode 25, 18 July 2023.
9. Hustwaite, B., 'Queer parenting with Sean Szeps', *Figuring Out 30* [podcast], season 3, episode 1, 29 August 2023.
10. Hustwaite, B., 'Gabriella Labucci is 31 and couldn't be happier', *Figuring Out 30* [podcast], season 3, episode 5, 26 September 2023.

Thirty-three
1. Hughes, S., 'Helen Gurley Brown: How to have it all', *The Guardian*, 15 August 2012.
2. Mousa, D., 'Young adulthood is no longer one of life's happiest times', *Scientific American*, 12 July 2024; scientificamerican.com/article/young-adulthood-is-no-longer-one-of-lifes-happiest-times/.

ABOUT THE AUTHOR

Bridget Hustwaite is a presenter, bestselling author, podcaster and content creator. In her twenties, Hustwaite spent seven years at triple j including five years hosting her own national music program, *Good Nights*. Already a trusted voice in the Australian music industry, since entering her thirties, Bridget's interest areas have expanded to include commentary on love, sex, career, fertility and more – all of which she explores in her popular podcast *Figuring Out 30*.

Bridget's bestselling first book, *How to Endo*, details her experience with endometriosis. Bridget's writing has also featured in *Vogue Australia*, *Harper's Bazaar Australia* and the *Sydney Morning Herald*, and she makes regular appearances on national television programs such as the *Today Show*, *Today Extra* and *The Project*.

Originally from Ballarat, Bridget spent most of her twenties in Melbourne and recently relocated to sunny Fremantle, Western Australia.